Bruce Springsteen's America
Lives of Moral Leadership
The Moral Intelligence of Children
Children of Crisis, I: A Study of Courage
and Fear
Still Hungry in America
The Image Is You
Uprooted Children
Teachers and the Children of Poverty
Wages of Neglect (*with Maria Piers*)
Drugs and Youth (*with Joseph Brenner and
Dermont Meagher*)
Erik H. Erikson: The Growth of His Work
The Middle Americans (*with Jon Erikson*)
The Geography of Faith (*with Daniel
Berrigan*)
Migrants, Sharecroppers, Mountaineers
(*Volume II of* Children of Crisis)
The South Goes North (*Volume III of*
Children of Crisis)
Farewell to the South
Twelve to Sixteen: Early Adolescence
(*with Jerome Kagan*)
A Spectacle unto the World: The Catholic
Worker Movement (*with Jon Erikson*)
The Old Ones of New Mexico
(*with Alex Harris*)
The Buses Roll (*with Carol Baldwin*)
The Darkness and the Light
(*with Doris Ulmann*)
Irony in the Mind's Life: Essays on Novels
by James Agee, Elizabeth Bowen, and
George Eliot
William Carlos Williams: The Knack of
Survival in America
The Mind's Fate: Ways of Seeing Psychiatry
and Psychoanalysis
Eskimos, Chicanos, Indians (*Volume IV of*
Children of Crisis)
Privileged Ones: The Well-Off and the Rich
in America (*Volume V of* Children of
Crisis)
A Festering Sweetness (*poems*)
The Last and First Eskimos
(*with Alex Harris*)

Women of Crisis, I: Lives of Struggle and
Hope (*with Jane Coles*)
Walker Percy: An American Search
Flannery O'Connor's South
Women of Crisis, II: Lives of Work and
Dreams (*with Jane Coles*)
Dorothea Lange
The Doctor Stories of William Carlos
Williams (*editor*)
Agee (*with Ross Spears*)
The Moral Life of Children
The Political Life of Children
Simone Weil: A Modern Pilgrimage
Dorothy Day: A Radical Devotion
In the Streets (*with Helen Levitt*)
Times of Surrender: Selected Essays
Harvard Diary: Reflections on the Sacred
and the Secular
That Red Wheelbarrow: Selected Literary
Essays
The Child in Our Times: Studies in the
Development of Resiliency
(*edited with Timothy Dugan*)
Anna Freud: The Dream of Psychoanalysis
Rumors of Separate Worlds (*poems*)
The Spiritual Life of Children
The Call of Stories: Teaching and the Moral
Imagination
Their Eyes Meeting the World:
The Drawings and Paintings of Children
(*with Margaret Sartor*)
The Call of Service: A Witness to Idealism
Doing Documentary Work
The Secular Mind
When They Were Young

FOR CHILDREN

Dead End School
The Grass Pipe
Saving Face
Riding Free
Headsparks

TEACHING STORIES

TEACHING STORIES

AN ANTHOLOGY ON THE POWER OF LEARNING AND LITERATURE

Selected by Robert Coles, with
Trevor B. Hall, Ernest Patterson, and
Michael Coles

THE MODERN LIBRARY

NEW YORK

2004 Modern Library Paperback Edition

Copyright © 2004 by Robert Coles

All rights reserved under International and Pan-American Copyright
Conventions. Published in the United States by Modern Library,
an imprint of The Random House Publishing Group, a division
of Random House, Inc., New York, and simultaneously in
Canada by Random House of Canada Limited, Toronto.

Permission acknowledgments for previously published material
can be found on page 285.

LIBRARY OF CONGRESS CATALOGING-IN-PUBLICATION DATA
Teaching stories: an anthology on the power of learning and literature/
selected by Robert Coles with Trevor Hall, Ernest Patterson,
and Michael Coles.—2004 Modern Library pbk. ed.
p. cm.
ISBN 0-8129-7169-8
1. Education—Fiction. 2. Teacher-student relationships—Fiction.
3. Teachers—Fiction. 4. Students—Fiction. 5. American fiction.
I. Coles, Robert.

PS648.E33T43 2004
813′.01083557—dc22   2004048294

Modern Library website address: www.modernlibrary.com

Printed in the United States of America

2 4 6 8 9 7 5 3 1

We dedicate this book to our teachers and to our teaching colleagues. Many thanks to our friends at *DoubleTake* magazine, and special thanks to Beetna Kim.

Contents

IV. PERSONAL EXPERIENCE AND COMMENTARY

V. POSTLUDE

INTRODUCTION

Robert Coles

What follow in the pages ahead are stories that in one way or another take the reader into a schoolroom, or ask the reader to think about all that happens when a person known as a teacher and other persons come together as students, find themselves listening, speaking, watching, writing, musing, and giving or taking tests—the activity of mind and heart and soul (and of body) that occurs in the name of learning, of acquiring what gets called an "education." What follows can also be described as the efforts of storytellers (essayists and novelists and poets) to render school life in all its complexity and variety—to render, as well, the ironies and paradoxes, the surprises, the baffling moments, or the revelatory ones, that visit teachers and those being taught as they collectively go through a day's school routine. What follow, finally, are the readings that made up a course offered for twenty years at a graduate school of education—a seminar attended by men and women who were already teachers, who aimed to learn more so that their work might take on new or alternative directions. That course, called "Writers in the Classroom," offered weekly readings in the same sequence that this book renders them: A seminar's curriculum, and yes, its point of view, explicit or implied, now becomes a book for readers across time and space to consider.

In a sense this book is a novel, which might be titled *A Classroom's World*. The parts feature particular writers whose voices, in their sum, address the reader inclined to take an interest; contemplate what sometimes happens as people read; and together have their say in response to what a writer, at a different time and place, has sent forth as her or his say. In a sense, too, this book is a play, divided into a series of acts and scenes: The drama (occasionally the melodrama or the tragicomedy or the humdrum light and amusing moments freighted now and then with tearful regret, alarm, bemusement) that unfolds is what takes place in the course of a classroom's daily life. The playwrights of such expression send words our way meant to ask or answer, to declare or refute, to push a matter further or second-guess it, all in the name of communication, exploration, discussion: those nouns meant to signify the activity that happens as we mortals address ourselves, then one another, in our time together—even as the writers in the pages ahead, through the words they have offered, are keeping us company, giving us the food for thought we so often ache to have available.

One year, at the end of the seminar Writers in the Classroom, an experienced high school teacher from Illinois spoke of what she had experienced "meeting," as she put it, Chekhov and Tolstoy, from nineteenth-century and early-twentieth-century Russia, Hardy, from the England of that time, and of course, in various degrees, a host of American writers who are nearer to us by virtue of when they lived and where they chose to locate their stories—under what set of social, cultural, and historical circumstances. Here are that teacher's concluding remarks. For us who have taught that seminar's curriculum again and again, it is an apt and stirring way to introduce this book (a class's ending remarks become a book's beginning aria).

We've been experiencing an opera here in this classroom: the writers singing to us about the music that teachers and students make as they learn together, and we singing our own songs, which tell of memories, of successful leaps and big letdowns. These writers sing *of* themselves [as Walt Whitman put it], but they sing *to* us, and *about* us [teachers and students alike become a classroom's *we*]. No big-deal theories in this seminar, no paradigms, no concepts—only our memories, our observations and participation, our concerns: *ourselves*, as the writers we've met, through their works, have become part of our way of seeing things, responding to one another. [A pause, then her final, brief, affecting summary:] These writers in their classrooms have given us our classrooms: to recall, to know, to anticipate coming to us, and being with us, over the years ahead.

The stories ahead were called "The Teacher Stories" by some who took the course—as in "The Doctor Stories," which the physician and poet and storyteller William Carlos Williams once gathered for his attentive readers. Still, some of the writers whose work is presented here knew well that teachers' stories, in one or another way, are also students' stories; so we all reminded ourselves—the two of us, me and Trevor Hall, who taught the course, the one of us, Michael Coles, a Montana teacher and photographer, who helped choose the stories, and Ernest Patterson, who took the course while on leave from his position as the principal of a Colorado school. For all of us over the years, these fictional narratives have been mainstays of educational enlightenment—so much so well and suggestively told. For all of us, too, the concluding remarks of Erik H. Erikson and Anna Freud have been a constant presence: Their wisdom is a pointed summons to the important task a classroom presents, as the writer Mark Edmundson makes clear in his memoir *The Teacher.*

I

CHALLENGES, IRONIES, POSSIBILITIES

Here are stories of teachers trying to make do, to understand the complexity of what they are meant to offer their students, whose variousness is a constant presence, a challenge. Here, also, are moments of moral and psychological scrutiny and, on occasion, of outright confession: We see them through Baxter's Miss Ferenczi, Yates's Miss Price, Wolff's portrait of academic life, Tolstoy's willingness to turn the tables on himself as a teacher, and Nemerov's ode, bidding an affectionate good-bye as a prelude to his son's new life.

Gryphon

Charles Baxter

On Wednesday afternoon, between the geography lesson on ancient Egypt's hand-operated irrigation system and an art project that involved drawing a model city next to a mountain, our fourth-grade teacher, Mr. Hibler, developed a cough. This cough began with a series of muffled throat-clearings and progressed to propulsive noises contained within Mr. Hibler's closed mouth. "Listen to him," Carol Peterson whispered to me. "He's gonna blow up." Mr. Hibler's laughter—dazed and infrequent—sounded a bit like his cough, but as we worked on our model cities we would look up, thinking he was enjoying a joke, and see Mr. Hibler's face turning red, his cheeks puffed out. This was not laughter. Twice he bent over, and his loose tie, like a plumb line, hung down straight from his neck as he exploded himself into a Kleenex. He would excuse himself, then go on coughing. "I'll bet you a dime," Carol Peterson whispered, "we get a substitute tomorrow."

Carol sat at the desk in front of mine and was a bad person—when she thought no one was looking she would blow her nose on notebook paper, then crumple it up and throw it into the wastebasket—but at times of crisis she spoke the truth. I knew I'd lose the dime.

"No deal," I said.

When Mr. Hibler stood us in formation at the door just prior to the final bell, he was almost incapable of speech. "I'm sorry, boys and girls," he said. "I seem to be coming down with something."

"I hope you feel better tomorrow, Mr. Hibler," Bobby Kryzanowicz, the faultless brown-noser, said, and I heard Carol Peterson's evil giggle. Then Mr. Hibler opened the door and we walked out to the buses, a clique of us starting noisily to hawk and laugh as soon as we thought we were a few feet beyond Mr. Hibler's earshot.

———

Since Five Oaks was a rural community, and in Michigan, the supply of substitute teachers was limited to the town's unemployed community college graduates, a pool of about four mothers. These ladies fluttered, provided easeful class days, and nervously covered material we had mastered weeks earlier. Therefore it was a surprise when a woman we had never seen came into the class the next day, carrying a purple purse, a checkerboard lunchbox, and a few books. She put the books on one side of Mr. Hibler's desk and the lunchbox on the other, next to the Voice of Music phonograph. Three of us in the back of the room were playing with Heever, the chameleon that lived in a terrarium and on one of the plastic drapes, when she walked in.

She clapped her hands at us. "Little boys," she said, "why are you bent over together like that?" She didn't wait for us to answer. "Are you tormenting an animal? Put it back. Please sit down at your desks. I want no cabals this time of the day." We just stared at her. "Boys," she repeated, "I asked you to sit down."

I put the chameleon in his terrarium and felt my way to my desk, never taking my eyes off the woman. With white and green chalk, she had started to draw a tree on the left side of the blackboard. She didn't look usual. Furthermore, her tree was outsized, disproportionate, for some reason.

"This room needs a tree," she said, with one line drawing the suggestion of a leaf. "A large, leafy, shady, deciduous . . . oak."

Her fine, light hair had been done up in what I would learn years later was called a chignon, and she wore gold-rimmed glasses whose lenses seemed to have the faintest blue tint. Harold Knardahl, who sat across from me, whispered, "Mars," and I nodded slowly, savoring the imminent weirdness of the day. The substitute drew another branch with an extravagant arm gesture, then turned around and said, "Good morning. I don't believe I said good morning to all of you yet."

Facing us, she was no special age—an adult is an adult—but her face had two prominent lines, descending vertically from the sides of her mouth to her chin. I knew where I had seen those lines before: *Pinocchio*. They were marionette lines. "You may stare at me," she said to us, as a few more kids from the last bus came into the room, their eyes fixed on her, "for a few more seconds, until the bell rings. Then I will permit no more staring. Looking I will permit. Staring, no. It is impolite to stare, and a sign of bad breeding. You cannot make a social effort while staring."

Harold Knardahl did not glance at me, or nudge, but I heard him whisper "Mars" again, trying to get more mileage out of his single joke with the kids who had just come in.

When everyone was seated, the substitute teacher finished her tree, put down her chalk fastidiously on the phonograph, brushed her hands, and faced us. "Good morning," she said. "I am Miss Ferenczi, your teacher for the day. I am fairly new to your community, and I don't believe any of you know me. I will therefore start by telling you a story about myself."

While we settled back, she launched into her tale. She said her grandfather had been a Hungarian prince; her mother had been born in some place called Flanders, had been a pianist, and had played concerts for people Miss Ferenczi referred to as "crowned heads." She gave us a knowing look. "Grieg," she said, "the Norwegian master, wrote a concerto for piano that was..."—she paused —"my mother's triumph at her debut concert in London." Her eyes searched the ceiling. Our eyes followed. Nothing up there but ceiling tile. "For reasons that I shall not go into, my family's fortunes took us to Detroit, then north to dreadful Saginaw, and now here I am in Five Oaks, as your substitute teacher, for today, Thursday, October the eleventh. I believe it will be a good day: all the forecasts coincide. We shall start with your reading lesson. Take out your reading book. I believe it is called *Broad Horizons*, or something along those lines."

Jeannie Vermeesch raised her hand. Miss Ferenczi nodded at her. "Mr. Hibler always starts the day with the Pledge of Allegiance," Jeannie whined.

"Oh, does he? In that case," Miss Ferenczi said, "you must know it *very* well by now, and we certainly need not spend our time on it. No, no allegiance pledging on the premises today, by my reckoning. Not with so much sunlight coming into the room. A pledge does not suit my mood." She glanced at her watch. "Time *is* flying. Take out *Broad Horizons.*"

———

She disappointed us by giving us an ordinary lesson, complete with vocabulary and drills, comprehension questions, and recitation. She didn't seem to care for the material, however. She sighed every few minutes and rubbed her glasses with a frilly handkerchief that she withdrew, magician-style, from her left sleeve.

After reading we moved on to arithmetic. It was my favorite time of the morning, when the lazy autumn sunlight dazzled its way through ribbons of clouds past the windows on the east side of the classroom and crept across the linoleum floor. On the playground the first group of children, the kindergartners, were running on the quack grass just beyond the monkey bars. We were doing multiplication tables. Miss Ferenczi had made John Wazny stand up at his desk in the front row. He was supposed to go through the tables of six. From where I was sitting, I could smell the Vitalis soaked into John's plastered hair. He was doing fine until he came to six times eleven and six times twelve. "Six times eleven," he said, "is sixty-eight. Six times twelve is..." He put his fingers to his head, quickly and secretly sniffed his fingertips, and said, "...seventy-two." Then he sat down.

"Fine," Miss Ferenczi said. "Well now. That was very good."

"Miss Ferenczi!" One of the Eddy twins was waving her hand desperately in the air. "Miss Ferenczi! Miss Ferenczi!"

"Yes?"

"John said that six times eleven is sixty-eight and you said he was right!"

"*Did* I?" She gazed at the class with a jolly look breaking across her marionette's face. "Did I say that? Well, what *is* six times eleven?"

"It's sixty-six!"

She nodded. "Yes. So it is. But, and I know some people will not entirely agree with me, at some times it is sixty-eight."

"When? When is it sixty-eight?"

We were all waiting.

"In higher mathematics, which you children do not yet understand, six times eleven can be considered to be sixty-eight." She laughed through her nose. "In higher mathematics numbers are . . . more fluid. The only thing a number does is contain a certain amount of something. Think of water. A cup is not the only way to measure a certain amount of water, is it?" We were staring, shaking our heads. "You could use saucepans or thimbles. In either case, the water *would be the same.* Perhaps," she started again, "it would be better for you to think that six times eleven is sixty-eight only when I am in the room."

"Why is it sixty-eight," Mark Poole asked, "when you're in the room?"

"Because it's more interesting that way," she said, smiling very rapidly behind her blue-tinted glasses. "Besides, I'm your substitute teacher, am I not?" We all nodded. "Well, then, think of six times eleven equals sixty-eight as a substitute fact."

"A substitute fact?"

"Yes." Then she looked at us carefully. "Do you think," she asked, "that anyone is going to be hurt by a substitute fact?"

We looked back at her.

"Will the plants on the windowsill be hurt?" We glanced at them. There were sensitive plants thriving in a green plastic tray, and several wilted ferns in small clay pots. "Your dogs and cats, or your moms and dads?" She waited. "So," she concluded, "what's the problem?"

"But it's wrong," Janice Weber said, "isn't it?"

"What's your name, young lady?"

"Janice Weber."

"And you think it's wrong, Janice?"

"I was just asking."

"Well, all right. You were just asking. I think we've spent enough time on this matter by now, don't you, class? You are free to think what you like. When your teacher, Mr. Hibler, returns, six times eleven will be sixty-six again, you can rest assured. And it will be that for the rest of your lives in Five Oaks. Too bad, eh?" She raised her eyebrows and glinted herself at us. "But for now, it wasn't. So much for that. Let us go on to your assigned problems for today, as painstakingly outlined, I see, in Mr. Hibler's lesson plan. Take out a sheet of paper and write your names on the upper left-hand corner."

For the next half hour we did the rest of our arithmetic problems. We handed them in and then went on to spelling, my worst subject. Spelling always came before lunch. We were taking spelling dictation and looking at the clock. "Thorough," Miss Ferenczi said. "Boundary." She walked in the aisles between the desks, holding the spelling book open and looking down at our papers. "Balcony." I clutched my pencil. Somehow, the way she said those words, they seemed foreign, mis-voweled and mis-consonated. I stared down at what I had spelled. *Balconie.* I turned the pencil upside down and erased my mistake. *Balconey.* That looked better, but still incorrect. I cursed the world of spelling and tried erasing it again and saw the paper beginning to wear away. *Balkony.* Suddenly I felt a hand on my shoulder.

"I don't like that word either," Miss Ferenczi whispered, bent over, her mouth near my ear. "It's ugly. My feeling is, if you don't like a word, you don't have to use it." She straightened up, leaving behind a slight odor of Clorets.

At lunchtime we went out to get our trays of sloppy joes, peaches in heavy syrup, coconut cookies, and milk, and brought them back to the classroom, where Miss Ferenczi was sitting at the desk, eating a brown sticky thing she had unwrapped from tightly rubber-banded waxed paper. "Miss Ferenczi," I said, raising my hand. "You don't have to eat with us. You can eat with the other teachers. There's a teacher's lounge," I ended up, "next to the principal's office."

"No, thank you," she said. "I prefer it here."

"We've got a room monitor," I said. "Mrs. Eddy." I pointed to where Mrs. Eddy, Joyce and Judy's mother, sat silently at the back of the room, doing her knitting.

"That's fine," Miss Ferenczi said. "But I shall continue to eat here, with you children. I prefer it," she repeated.

"How come?" Wayne Razmer asked without raising his hand.

"I talked to the other teachers before class this morning," Miss Ferenczi said, biting into her brown food. "There was a great rattling of the words for the fewness of the ideas. I didn't care for their brand of hilarity. I don't like ditto-machine jokes."

"Oh," Wayne said.

"What's that you're eating?" Maxine Sylvester asked, twitching her nose. "Is it food?"

"It most certainly *is* food. It's a stuffed fig. I had to drive almost down to Detroit to get it. I also brought some smoked sturgeon. And this," she said, lifting some green leaves out of her lunchbox, "is raw spinach, cleaned this morning."

"Why're you eating raw spinach?" Maxine asked.

"It's good for you," Miss Ferenczi said. "More stimulating than soda pop or smelling salts." I bit into my sloppy joe and stared blankly out the window. An almost invisible moon was faintly silvered in the daytime autumn sky. "As far as food is concerned," Miss Ferenczi was saying, "you have to shuffle the pack. Mix it up. Too many people eat... well, never mind."

"Miss Ferenczi," Carol Peterson said, "what are we going to do this afternoon?"

"Well," she said, looking down at Mr. Hibler's lesson plan, "I see that your teacher, Mr. Hibler, has you scheduled for a unit on the

Egyptians." Carol groaned. "Yessss," Miss Ferenczi continued, "that is what we will do: the Egyptians. A remarkable people. Almost as remarkable as the Americans. But not quite." She lowered her head, did her quick smile, and went back to eating her spinach.

———

After noon recess we came back into the classroom and saw that Miss Ferenczi had drawn a pyramid on the blackboard close to her oak tree. Some of us who had been playing baseball were messing around in the back of the room, dropping the bats and gloves into the playground box, and Ray Schontzeler had just slugged me when I heard Miss Ferenczi's high-pitched voice, quavering with emotions. "Boys," she said, "come to order right this minute and take your seats. I do not wish to waste a minute of class time. Take out your geography books." We trudged to our desks and, still sweating, pulled out *Distant Lands and Their People*. "Turn to page forty-two." She waited for thirty seconds, then looked over at Kelly Munger. "Young man," she said, "why are you still fossicking in your desk?"

Kelly looked as if his foot had been stepped on. "Why am I what?"

"Why are you ... burrowing in your desk like that?"

"I'm lookin' for the book, Miss Ferenczi."

Bobby Kryzanowicz, the faultless brown-noser who sat in the first row by choice, softly said, "His name is Kelly Munger. He can't ever find his stuff. He always does that."

"I don't care what his name is, especially after lunch," Miss Ferenczi said. *"Where is your book?"*

"I just found it." Kelly was peering into his desk and with both hands pulled at the book, shoveling along in front of it several pencils and crayons, which fell into his lap and then to the floor.

"I hate a mess," Miss Ferenczi said. "I hate a mess in a desk or a mind. It's ... unsanitary. You wouldn't want your house at home to look like your desk at school, now, would you?" She didn't wait for an answer. "I should think not. A house at home should be as neat as human hands can make it. What were we talking about? Egypt. Page forty-two. I note from Mr. Hibler's lesson plan that you have been discussing the modes of Egyptian irrigation. Interesting, in my view, but not so interesting as what we are about to cover. The pyramids, and Egyptian slave labor. A plus on one side, a minus on the other." We had our books open to page forty-two, where there was a picture of a pyramid, but Miss Ferenczi wasn't looking at the book. Instead, she was staring at some object just outside the window.

"Pyramids," Miss Ferenczi said, still looking past the window. "I want you to think about pyramids. And what was inside. The bodies of the pharaohs, of course, and their attendant treasures. Scrolls. Perhaps," Miss Ferenczi said, her face gleeful but unsmiling, "these scrolls were novels for the pharaohs, helping them to pass the time in their long voyage through the centuries. But then, I am joking." I was looking at the lines on Miss Ferenczi's skin. "Pyramids," Miss Ferenczi went on, "were the repositories of special cosmic powers. The nature of a pyramid is to guide cosmic energy forces into a concentrated point. The Egyptians knew that; we have generally forgotten it. Did you know," she asked, walking to the side of the room so that she was standing by the coat closet, "that George Washington had Egyptian blood, from his grandmother? Certain features of the Constitution of the United States are notable for their Egyptian ideas."

Without glancing down at the book, she began to talk about the movement of souls in Egyptian religion. She said that when people die, their souls return to Earth in the form of carpenter ants or walnut trees, depending on how they behaved—"well or ill"—in life. She said that the Egyptians believed that people act the way they do because of magnetism produced by tidal forces in the solar system, forces produced by the sun and by its "planetary ally," Jupiter. Jupiter, she said, was a planet, as we had been told, but had "certain properties of stars." She was speaking very fast. She said that the Egyptians were great explorers and conquerors. She said that the greatest of all the conquerors, Genghis Khan, had had forty horses and forty young women killed on the site of his grave. We listened. No one tried to stop her. "I myself have been in Egypt," she said, "and have witnessed much dust and many brutalities." She said that an old man in Egypt who worked for a circus had personally shown her an animal in a cage, a monster, half bird and half lion. She said that this monster was called a gryphon and that she had heard about them but never seen them until she traveled to the outskirts of Cairo. She wrote the word out on the blackboard in large capital letters: GRYPHON. She said that Egyptian astronomers had discovered the planet Saturn but had not seen its rings. She said that the Egyptians were the first to discover that dogs, when they are ill, will not drink from rivers, but wait for rain, and hold their jaws open to catch it.

———

"She lies."

We were on the school bus home. I was sitting next to Carl Whiteside, who had bad breath and a huge collection of marbles. We were arguing. Carl thought she was lying. I said she wasn't, probably.

"I didn't believe that stuff about the bird," Carl said, "and what she told us about the pyramids? I didn't believe that, either. She didn't know what she was talking about."

"Oh yeah?" I had liked her. She was strange. I thought I could nail him. "If she was lying," I said, "what'd she say that was a lie?"

"Six times eleven isn't sixty-eight. It isn't ever. It's sixty-six, I know for a fact."

"She said so. She admitted it. What else did she lie about?"

"I don't know," he said. "Stuff."

"What stuff?"

"Well." He swung his legs back and forth. "You ever see an animal that was half lion and half bird?" He crossed his arms. "It sounded real fakey to me."

"It could happen," I said. I had to improvise, to outrage him. "I read in this newspaper my mom bought in the IGA about this scientist, this mad scientist in the Swiss Alps, and he's been putting genes and chromosomes and stuff together in test tubes, and he combined a human being and a hamster." I waited, for effect. "It's called a humster."

"You never." Carl was staring at me, his mouth open, his terrible bad breath making its way toward me. "What newspaper was it?"

"The National Enquirer," I said, "that they sell next to the cash registers." When I saw his look of recognition, I knew I had him. "And this mad scientist," I said, "his name was, um, Dr. Frankenbush." I realized belatedly that this name was a mistake and waited for Carl to notice its resemblance to the name of the other famous mad master of permutations, but he only sat there.

"A man and a hamster?" He was staring at me, squinting, his mouth opening in distaste. "Jeez. What'd it look like?"

———

When the bus reached my stop, I took off down our dirt road and ran up through the backyard, kicking the tire swing for good luck. I dropped my books on the back steps so I could hug and kiss our dog, Mr. Selby. Then I hurried inside. I could smell brussels sprouts cooking, my unfavorite vegetable. My mother was washing other vegetables in the kitchen sink, and my baby brother was hollering in his yellow playpen on the kitchen floor.

"Hi, Mom," I said, hopping around the playpen to kiss her. "Guess what?"

"I have no idea."

"We had this substitute today, Miss Ferenczi, and I'd never seen her before, and she had all these stories and ideas and stuff."

"Well. That's good." My mother looked out the window in front of the sink, her eyes on the pine woods west of our house. That time of the afternoon her skin always looked so white to me. Strangers always said my mother looked like Betty Crocker, framed by the giant spoon on the side of the Bisquick box. "Listen, Tommy," she said. "Would you please go upstairs and pick your clothes off the floor in the bathroom, and then go outside to the shed and put the shovel and ax away that your father left outside this morning?"

"She said that six times eleven was sometimes sixty-eight!" I said. "And she said she once saw a monster that was half lion and half bird." I waited. "In Egypt."

"Did you hear me?" my mother asked, raising her arm to wipe her forehead with the back of her hand. "You have chores to do."

"I know," I said. "I was just telling you about the substitute."

"It's very interesting," my mother said, quickly glancing down at me, "and we can talk about it later when your father gets home. But right now you have some work to do."

"Okay, Mom." I took a cookie out of the jar on the counter and was about to go outside when I had a thought. I ran into the living room, pulled out a dictionary next to the TV stand, and opened it to the Gs. After five minutes I found it. *Gryphon:* variant of griffin. *Griffin:* "a fabulous beast with the head and wings of an eagle and the body of a lion." Fabulous was right. I shouted with triumph and ran outside to put my father's tools in their proper places.

———

Miss Ferenczi was back the next day, slightly altered. She had pulled her hair down and twisted it into pigtails, with red rubber bands holding them tight one inch from the ends. She was wearing a green blouse and pink scarf, making her difficult to look at for a full class day. This time there was no pretense of doing a reading lesson or moving on to arithmetic. As soon as the bell rang, she simply began to talk.

She talked for forty minutes straight. There seemed to be less connection between her ideas, but the ideas themselves were, as the dictionary would say, fabulous. She said she had heard of a huge jewel, in what she called the antipodes, that was so brilliant that when light shone into it at a certain angle it would blind whoever was looking at its center. She said the biggest diamond in the world was cursed and had killed everyone who owned it, and that by a trick of fate it was called the Hope Diamond. Diamonds are magic, she said, and this is why women wear them on their fingers, as a sign of the magic of womanhood. Men have strength, Miss Ferenczi said, but no true magic. That is why men fall in love with women but women do not fall in love with men: they just love being loved. George Washington had died because of a mistake he made about a diamond. Washington was not the first *true* President, but she didn't say who was. In some places in the world, she said, men and women still live in the trees and eat monkeys for breakfast. Their doctors are magicians. At the bottom of the sea are creatures thin as pancakes who have never been studied by scientists because when you take them up to air, the fish explode.

There was not a sound in the classroom, except for Miss Ferenczi's voice, and Donna DeShano's coughing. No one even went to the bathroom.

Beethoven, she said, had not been deaf; it was a trick to make himself famous, and it worked. As she talked, Miss Ferenczi's pigtails swung back and forth. There are trees in the world, she said, that eat meat: their leaves are sticky and close up on bugs like hands. She lifted her hands and brought them together, palm to palm. Venus, which most people think is the next closest planet to the sun, is not always closer, and, besides, it is the planet of greatest mystery because of its thick cloud cover. "I know what lies underneath those clouds," Miss Ferenczi said, and waited. After the silence, she said, "Angels. Angels live under those clouds." She said that angels were not invisible to everyone and were in fact smarter than most people. They did not dress in robes as was often claimed but instead wore formal evening clothes, as if they were about to attend a concert. Often angels *do* attend concerts and sit in the aisles, where, she said, most people pay no attention to them. She said the most terrible angel had the shape of the Sphinx. "There is no running away from that one," she said. She said that unquenchable fires burn just under the surface of the earth in Ohio, and that the baby Mozart fainted dead away in his cradle when he first heard the sound of a trumpet. She said that someone named Narzim al Harrardim was the greatest writer who ever lived. She said that planets control behavior, and anyone conceived during a solar eclipse would be born with webbed feet.

"I know you children like to hear these things," she said, "these secrets, and that is why I am telling you all this." We nodded. It was better than doing comprehension questions for the readings in *Broad Horizons*.

"I will tell you one more story," she said, "and then we will have to do arithmetic." She leaned over, and her voice grew soft. "There is no death," she said. "You must never be afraid. Never. That which is, cannot die. It will change into different earthly and unearthly elements, but I know this as sure as I stand here in front of you, and I swear it: you must not be afraid. I have seen this truth with these eyes. I know it because in a dream God kissed me. Here." And she pointed with her right index finger to the side of her head, below the mouth where the vertical lines were carved into her skin.

———

Absentmindedly we all did our arithmetic problems. At recess the class was out on the playground, but no one was playing. We were all standing in small groups, talking about Miss Ferenczi. We didn't know if she was crazy, or what. I looked out beyond the playground, at the rusted cars piled in a small heap behind a clump of sumac, and I wanted to see shapes there, approaching me.

———

On the way home, Carl sat next to me again. He didn't say much, and I didn't either. At last he turned to me. "You know what she said about the leaves that close up on bugs?"

"Huh?"

"The leaves," Carl insisted. "The meat-eating plants. I know it's true. I saw it on television. The leaves have this icky glue that the plants have got smeared all over them and the insects can't get off 'cause they're stuck. I saw it." He seemed demoralized. "She's tellin' the truth."

"Yeah."

"You think she's seen all those angels?"

I shrugged.

"I don't think she has," Carl informed me. "I think she made that part up."

"There's a tree," I suddenly said. I was looking out the window at the farms along County Road H. I knew every barn, every broken windmill, every fence, every anhydrous ammonia tank, by heart. "There's a tree that's . . . that I've seen . . ."

"Don't you try to do it," Carl said. "You'll just sound like a jerk."

I kissed my mother. She was standing in front of the stove. "How was your day?" she asked.

"Fine."

"Did you have Miss Ferenczi again?"

"Yeah."

"Well?"

"She was fine. Mom," I asked, "can I go to my room?"

"No," she said, "not until you've gone out to the vegetable garden and picked me a few tomatoes." She glanced at the sky. "I think it's going to rain. Skedaddle and do it now. Then you come back inside and watch your brother for a few minutes while I go upstairs. I need to clean up before dinner." She looked down at me. "You're looking a little pale, Tommy." She touched the back of her hand to my forehead and I felt her diamond ring against my skin. "Do you feel all right?"

"I'm fine," I said, and went out to pick the tomatoes.

Coughing mutedly, Mr. Hibler was back the next day, slipping lozenges into his mouth when his back was turned at forty-five-minute intervals and asking us how much of his prepared lesson plan Miss Ferenczi had followed. Edith Atwater took the responsibility for the class of explaining to Mr. Hibler that the substitute hadn't always done exactly what he, Mr. Hibler, would have done, but we had worked hard even though she talked a lot. About what? he asked. All kinds of things, Edith said. I sort of forgot. To our relief, Mr. Hibler seemed not at all interested in what Miss Ferenczi had said to fill the day. He probably thought it was woman's talk: unserious and not suited for school. It was enough that he had a pile of arithmetic problems from us to correct.

For the next month, the sumac turned a distracting red in the field, and the sun traveled toward the southern sky, so that its rays reached Mr. Hibler's Halloween display on the bulletin board in the back of the room, fading the pumpkin head scarecrow from orange to tan. Every three days I measured how much farther the sun had moved toward the southern horizon by making small marks with my black Crayola on the north wall, ant-sized marks only I knew were there.

And then in early December, four days after the first permanent snowfall, she appeared again in our classroom. The minute she came in the door, I felt my heart begin to pound. Once again, she was different: this time, her hair hung straight down and seemed hardly to have been combed. She hadn't brought her lunchbox with her, but she was carrying what seemed to be a small box. She greeted all of us and talked about the weather. Donna DeShano had to remind her to take her overcoat off.

When the bell to start the day finally rang, Miss Ferenczi looked out at all of us and said, "Children, I have enjoyed your company in the past, and today I am going to reward you." She held up the small box. "Do you know what this is?" She waited. "Of course you don't. It is a Tarot pack."

Edith Atwater raised her hand. "What's a Tarot pack, Miss Ferenczi?"

"It is used to tell fortunes," she said. "And that is what I shall do this morning. I shall tell your fortunes, as I have been taught to do."

"What's fortune?" Bobby Kryzanowicz asked.

"The future, young man. I shall tell you what your future will be. I can't do your whole future, of course. I shall have to limit myself to the five-card system, the wands, cups, swords, pentacles, and the higher arcanes. Now who wants to be first?"

There was a long silence. Then Carol Peterson raised her hand.

"All right," Miss Ferenczi said. She divided the pack into five smaller packs and walked back to Carol's desk, in front of mine. "Pick one card from each one of these packs," she said. I saw that Carol had a four of cups and a six of swords, but I couldn't see the other cards. Miss Ferenczi studied the cards on Carol's desk for a minute. "Not bad," she said. "I do not see much higher education. Probably an early marriage. Many children. There's something bleak and dreary here, but I can't tell what. Perhaps just the tasks of a housewife life. I think you'll do very well, for the most part." She smiled at Carol, a smile with a certain lack of interest. "Who wants to be next?"

Carl Whiteside raised his hand slowly.

"Yes," Miss Ferenczi said, "let's do a boy." She walked over to where Carl sat. After he picked his five cards, she gazed at them for a long time. "Travel," she said. "Much distant travel. You might go into the army. Not too much romantic interest here. A late marriage, if at all. But the Sun in your major arcana, that's a very good card." She giggled. "You'll have a happy life."

Next I raised my hand. She told me my future. She did the same with Bobby Kryzanowicz, Kelly Munger, Edith Atwater, and Kim Foor. Then she came to Wayne Razmer. He picked his five cards, and I could see that the Death card was one of them.

"What's your name?" Miss Ferenczi asked.

"Wayne."

"Well, Wayne," she said, "you will undergo a great metamorphosis, a change, before you become an adult. Your earthly element will no doubt leap higher, because you seem to be a sweet boy. This card, this nine of swords, tells me of suffering and desolation. And this ten of wands, well, that's a heavy load."

"What about this one?" Wayne pointed at the Death card.

"It means, my sweet, that you will die soon." She gathered up the cards. We were all looking at Wayne. "But do not fear," she said. "It is not really death. Just change. Out of your earthly shape." She put the cards on Mr. Hibler's desk. "And now, let's do some arithmetic."

———

At lunchtime Wayne went to Mr. Faegre, the principal, and informed him of what Miss Ferenczi had done. During the noon recess, we saw Miss Ferenczi drive out of the parking lot in her rusting green Rambler American. I stood under the slide, listening to the other kids coasting down and landing in the little depressive bowls at the bottom. I was kicking stones and tugging at my hair right up to the moment when I saw Wayne come out to the playground. He smiled, the dead fool, and with the fingers of his right hand he was showing everyone how he had told on Miss Ferenczi.

I made my way toward Wayne, pushing myself past two girls from another class. He was watching me with his little pinhead eyes.

"You told," I shouted at him. "She was just kidding."

"She shouldn't have," he shouted back. "We were supposed to be doing arithmetic."

"She just scared you," I said. "You're a chicken. You're a chicken, Wayne. You are. Scared of a little card," I singsonged.

Wayne fell at me, his two fists hammering down on my nose. I gave him a good one in the stomach and then I tried for his head. Aiming my fist, I saw that he was crying. I slugged him.

"She was right," I yelled. "She was always right! She told the truth!" Other kids were whooping. "You were just scared, that's all!"

And then large hands pulled at us, and it was my turn to speak to Mr. Faegre.

———

In the afternoon Miss Ferenczi was gone, and my nose was stuffed with cotton clotted with blood, and my lip had swelled, and our class had been combined with Mrs. Mantei's sixth-grade class for a crowded afternoon science unit on insect life in ditches and swamps. I knew where Mrs. Mantei lived: she had a new house trailer just down the road from us, at the Clearwater Park. She was no mystery. Somehow she and Mr. Bodine, the other fourth-grade teacher, had managed to fit forty-five desks into the room. Kelly Munger asked if Miss Ferenczi had been arrested, and Mrs. Mantei said no, of course not. All that afternoon, until the buses came to pick us up, we learned about field crickets and two-striped grasshoppers, water bugs, cicadas, mosquitoes, flies, and moths. We learned about insects' hard outer shell, the exoskeleton, and the usual parts of the mouth, including the labrum, mandible, maxilla, and glossa. We learned about compound eyes, and the four-stage metamorphosis from egg to larva to pupa to adult. We learned something, but not much, about mating. Mrs. Mantei drew, very skillfully, the internal anatomy of the grasshopper on the blackboard. We learned about the dance of the honeybee, directing other bees in the hive to pollen. We found out about which insects were pests to man, and which were not. On lined white pieces of paper we made lists of insects we might actually see, then a list of insects too small to be clearly visible, such as fleas; Mrs. Mantei said that our assignment would be to memorize these lists for the next day, when Mr. Hibler would certainly return and test us on our knowledge.

———

CHARLES BAXTER was born in Minneapolis in 1947. He teaches in the English department at the University of Minnesota.

DOCTOR JACK-O'-LANTERN

Richard Yates

All Miss Price had been told about the new boy was that he'd spent most of his life in some kind of orphanage, and that the gray-haired "aunt and uncle" with whom he now lived were really foster parents, paid by the Welfare Department of the City of New York. A less dedicated or less imaginative teacher might have pressed for more details, but Miss Price was content with the rough outline. It was enough, in fact, to fill her with a sense of mission that shone from her eyes, as plain as love, from the first morning he joined the fourth grade.

He arrived early and sat in the back row—his spine very straight, his ankles crossed precisely under the desk and his hands folded on the very center of its top, as if symmetry might make him less conspicuous—and while the other children were filing in and settling down, he received a long, expressionless stare from each of them.

"We have a new classmate this morning," Miss Price said, laboring the obvious in a way that made everybody want to giggle. "His name is Vincent Sabella and he comes from New York City. I know we'll all do our best to make him feel at home."

This time they all swung around to stare at once, which caused him to duck his head slightly and shift his weight from one buttock to the other. Ordinarily, the fact of someone's coming from New York might have held a certain prestige, for to most of the children the city was an awesome, adult place that swallowed up their fathers every day, and which they themselves were permitted to visit only rarely, in their best clothes, as a treat. But anyone could see at a glance that Vincent Sabella had nothing whatever to do with skyscrapers. Even if you could ignore his tangled black hair and gray skin, his clothes would have given him away: absurdly new corduroys, absurdly old sneakers and a yellow sweatshirt, much too small, with the shredded remains of a Mickey Mouse design stamped on its chest. Clearly, he was from the part of New York that you had to pass through on the train to Grand Central—the part where people hung bedding over their windowsills and leaned out on it all day in a trance of boredom, and where you got vistas of straight, deep streets, one after another, all alike in the clutter of their sidewalks and all swarming with gray boys at play in some desperate kind of ball game.

The girls decided that he wasn't very nice and turned away, but the boys lingered in their scrutiny, looking him up and down with faint smiles. This was the kind of kid they were accustomed to thinking of as "tough," the kind whose stares had made all of them uncomfortable at one time or another in unfamiliar neighborhoods; here was a unique chance for retaliation.

"What would you like us to call you, Vincent?" Miss Price inquired. "I mean, do you prefer Vincent, or Vince, or—or what?" (It was purely an academic question; even Miss Price knew that the boys would call him "Sabella" and that the girls wouldn't call him anything at all.)

"Vinny's okay," he said in a strange, croaking voice that had evidently yelled itself hoarse down the ugly streets of his home.

"I'm afraid I didn't hear you," she said, craning her pretty head forward and to one side so that a heavy lock of hair swung free of one shoulder. "Did you say 'Vince'?"

"Vinny, I said," he said again, squirming.

"Vincent, is it? All right, then, Vincent." A few of the class giggled, but nobody bothered to correct her; it would be more fun to let the mistake continue.

"I won't take time to introduce you to everyone by name, Vincent," Miss Price went on, "because I think it would be simpler just to let you learn the names as we go along, don't you? Now, we won't expect you to take any real part in the work for the first day or so; just take your time, and if there's anything you don't understand, why, don't be afraid to ask."

He made an unintelligible croak and smiled fleetingly, just enough to show that the roots of his teeth were green.

"Now then," Miss Price said, getting down to business. "This is Monday morning, and so the first thing on the program is reports. Who'd like to start off?"

Vincent Sabella was momentarily forgotten as six or seven hands went up, and Miss Price drew back in mock confusion. "Goodness, we do have a lot of reports this morning," she said. The idea of the reports—a fifteen-minute period every Monday in which the children were encouraged to relate their experiences over the weekend—was Miss Price's own, and she took a pardonable pride in it. The principal had commended her on it at a recent staff meeting, pointing out that it made a splendid bridge between the worlds of school and home, and that it was a fine way for children to learn poise and assurance. It called for intelligent supervision—the shy children had to be drawn out and the show-offs curbed—but in general, as Miss Price had assured the principal, it was fun for everyone. She particularly hoped it would be fun today, to help put Vincent Sabella at ease, and that was why she chose Nancy Parker to start off; there was nobody like Nancy for holding an audience.

The others fell silent as Nancy moved gracefully to the head of the room; even the two or three girls who secretly despised her had to feign enthrallment when she spoke (she was that popular), and every boy in the class, who at recess liked nothing better than to push her shrieking into the mud, was unable to watch her without an idiotically tremulous smile.

"Well—" she began, and then she clapped a hand over her mouth while everyone laughed.

"Oh, *Nancy*," Miss Price said. "You *know* the rule about starting a report with 'well.'"

Nancy knew the rule; she had only broken it to get the laugh. Now she let her fit of giggles subside, ran her fragile forefingers down the side seams of her skirt, and began again in the proper way. "On Friday my whole family went for a ride in my brother's new car. My brother bought this new Pontiac last week, and he wanted to take us all for a ride—you know, to try it out and everything? So we went into White Plains and had dinner in a restaurant there, and then we all wanted to go see this movie, 'Doctor Jekyll and Mr. Hyde,' but my brother said it was too horrible and everything, and I wasn't old enough to enjoy it—oh, he made me so mad! And then, let's see. On Saturday I stayed home all day and helped my mother make my sister's wedding dress. My sister's engaged to be married, you see, and my mother's making this wedding dress for her? So we did that, and then on Sunday this friend of my brother's came over for dinner, and then they both had to get back to college that night, and I was allowed to stay up late and say goodbye to them and everything, and I guess that's all." She always had a sure instinct for keeping her performance brief—or rather, for making it seem briefer than it really was.

"Very good, Nancy," Miss Price said. "Now, who's next?"

Warren Berg was next, elaborately hitching up his pants as he made his way down the aisle. "On Saturday I went over to Bill Stringer's house for lunch," he began in his direct, man-to-man style, and Bill Stringer wriggled bashfully in the front row. Warren Berg and Bill Stringer were great friends, and their reports often overlapped. "And then after lunch we went into White Plains, on our bikes. Only we *saw* 'Doctor Jekyll and Mr. Hyde.'" Here he nodded his head in Nancy's direction, and Nancy got another laugh by making a little whimper of envy. "It was real good, too," he went on, with mounting excitement. "It's all about this guy who—"

"About *a man* who," Miss Price corrected.

"About a man who mixes up this chemical, like, that he drinks? And whenever he drinks this chemical, he changes into this real monster, like? You see him drink this chemical, and then you see his hands start to get all scales all over them, like a reptile and everything, and then you see his face start to change into this real horrible-looking face—with fangs and all? Sticking out of his mouth?"

All the girls shuddered in pleasure. "Well," Miss Price said, "I think Nancy's brother was probably wise in not wanting her to see it. What did you do *after* the movie, Warren?"

There was a general *"Aw-w-w!"* of disappointment—everyone wanted to hear more about the scales and fangs—but Miss Price never liked to let the reports degenerate into accounts of movies. Warren continued without much enthusiasm: all they had done after the movie was fool around Bill Stringer's yard until suppertime. "And then on Sunday," he said, brightening again, "Bill Stringer came over to *my* house, and my dad helped us rig up this old tire on this long rope? From a tree? There's this steep hill down behind my house, you see—this ravine, like?—and we hung this tire so that what you do is, you take the tire and run a little ways and then lift your feet, and you go swinging way, way out over the ravine and back again."

"That sounds like fun," Miss Price said, glancing at her watch.

"Oh, it's *fun,* all right," Warren conceded. But then he hitched up his pants again and added, with a puckering of his forehead, "'Course, it's pretty dangerous. You let go of that tire or anything, you'd get a bad fall. Hit a rock or anything, you'd probably break your leg, or your spine. But my dad said he trusted us both to look out for our own safety."

"Well, I'm afraid that's all we'll have time for, Warren," Miss Price said. "Now, there's just time for one more report. Who's ready? Arthur Cross?"

There was a soft groan, because Arthur Cross was the biggest dope in class and his reports were always a bore. This time it turned out to be something tedious about going to visit his uncle on Long Island. At one point he made a slip—he said "botormoat" instead of "motorboat"—and everyone laughed with the particular edge of scorn they reserved for Arthur Cross. But the laughter died abruptly when it was joined by a harsh, dry croaking from the back of the room. Vincent Sabella was laughing too, green teeth and all, and they all had to glare at him until he stopped.

When the reports were over, everyone settled down for school. It was recess time before any of the children thought much about Vincent Sabella again, and then they thought of him only to make sure he was left out of everything. He wasn't in the group of boys that clustered around the horizontal bar to take turns at skinning-the-cat, or the group that whispered in a far corner of the playground, hatching a plot to push Nancy Parker in the mud. Nor was he in the larger group, of which even Arthur Cross was a member, that chased itself in circles in a frantic variation of the game of tag. He couldn't join the girls, of course, or the boys from other classes, and so he joined nobody. He stayed on the apron of the playground, close to school, and for the first part of the recess he pretended to be very busy with the laces of his sneakers. He would squat to undo and retie them, straighten up and take a few experimental steps in a springy, athletic way, and then get down and go to work on them again. After five minutes of this he gave it up, picked up a handful of pebbles and began shying them at an invisible target several yards away. That was good for another five minutes, but then there were still five minutes left, and he could think of nothing to do but stand there, first with his hands in his pockets, then with his hands on his hips, and then with his arms folded in a manly way across his chest.

Miss Price stood watching all this from the doorway, and she spent the full recess wondering if she ought to go out and do something about it. She guessed it would be better not to.

She managed to control the same impulse at recess the next day, and every other day that week, though every day it grew more difficult. But one thing she could not control was a tendency to let her anxiety show in class. All Vincent Sabella's errors in schoolwork were publicly excused, even those having nothing to do with his newness, and all his accomplishments were singled out for special mention. Her campaign to build him up was painfully obvious, and never more so than when she tried to make it subtle; once, for instance, in explaining an arithmetic problem, she said, "Now, suppose Warren Berg and Vincent Sabella went to the store with fifteen cents each, and candy bars cost ten cents. How many candy bars would each boy have?" By the end of the week he was well on the way to becoming the worst possible kind of teacher's pet, a victim of the teacher's pity.

On Friday she decided the best thing to do would be to speak to him privately, and try to draw him out. She could say something about the pictures he had painted in art class—that would do for an opening—and she decided to do it at lunchtime.

The only trouble was that lunchtime, next to recess, was the most trying part of Vincent Sabella's day. Instead of going home for an hour as the other children did, he brought his lunch to school in a wrinkled paper bag and ate it in the classroom, which always made for a certain amount of awkwardness. The last children to leave would see him still seated apologetically at his desk, holding his paper bag, and anyone who happened to straggle back later for a forgotten hat or sweater would surprise him in the middle of his meal—perhaps shielding a hard-boiled egg from view or wiping mayonnaise from his mouth with a furtive hand. It was a situation that Miss Price did not improve by walking up to him while the room was still half full of children and sitting prettily on the edge of the desk beside his, making it clear that she was cutting her own lunch hour short in order to be with him.

"Vincent," she began, "I've been meaning to tell you how much I enjoyed those pictures of yours. They're really very good."

He mumbled something and shifted his eyes to the cluster of departing children at the door. She went right on talking and smiling, elaborating on her praise of the pictures; and finally, after the door had closed behind the last child, he was able to give her his attention. He did so tentatively at first; but the more she talked, the more he seemed to relax, until she realized she was putting him at ease. It was as simple and as gratifying as stroking a cat. She had finished with the pictures now and moved on, triumphantly, to broader fields of praise. "It's never easy," she was saying, "to come to a new school and adjust yourself to the—well, the new work, and new working methods, and I think you've done a splendid job so far. I really do. But tell me, do you think you're going to like it here?"

He looked at the floor just long enough to make his reply—"It's awright"—and then his eyes stared into hers again.

"I'm so glad. Please don't let me interfere with your lunch, Vincent. Do go ahead and eat, that is, if you don't mind my sitting here with you." But it was now abundantly clear that he didn't mind at all, and he began to unwrap a bologna sandwich with what she felt sure was the best appetite he'd had all week. It wouldn't even have mattered very much now if someone from the class had come in and watched, though it was probably just as well that no one did.

Miss Price sat back more comfortably on the desk top, crossed her legs and allowed one slim stockinged foot to slip part of the way out of its moccasin. "Of course," she went on, "it always does take a little time to sort of get your bearings in a new school. For one thing, well, it's never too easy for the new member of the class to make friends with the other members. What I mean is, you mustn't mind if the others seem a little rude to you at first. Actually, they're just as anxious to make friends as you are, but they're shy. All it takes is a little time, and a little effort on your part as well as theirs. Not too much, of course, but a little. Now for instance, these reports we have Monday mornings—they're a fine way for people to get to know one another. A person never feels he has to make a report; it's just a thing he can do if he wants to. And that's only one way of helping others to know the kind of person you are; there are lots and lots of ways. The main thing to remember is that making friends is the most natural thing in the world, and it's only a question of time until you have all the friends you want. And in the meantime, Vincent, I hope you'll consider *me* your friend, and feel free to call on me for whatever advice or anything you might need. Will you do that?"

He nodded, swallowing.

"Good." She stood up and smoothed her skirt over her long thighs. "Now I must go or I'll be late for *my* lunch. But I'm glad we had this little talk, Vincent, and I hope we'll have others."

It was probably a lucky thing that she stood up when she did, for if she'd stayed on that desk a minute longer Vincent Sabella would have thrown his arms around her and buried his face in the warm gray flannel of her lap, and that might have been enough to confuse the most dedicated and imaginative of teachers.

———

At report time on Monday morning, nobody was more surprised than Miss Price when Vincent Sabella's smudged hand was among the first and most eager to rise. Apprehensively she considered letting someone else start off, but then, for fear of hurting his feelings, she said, "All right, Vincent," in as matter-of-fact a way as she could manage.

There was a suggestion of muffled titters from the class as he walked confidently to the head of the room and turned to face his audience. He looked, if anything, too confident: there were signs, in the way he held his shoulders and the way his eyes shone, of the terrible poise of panic.

"Saturday I seen that pitcha," he announced.

"Saw, Vincent," Miss Price corrected gently.

"That's what I mean," he said; "I sore that pitcha. 'Doctor Jack-o'-lantern and Mr. Hide.'"

There was a burst of wild, delighted laughter and a chorus of correction: "Doctor *Jekyll!*"

He was unable to speak over the noise. Miss Price was on her feet, furious. "It's a *perfectly natural mistake!*" she was saying. "There's no reason for any of you to be so rude. Go on, Vincent, and please excuse this very silly interruption." The laughter subsided, but the class continued to shake their heads derisively from side to side. It hadn't, of course, been a perfectly natural mistake at all; for one thing it proved that he was a hopeless dope, and for another it proved that he was lying.

"That's what I mean," he continued. "'Doctor Jackal and Mr. Hide.' I got it a little mixed up. Anyways, I seen all about where his teet' start comin' outa his mout' and all like that, and I thought it was very good. And then on Sunday my mudda and fodda come out to see me in this car they got. This Buick. My fodda siz, 'Vinny, wanna go for a little ride?' I siz, 'Sure, where yiz goin'?' He siz, 'Anyplace ya like.' So I siz, 'Let's go out in the country a ways, get on one of them big roads and make some time.' So we go out—oh, I guess fifty, sixty miles—and we're cruisin' along this highway, when this cop starts tailin' us? My fodda siz, 'Don't worry, we'll shake him,' and he steps on it, see? My mudda's gettin' pretty scared, but my fodda siz, 'Don't worry, dear.' He's tryin' to make this turn, see, so he can get off the highway and shake the cop? But just when he's makin' the turn, the cop opens up and starts shootin', see?"

By this time the few members of the class who could bear to look at him at all were doing so with heads on one side and mouths partly open, the way you look at a broken arm or a circus freak.

"We just barely made it," Vincent went on, his eyes gleaming, "and this one bullet got my fodda in the shoulder. Didn't hurt him bad—just grazed him, like—so my mudda bandaged it up for him and all, but he couldn't do no more drivin' after that, and we had to get him to a doctor, see? So my fodda siz, 'Vinny, think you can drive a ways?' I siz, 'Sure, if you show me how.' So he showed me how to work the gas and the brake, and all like that, and I drove to the doctor. My mudda siz, 'I'm prouda you, Vinny, drivin' all by yourself.' So anyways, we got to the doctor, got my fodda fixed up and all, and then he drove us back home." He was breathless. After an uncertain pause he said, "And that's all." Then he walked quickly back to his desk, his stiff new corduroy pants whistling faintly with each step.

"Well, that was very—entertaining, Vincent," Miss Price said, trying to act as if nothing had happened. "Now, who's next?" But nobody raised a hand.

Recess was worse than usual for him that day; at least it was until he found a place to hide—a narrow concrete alley, blind except for several closed fire-exit doors, that cut between two sections of the school building. It was reassuringly dismal and cool in there—he could stand with his back to the wall and his eyes guarding the entrance, and the noises of recess were as remote as the sunshine. But when the bell rang he had to go back to class, and in another hour it was lunchtime.

Miss Price left him alone until her own meal was finished. Then, after standing with one hand on the doorknob for a full minute to gather courage, she went in and sat beside him for another little talk, just as he was trying to swallow the last of a pimento-cheese sandwich.

"Vincent," she began, "we all enjoyed your report this morning, but I think we would have enjoyed it more—a great deal more—if you'd told us something about your real life instead. I mean," she hurried on, "for instance, I noticed you were wearing a nice new windbreaker this morning. It *is* new, isn't it? And did your aunt buy it for you over the weekend?"

He did not deny it.

"Well then, why couldn't you have told us about going to the store with your aunt, and buying the windbreaker, and whatever you did afterwards. That would have made a perfectly good report." She paused, and for the first time looked steadily into his eyes. "You do understand what I'm trying to say, don't you, Vincent?"

He wiped crumbs of bread from his lips, looked at the floor, and nodded.

"And you'll remember next time, won't you?"

He nodded again. "Please may I be excused, Miss Price?"

"Of course you may."

He went to the boys' lavatory and vomited. Afterwards he washed his face and drank a little water, and then he returned to the classroom. Miss Price was busy at her desk now, and didn't look up. To avoid getting involved with her again, he wandered out to the cloakroom and sat on one of the long benches, where he picked up someone's discarded overshoe and turned it over and over in his hands. In a little while he heard the chatter of returning children, and to avoid being discovered there, he got up and went to the fire-exit door. Pushing it open, he found that it gave onto the alley he had hidden in that morning, and he slipped outside. For a minute or two he just stood there, looking at the blankness of the concrete wall; then he found a piece of chalk in his pocket and wrote out all the dirty words he could think of, in block letters a foot high. He had put down four words and was trying to remember a fifth when he heard a shuffling at the door behind him. Arthur Cross was there, holding the door open and reading the words with wide eyes. "Boy," he said in an awed half-whisper. "Boy, you're gonna get it. You're really gonna *get* it."

Startled, and then suddenly calm, Vincent Sabella palmed his chalk, hooked his thumbs in his belt and turned on Arthur Cross with a menacing look. "Yeah?" he inquired. "Who's gonna squeal on me?"

"Well, nobody's gonna *squeal* on you," Arthur Cross said uneasily, "but you shouldn't go around writing—"

"Arright," Vincent said, advancing a step. His shoulders were slumped, his head thrust forward and his eyes narrowed, like Edward G. Robinson. "Arright. That's all I wanna know. I don't like squealers, unnastand?"

While he was saying this, Warren Berg and Bill Stringer appeared in the doorway—just in time to hear it and to see the words on the wall before Vincent turned on them. "And that goes fa you too, unnastand?" he said. "Both a yiz."

And the remarkable thing was that both their faces fell into the same foolish, defensive smile that Arthur Cross was wearing. It wasn't until they had glanced at each other that they were able to meet his eyes with the proper degree of contempt, and by then it was too late. "Think you're pretty smart, don'tcha, Sabella?" Bill Stringer said.

"Never mind what I think," Vincent told him. "You heard what I said. Now let's get back inside."

And they could do nothing but move aside to make way for him, and follow him dumfounded into the cloakroom.

It was Nancy Parker who squealed—although, of course, with someone like Nancy Parker you didn't think of it as squealing. She had heard everything from the cloakroom; as soon as the boys came in she peeked into the alley, saw the words and, setting her face in a prim frown, went straight to Miss Price. Miss Price was just about to call the class to order for the afternoon when Nancy came up and whispered in her ear. They both disappeared into the cloak-room—from which, after a moment, came the sound of the fire-exit door being abruptly slammed—and when they returned to class Nancy was flushed with righteousness, Miss Price very pale. No announcement was made. Classes proceeded in the ordinary way all afternoon, though it was clear that Miss Price was upset, and it wasn't until she was dismissing the children at three o'clock that she brought the thing into the open. "Will Vincent Sabella please remain seated?" She nodded at the rest of the class. "That's all."

While the room was clearing out she sat at her desk, closed her eyes and massaged the frail bridge of her nose with thumb and fore-finger, sorting out half-remembered fragments of a book she had once read on the subject of seriously disturbed children. Perhaps, after all, she should never have undertaken the responsibility of Vincent Sabella's loneliness. Perhaps the whole thing called for the attention of a specialist. She took a deep breath.

"Come over here and sit beside me, Vincent," she said, and when he had settled himself, she looked at him. "I want you to tell me the truth. Did you write those words on the wall outside?"

He stared at the floor.

"Look at me," she said, and he looked at her. She had never looked prettier: her cheeks slightly flushed, her eyes shining and her sweet mouth pressed into a self-conscious frown. "First of all," she said, handing him a small enameled basin streaked with poster paint, "I want you to take this to the boys' room and fill it with hot water and soap."

He did as he was told, and when he came back, carrying the basin carefully to keep the suds from spilling, she was sorting out some old rags in the bottom drawer of her desk. "Here," she said, selecting one and shutting the drawer in a businesslike way. "This will do. Soak this up." She led him back to the fire exit and stood in the alley watching him, silently, while he washed off all the words.

When the job had been done, and the rag and basin put away, they sat down at Miss Price's desk again. "I suppose you think I'm angry with you, Vincent," she said. "Well, I'm not. I almost wish I could be angry—that would make it much easier—but instead I'm hurt. I've tried to be a good friend to you, and I thought you wanted to be my friend too. But this kind of thing—well, it's very hard to be friendly with a person who'd do a thing like that."

She saw, gratefully, that there were tears in his eyes. "Vincent, perhaps I understand some things better than you think. Perhaps I understand that sometimes, when a person does a thing like that, it isn't really because he wants to hurt anyone, but only because he's unhappy. He knows it isn't a good thing to do, and he even knows it isn't going to make him any happier afterwards, but he goes ahead and does it anyway. Then when he finds he's lost a friend, he's terribly sorry, but it's too late. The thing is done."

She allowed this somber note to reverberate in the silence of the room for a little while before she spoke again. "I won't be able to forget this, Vincent. But perhaps, just this once, we can still be friends—as long as I understand that you didn't mean to hurt me. But you must promise me that you won't forget it either. Never forget that when you do a thing like that, you're going to hurt people who want very much to like you, and in that way you're going to hurt yourself. Will you promise me to remember that, dear?"

The "dear" was as involuntary as the slender hand that reached out and held the shoulder of his sweatshirt; both made his head hang lower than before.

"All right," she said. "You may go now."

He got his windbreaker out of the cloakroom and left, avoiding the tired uncertainty of her eyes. The corridors were deserted, and dead silent except for the hollow, rhythmic knocking of a janitor's push-broom against some distant wall. His own rubber-soled tread only added to the silence; so did the lonely little noise made by the zipping-up of his windbreaker, and so did the faint mechanical sigh of the heavy front door. The silence made it all the more startling when he found, several yards down the concrete walk outside, that two boys were walking beside him: Warren Berg and Bill Stringer. They were both smiling at him in an eager, almost friendly way.

"What'd she do to ya, anyway?" Bill Stringer asked.

Caught off guard, Vincent barely managed to put on his Edward G. Robinson face in time. "Nunnya business," he said, and walked faster.

"No, listen—wait up, hey," Warren Berg said, as they trotted to keep up with him. "What'd she do, anyway? She bawl ya out, or what? Wait up, hey, Vinny."

The name made him tremble all over. He had to jam his hands in his windbreaker pockets and force himself to keep on walking; he had to force his voice to be steady when he said "Nunnya *business,* I told ya. Lea' me alone."

But they were right in step with him now. "Boy, she must of given you the works," Warren Berg persisted. "What'd she say, anyway? C'mon, tell us, Vinny."

This time the name was too much for him. It overwhelmed his resistance and made his softening knees slow down to a slack, conversational stroll. "She din say nothin'" he said at last; and then after a dramatic pause he added, "She let the ruler do her talkin' for her."

"The *ruler?* Ya mean she used a *ruler* on ya?" Their faces were stunned, either with disbelief or admiration, and it began to look more and more like admiration as they listened.

"On the knuckles," Vincent said through tightening lips. "Five times on each hand. She siz, 'Make a fist. Lay it out here on the desk.' Then she takes the ruler and *Whop! Whop! Whop!* Five times. Ya think that don't hurt, you're crazy."

Miss Price, buttoning her polo coat as the front door whispered shut behind her, could scarcely believe her eyes. This couldn't be Vincent Sabella—this perfectly normal, perfectly happy boy on the sidewalk ahead of her, flanked by attentive friends. But it was, and the scene made her want to laugh aloud with pleasure and relief. He was going to be all right, after all. For all her well-intentioned groping in the shadows she could never have predicted a scene like this, and certainly could never have caused it to happen. But it was happening, and it just proved, once again, that she would never understand the ways of children.

She quickened her graceful stride and overtook them, turning to smile down at them as she passed. "Goodnight, boys," she called, intending it as a kind of cheerful benediction; and then, embarrassed by their three startled faces, she smiled even wider and said, "Goodness, it *is* getting colder, isn't it? That windbreaker of yours looks nice and warm, Vincent. I envy you." Finally they nodded bashfully at her; she called goodnight again, turned, and continued on her way to the bus stop.

She left a profound silence in her wake. Staring after her, Warren Berg and Bill Stringer waited until she had disappeared around the corner before they turned on Vincent Sabella.

"Ruler, my eye!" Bill Stringer said. "Ruler, my eye!" He gave Vincent a disgusted shove that sent him stumbling against Warren Berg, who shoved him back.

"Jeez, you lie about *everything,* don'tcha, Sabella? You lie about *everything*!"

Jostled off balance, keeping his hands tight in the windbreaker pockets, Vincent tried in vain to retain his dignity. "Think *I* care if yiz believe me?" he said, and then because he couldn't think of anything else to say, he said it again. "Think *I* care if yiz believe me?"

But he was walking alone. Warren Berg and Bill Stringer were drifting away across the street, walking backwards in order to look back on him with furious contempt. "Just like the lies you told about the policeman shooting your father," Bill Stringer called.

"Even *movies* he lies about," Warren Berg put in; and suddenly doubling up with artificial laughter he cupped both hands to his mouth and yelled, "Hey, Doctor Jack-o'-lantern!"

It wasn't a very good nickname, but it had an authentic ring to it—the kind of a name that might spread around, catch on quickly, and stick. Nudging each other, they both took up the cry:

"What's the matter, Doctor Jack-o'-lantern?"

"Why don'tcha run on home with Miss Price, Doctor Jack-o'-lantern?"

"So long, Doctor Jack-o'-lantern!"

Vincent Sabella went on walking, ignoring them, waiting until they were out of sight. Then he turned and retraced his steps all the way back to school, around through the playground and back to the alley, where the wall was still dark in spots from the circular scrubbing of his wet rag.

Choosing a dry place, he got out his chalk and began to draw a head with great care, in profile, making the hair long and rich and taking his time over the face, erasing it with moist fingers and reworking it until it was the most beautiful face he had ever drawn: a delicate nose, slightly parted lips, an eye with lashes that curved as gracefully as a bird's wing. He paused to admire it with a lover's solemnity; then from the lips he drew a line that connected with a big speech balloon, and in the balloon he wrote, so angrily that the chalk kept breaking in his fingers, every one of the words he had written that noon. Returning to the head, he gave it a slender neck and gently sloping shoulders, and then, with bold strikes, he gave it the body of a naked woman: great breasts with hard little nipples, a trim waist, a dot for a navel, wide hips and thighs that flared around a triangle of fiercely scribbled pubic hair. Beneath the picture he printed its title: "Miss Price."

He stood there looking at it for a little while, breathing hard, and then he went home.

———

RICHARD YATES (1926–1992) published his short-story collection *Eleven Kinds of Loneliness* in 1962—a group of stories that includes "Doctor Jack-o'-lantern" and is insistent in its efforts to convey an America at once strong and jittery. The vulnerability of being with people yet at some moments being decisively detached and alone is a common theme in each "kind" of life presented.

In the Garden of the
North American Martyrs

Tobias Wolff

When she was young, Mary saw a brilliant and original man lose his job because he had expressed ideas that were offensive to the trustees of the college where they both taught. She shared his views, but did not sign the protest petition. She was, after all, on trial herself—as a teacher, as a woman, as an interpreter of history.

Mary watched herself. Before giving a lecture she wrote it out in full, using the arguments and often the words of other, approved writers, so that she would not by chance say something scandalous. Her own thoughts she kept to herself, and the words for them grew faint as time went on; without quite disappearing they shrank to remote, nervous points, like birds flying away.

When the department turned into a hive of cliques, Mary went about her business and pretended not to know that people hated each other. To avoid seeming bland she let herself become eccentric in harmless ways. She took up bowling, which she learned to love, and founded the Brandon College chapter of a society dedicated to restoring the good name of Richard III. She memorized comedy routines from records and jokes from books; people groaned when she rattled them off, but she did not let that stop her, and after a time the groans became the point of the jokes. They were a kind of tribute to Mary's willingness to expose herself.

In fact no one at the college was safer than Mary, for she was making herself into something institutional, like a custom, or a mascot—part of the college's idea of itself.

Now and then she wondered whether she had been too careful. The things she said and wrote seemed flat to her, pulpy, as though someone else had squeezed the juice out of them. And once, while talking with a senior professor, Mary saw herself reflected in a window: she was leaning toward him and had her head turned so that her ear was right in front of his moving mouth. The sight disgusted her. Years later, when she had to get a hearing aid, Mary suspected that her deafness was a result of always trying to catch everything everyone said.

In the second half of Mary's fifteenth year at Brandon the provost called a meeting of all faculty and students to announce that the college was bankrupt and would not open its gates again. He was every bit as much surprised as they; the report from the trustees had reached his desk only that morning. It seemed that Brandon's financial manager had speculated in some kind of futures and lost everything. The provost wanted to deliver the news in person before it reached the papers. He wept openly and so did the students and teachers, with only a few exceptions—some cynical upperclassmen who claimed to despise the education they had received.

Mary could not rid her mind of the word "speculate." It meant to guess, in terms of money to gamble. How could a man gamble a college? Why would he want to do that, and how could it be that no one stopped him? To Mary, it seemed to belong to another time; she thought of a drunken plantation owner gaming away his slaves. She applied for jobs and got an offer from a new experimental college in Oregon. It was her only offer so she took it.

The college was in one building. Bells rang all the time, lockers lined the hallways, and at every corner stood a buzzing water fountain. The student newspaper came out twice a month on mimeograph paper which felt wet. The library, which was next to the band room, had no librarian and no books.

The countryside was beautiful, though, and Mary might have enjoyed it if the rain had not caused her so much trouble. There was something wrong with her lungs that the doctors couldn't agree on, and couldn't cure; whatever it was, the dampness made it worse. On rainy days condensation formed in Mary's hearing aid and shorted it out. She began to dread talking with people, never knowing when she would have to take out her control box and slap it against her leg.

It rained nearly every day. When it was not raining it was getting ready to rain, or clearing. The ground glinted under the grass, and the light had a yellow undertone that flared up during storms.

There was water in Mary's basement. Her walls sweated, and she had found toadstools growing behind the refrigerator. She felt as though she were rusting out, like one of those old cars people thereabouts kept in their front yards, on pieces of wood. Mary knew that everyone was dying, but it did seem to her that she was dying faster than most.

She continued to look for another job, without success. Then, in the fall of her third year in Oregon, she got a letter from a woman named Louise who'd once taught at Brandon. Louise had scored a great success with a book on Benedict Arnold and was now on the faculty of a famous college in upstate New York. She said that one of her colleagues would be retiring at the end of the year and asked whether Mary would be interested in the position.

The letter surprised Mary. Louise thought of herself as a great historian and of almost everyone else as useless; Mary had not known that she felt differently about her. Moreover, enthusiasm for other people's causes did not come easily to Louise, who had a way of sucking in her breath when familiar names were mentioned, as though she knew things that friendship kept her from disclosing.

Mary expected nothing, but sent a résumé and copies of her two books. Shortly after that Louise called to say that the search committee, of which she was chairwoman, had decided to grant Mary an interview in early November. "Now don't get your hopes *too* high," Louise said.

"Oh, no," Mary said, but thought: Why shouldn't I hope? They would not go to the bother and expense of bringing her to the college if they weren't serious. And she was certain that the interview would go well. She would make them like her, or at least give them no cause to dislike her.

She read about the area with a strange sense of familiarity, as if the land and its history were already known to her. And when her plane left Portland and climbed easterly into the clouds, Mary felt like she was going home. The feeling stayed with her, growing stronger when they landed. She tried to describe it to Louise as they left the airport at Syracuse and drove toward the college, an hour or so away. "It's like *déjà vu*," she said.

"*Déjà vu* is a hoax," Louise said. "It's just a chemical imbalance of some kind."

"Maybe so," Mary said, "but I still have this sensation."

"Don't get serious on me," Louise said. "That's not your long suit. Just be your funny, wisecracking old self. Tell me now—honestly—how do I look?"

It was night, too dark to see Louise's face well, but in the airport she had seemed gaunt and pale and intense. She reminded Mary of a description in the book she'd been reading, of how Iroquois warriors gave themselves visions by fasting. She had that kind of look about her. But she wouldn't want to hear that. "You look wonderful," Mary said.

"There's a reason," Louise said. "I've taken a lover. My concentration has improved, my energy level is up, and I've lost ten pounds. I'm also getting some color in my cheeks, though that could be the weather. I recommend the experience highly. But you probably disapprove."

Mary didn't know what to say. She said that she was sure Louise knew best, but that didn't seem to be enough. "Marriage is a great institution," she added, "but who wants to live in an institution?"

Louise groaned. "I know you," she said, "and I know that right now you're thinking 'But what about Ted? What about the children?' The fact is, Mary, they aren't taking it well at all. Ted has become a nag." She handed Mary her purse. "Be a good girl and light me a cigarette, will you? I know I told you I quit, but this whole thing has been very hard on me, very hard, and I'm afraid I've started again."

They were in the hills now, heading north on a narrow road. Tall trees arched above them. As they topped a rise Mary saw the forest all around, deep black under the plum-colored sky. There were a few lights and these made the darkness seem even greater.

"Ted has succeeded in completely alienating the children from me," Louise was saying. "There is no reasoning with any of them. In fact, they refuse to discuss the matter at all, which is very ironical because over the years I have tried to instill in them a willingness to see things from the other person's point of view. If they could just *meet* Jonathan I know they would feel differently. But they won't hear of it. Jonathan," she said, "is my lover."

"I see," Mary said, and nodded.

Coming around a curve they caught two deer in the headlights. Their eyes lit up and their hindquarters tensed; Mary could see them trembling as the car went by. "Deer," she said.

"I don't know," Louise said, "I just don't know. I do my best and it never seems to be enough. But that's enough about me—let's talk about you. What did you think of my latest book?" She squawked and beat her palms on the steering wheel. "God, I love that joke," she said. "Seriously, though, what about you? It must have been a real shockeroo when good old Brandon folded."

"It was hard. Things haven't been good but they'll be a lot better if I get this job."

"At least you have work," Louise said. "You should look at it from the bright side."

"I try."

"You seem so gloomy. I hope you're not worrying about the interview, or the class. Worrying won't do you a bit of good. Be happy."

"Class? What class?"

"The class you're supposed to give tomorrow, after the interview. Didn't I tell you? *Mea culpa*, hon, *mea maxima culpa*. I've been uncharacteristically forgetful lately."

"But what will I do?"

"Relax," Louise said. "Just pick a subject and wing it."

"Wing it?"

"You know, open your mouth and see what comes out. Extemporize."

"But I always work from a prepared lecture."

Louise sighed. "All right. I'll tell you what. Last year I wrote an article on the Marshall Plan that I got bored with and never published. You can read that."

Parroting what Louise had written seemed wrong to Mary, at first; then it occurred to her that she had been doing the same kind of thing for many years, and that this was not the time to get scruples. "Thanks," she said. "I appreciate it."

"Here we are," Louise said, and pulled into a circular drive with several cabins grouped around it. In two of the cabins lights were on; smoke drifted straight up from the chimneys. "This is the visitors' center. The college is another two miles thataway." Louise pointed down the road. "I'd invite you to stay at my house, but I'm spending the night with Jonathan and Ted is not good company these days. You would hardly recognize him."

She took Mary's bags from the trunk and carried them up the steps of a darkened cabin. "Look," she said, "they've laid a fire for you. All you have to do is light it." She stood in the middle of the room with her arms crossed and watched as Mary held a match under the kindling. "There," she said. "You'll be snugaroo in no time. I'd love to stay and chew the fat but I can't. You just get a good night's sleep and I'll see you in the morning."

Mary stood in the doorway and waved as Louise pulled out of the drive, spraying gravel. She filled her lungs, to taste the air: it was tart and clear. She could see the stars in their figurations, and the vague streams of light that ran among the stars.

She still felt uneasy about reading Louise's work as her own. It would be her first complete act of plagiarism. It would change her.

It would make her less—how much less, she did not know. But what else could she do? She certainly couldn't "wing it." Words might fail her, and then what? Mary had a dread of silence. When she thought of silence she thought of drowning, as if it were a kind of water she could not swim in.

"I want this job," she said, and settled deep into her coat. It was cashmere and Mary had not worn it since moving to Oregon, because people there thought you were pretentious if you had on anything but a Pendleton shirt or, of course, raingear. She rubbed her cheek against the upturned collar and thought of a silver moon shining through bare black branches, a white house with green shutters, red leaves falling in a hard blue sky.

———

Louise woke her a few hours later. She was sitting on the edge of the bed, pushing at Mary's shoulder and snuffling loudly. When Mary asked her what was wrong she said, "I want your opinion on something. It's very important. Do you think I'm womanly?"

Mary sat up. "Louise, can this wait?"

"No."

"Womanly?"

Louise nodded.

"You are very beautiful," Mary said, "and you know how to present yourself."

Louise stood and paced the room. "That son of a bitch," she said. She came back and stood over Mary. "Let's suppose someone said I have no sense of humor. Would you agree or disagree?"

"In some things you do. I mean, yes, you have a good sense of humor."

"What do you mean, 'in some things'? What kind of things?"

"Well, if you heard that someone had been killed in an unusual way, like by an exploding cigar, you would think that was funny."

Louise laughed.

"That's what I mean," Mary said.

Louise went on laughing. "Oh, Lordy," she said. "Now it's my turn to say something about you." She sat down beside Mary.

"Please," Mary said.

"Just one thing," Louise said.

Mary waited.

"You're trembling," Louise said. "I was just going to say—oh, forget it. Listen, do you mind if I sleep on the couch? I'm all in."

"Go ahead."

"Sure it's okay? You've got a big day tomorrow." She fell back on the sofa and kicked off her shoes. "I was just going to say, you should use some liner on those eyebrows of yours. They sort of disappear and the effect is disconcerting."

Neither of them slept. Louise chain-smoked cigarettes and Mary watched the coals burn down. When it was light enough that they could see each other Louise got up. "I'll send a student for you," she said. "Good luck."

———

The college looked the way colleges are supposed to look. Roger, the student assigned to show Mary around, explained that it was an exact copy of a college in England, right down to the gargoyles and stained-glass windows. It looked so much like a college that moviemakers sometimes used it as a set. *Andy Hardy Goes to College* had been filmed there, and every fall they had an Andy Hardy Goes to College Day, with raccoon coats and goldfish-swallowing contests.

Above the door of the Founder's Building was a Latin motto which, roughly translated, meant "God helps those who help themselves." As Roger recited the names of illustrious graduates Mary was struck by the extent to which they had taken this precept to heart. They had helped themselves to railroads, mines, armies, states; to empires of finance with outposts all over the world.

Roger took Mary to the chapel and showed her a plaque bearing the names of alumni who had been killed in various wars, all the way back to the Civil War. There were not many names. Here too, apparently, the graduates had helped themselves. "Oh yes," Roger said as they were leaving, "I forgot to tell you. The communion rail comes from some church in Europe where Charlemagne used to go."

They went to the gymnasium, and the three hockey rinks, and

the library, where Mary inspected the card catalogue, as though she would turn down the job if they didn't have the right books. "We have a little more time," Roger said as they went outside. "Would you like to see the power plant?"

Mary wanted to keep busy until the last minute, so she agreed.

Roger led her into the depths of the service building, explaining things about the machine, which was the most advanced in the country. "People think the college is really old-fashioned," he said, "but it isn't. They let girls come here now, and some of the teachers are women. In fact, there's a statute that says they have to interview at least one woman for each opening. There it is."

They were standing on an iron catwalk above the biggest machine Mary had ever beheld. Roger, who was majoring in Earth Sciences, said that it had been built from a design pioneered by a professor in his department. Where before he had been gabby Roger now became reverent. It was clear that for him this machine was the soul of the college, that the purpose of the college was to provide outlets for the machine. Together they leaned against the railing and watched it hum.

———

Mary arrived at the committee room exactly on time for her interview, but the room was empty. Her two books were on the table, along with a water pitcher and some glasses. She sat down and picked up one of the books. The binding cracked as she opened it. The pages were smooth, clean, unread. Mary turned to the first chapter, which began, "It is generally believed that..." How dull, she thought.

Nearly twenty minutes later Louise came in with several men. "Sorry we're late," she said. "We don't have much time so we'd better get started." She introduced Mary to the men, but with one exception the names and faces did not stay together. The exception was Dr. Howells, the department chairman, who had a porous blue nose and terrible teeth.

A shiny-faced man to Dr. Howells's right spoke first. "So," he said, "I understand you once taught at Brandon College."

"It was a shame that Brandon had to close," said a young man with a pipe in his mouth. "There is a place for schools like Brandon." As he talked the pipe wagged up and down.

"Now you're in Oregon," Dr. Howells said. "I've never been there. How do you like it?"

"Not very much," Mary said.

"Is that right?" Dr. Howells leaned toward her. "I thought everyone liked Oregon. I hear it's very green."

"That's true," Mary said.

"I suppose it rains a lot," he said.

"Nearly every day."

"I wouldn't like that," he said, shaking his head. "I like it dry. Of course it snows here, and you have your rain now and then, but it's a *dry* rain. Have you ever been to Utah? There's a state for you. Bryce Canyon. The Mormon Tabernacle Choir."

"Dr. Howells was brought up in Utah," said the young man with the pipe.

"It was a different place altogether in those days," Dr. Howells said. "Mrs. Howells and I have always talked about going back when I retire, but now I'm not so sure."

"We're a little short on time," Louise said.

"And here I've been going on and on," Dr. Howells said. "Before we wind things up, is there anything you want to tell us?"

"Yes. I think you should give me the job." Mary laughed when she said this, but no one laughed back, or even looked at her. They all looked away. Mary understood then that they were not really considering her for the position. She had been brought here to satisfy a rule. She had no hope.

The men gathered their papers and shook hands with Mary and told her how much they were looking forward to her class. "I can't get enough of the Marshall Plan," Dr. Howells said.

"Sorry about that," Louise said when they were alone. "I didn't think it would be so bad. That was a real bitcheroo."

"Tell me something," Mary said. "You already know who you're going to hire, don't you?"

Louise nodded.

"Then why did you bring me here?"

Louise began to explain about the statute and Mary interrupted. "I know all that. But why me? Why did you pick *me*?"

Louise walked to the window. She spoke with her back to Mary. "Things haven't been going very well for old Louise," she said. "I've been unhappy and I thought you might cheer me up. You used to be so funny, and I was sure you would enjoy the trip—it didn't cost you anything, and it's pretty this time of year with the leaves and everything. Mary, you don't know the things my parents did to me. And Ted is no barrel of laughs either. Or Jonathan, the son of a bitch. I deserve some love and friendship but I don't get any." She turned and looked at her watch. "It's almost time for your class. We'd better go."

"I would rather not give it. After all, there's not much point, is there?"

"But you *have* to give it. That's part of the interview." Louise handed Mary a folder. "All you have to do is read this. It isn't much, considering all the money we've laid out to get you here."

Mary followed Louise down the hall to the lecture room. The professors were sitting in the front row with their legs crossed. They smiled and nodded at Mary. Behind them the room was full of students, some of whom had spilled over into the aisles. One of the professors adjusted the microphone to Mary's height, crouching down as he went to the podium and back as though he would prefer not to be seen.

Louise called the room to order. She introduced Mary and gave the subject of the lecture. But Mary had decided to wing it after all. Mary came to the podium unsure of what she would say; sure only that she would rather die than read Louise's article. The sun poured through the stained glass onto the people around her, painting their faces. Thick streams of smoke from the young professor's pipe drifted through a circle of red light at Mary's feet, turning crimson and twisting like flames.

"I wonder how many of you know," she began, "that we are in the Long House, the ancient domain of the Five Nations of the Iroquois."

Two professors looked at each other.

"The Iroquois were without pity," Mary said. "They hunted people down with clubs and arrows and spears and nets, and blowguns made from elder stalks. They tortured their captives, sparing no one, not even the little children. They took scalps and practiced cannibalism and slavery. Because they had no pity they became powerful, so powerful that no other tribe dared to oppose them. They made the other tribes pay tribute, and when they had nothing more to pay the Iroquois attacked them."

Several of the professors began to whisper. Dr. Howells was saying something to Louise, and Louise was shaking her head.

"In one of their raids," Mary said, "they captured two Jesuit priests, Jean de Brébeuf and Gabriel Lalement. They covered Lalement with pitch and set him on fire in front of Brébeuf. When Brébeuf rebuked them they cut off his lips and put a burning iron down his throat. They hung a collar of red-hot hatchets around his neck, and poured boiling water over his head. When he continued to preach to them they cut strips of flesh from his body and ate them before his eyes. While he was still alive they scalped him and cut open his breast and drank his blood. Later, their chief tore out Brébeuf's heart and ate it, but just before he did this Brébeuf spoke to them one last time. He said—"

"That's enough!" yelled Dr. Howells, jumping to his feet.

Louise stopped shaking her head. Her eyes were perfectly round.

Mary had come to the end of her facts. She did not know what Brébeuf had said. Silence rose up around her; just when she thought she would go under and be lost in it she heard someone whistling in the hallway outside, trilling the notes like a bird, like many birds.

"Mend your lives," she said. "You have deceived yourselves in the pride of your hearts, and the strength of your arms. Though you soar aloft like the eagle, though your nest is set among the stars, thence I will bring you down, says the Lord. Turn from power to love. Be kind. Do justice. Walk humbly."

Louise was waving her arms. "Mary!" she shouted.

But Mary had more to say, much more; she waved back at

Louise, then turned off her hearing aid so that she would not be distracted again.

———

TOBIAS WOLFF was born on June 19, 1945, in Birmingham, Alabama. He served in Vietnam and described his experiences in a memoir titled *In Pharaoh's Army: Memories of the Lost War.* His first collection of short stories, *In the Garden of the North American Martyrs,* from which this story is taken, appeared in 1981.

Are the Peasant Children to Learn to Write from Us? Or, Are We to Learn from the Peasant Children?

Leo Tolstoy

In the fourth number of *Yásnaya Polyána,* in the department of children's compositions, there was printed by the editor's mistake "A Story of How a Boy Was Frightened in Túla." This story was not composed by a boy, but by the teacher from a boy's dream as related to him. Some of the readers, who follow the numbers of *Yásnaya Polyána,* have expressed their doubts as regards the authorship of this story. I hasten to beg the readers' indulgence for this oversight, and to remark that in such matters a falsification is impossible. This story was recognized, not because it was better, but because it was worse, infinitely worse, than all children's compositions. All the other stories belong to the children themselves. Two of them, "He Feeds with the Spoon, and Pricks the Eye with the Handle," and "A Soldier's Life," were composed in the following manner.

The chief art of the teacher, in the study of language, and the chief exercise with the aim in view of guiding children to write compositions consist in giving them themes, and not so much in furnishing them as in presenting a large choice, in pointing out the extent of the composition, and in indicating the initial steps. Many clever and talented pupils wrote nonsense; they wrote: "It began to burn, they began to drag out things, and I went into the street," and nothing came of it, although the subject was rich, and that which was described left a deep impression on the child. They did not understand, above all, why they should write, and what good there was in writing. They did not understand the art of expressing life by means of words, nor the charm of this art.

As I have already mentioned in the second number, I tried many different methods of giving them themes to write. I gave them, according to their inclinations, exact, artistic, touching, funny, epic themes—all to no purpose. Here is how I unexpectedly hit upon the present method.

The reading of the collection of Snegirév's proverbs has long formed one of my favourite occupations—nay, enjoyments. To every proverb I imagine individuals from among the people and their conflicts in the sense of the proverb. Among the number of unrealizable dreams, I always imagine a series of pictures, or stories, written to fit the proverbs. Once, last winter, I forgot everything after dinner in the reading of Snegirév's book, and even returned to the school with the book. It was the lesson in the Russian language.

"Well, write something on a proverb!" I said.

The best pupils, Fédka, Sémka, and others, pricked up their ears.

"What do you mean by 'on a proverb'? What is it? Tell us!" the questions ran.

I happened to open to the proverb: "He feeds with the spoon, and pricks the eye with the handle."

"Now, imagine," I said, "that a peasant has taken a beggar to his house, and then begins to rebuke him for the good he has done him, and you will get that 'he feeds with the spoon, and pricks the eye with the handle.'"

"But how are you going to write it up?" said Fédka and all the rest who had pricked up their ears. They retreated, having convinced themselves that this matter was above their strength, and betook themselves to the work which they had begun.

"Write it yourself," one of them said to me.

Everybody was busy with his work; I took a pen and inkstand, and began to write.

"Well," said I, "who will write it best? I am with you."

I began the story, printed in the fourth number of the *Yásnaya Polyána*, and wrote down the first page. Every unbiased man, who has the artistic sense and feels with the people, will, upon reading this first page, written by me, and the following pages of the story, written by the pupils themselves, separate this page from the rest, as he will take a fly out of the milk: it is so false, so artificial, and written in such a bad language. I must remark that in the original form it was even more monstrous, since much has been corrected, thanks to the indications of the pupils.

Fédka kept looking up from his copy-book to me, and, upon meeting my eyes, smiled, winked, and repeated: "Write, write, or I'll give it to you!" He was evidently amused to see a grown person write a theme.

Having finished his theme worse and faster than usual, he climbed on the back of my chair and began to read over my shoulders. I could not proceed; others came up to us, and I read to them what I had written.

They did not like it, and nobody praised it. I felt ashamed, and, to soothe my literary ambition, I began to tell them the plan of what was to follow. In the proportion as I advanced in my story, I became enthusiastic, corrected myself, and they kept helping me out. One would say that the old man should be a magician; another would remark: "No, that won't do—he will be just a soldier; the best thing will be if he steals from him; no, that won't go with the proverb," and so forth.

All were exceedingly interested. It was evidently a new and exciting sensation for them to be present at the process of creation, and to take part in it. Their judgments were all, for the most part, of the same kind, and they were just, both as to the very structure of the story and as to the details and characterizations of the persons. Nearly all of them took part in the composition; but, from the start, there distinguished themselves positive Sémka, by his clearly defined artistic quality of description, and Fédka, by the correctness of his poetical conceptions, and especially by the glow and rapidity of his imagination.

Their demands had so little of the accidental in them and were so definite, that more than once I debated with them, only to give way to them. I was strongly possessed by the demands of a regular structure and of an exact correspondence of the idea of the proverb to the story; while they, on the contrary, were only concerned about the demands of artistic truth. I, for example, wanted that the peasant, who had taken the old man to his house, should himself repent of his good deed—while they regarded this as impossible and created a cross old woman.

I said: "The peasant was at first sorry for the old man, and later he hated to give away the bread."

Fédka replied that that would be improbable: "He did not obey the old woman from the start and would not submit later."

"What kind of a man is he, according to you?" I asked.

"He is like Uncle Timoféy," said Fédka, smiling. "He has a scanty beard, goes to church, and he has bees."

"Is he good, but stubborn?" I asked.

"Yes," said Fédka, "he will not obey the old woman."

From the time that the old man was brought into the hut, the work became animated. They evidently for the first time felt the charm of clothing artistic details in words. Sémka distinguished himself more than the rest in this respect: the correctest details were poured forth one after the other. The only reproach that could be made to him was that these details sketched only minutes of the present, without connection with the general feeling of the story. I hardly could write as fast as they told me the incidents, and only asked them to wait and not forget what they had told me.

Sémka seemed to see and describe that which was before his eyes: the stiff, frozen bast shoes, and the dirt oozing from them, as they melted out, and the toast into which they were changed when the old woman threw them into the oven.

Fédka, on the contrary, saw only such details as evoked in him the particular feeling with which he looked upon a certain person. Fédka saw the snow drifting behind the peasant's leg-rags, and the feeling of compassion with which the peasant said: "Lord, how it snows!" (Fédka's face even showed how the peasant said it, and he swung his hands and shook his head.) He saw the overcoat, a mass of rags and patches, and the torn shirt, behind which could be seen the haggard body of the old man, wet from the thawing snow. He created the old woman, who growled as, at the command of her husband, she took off his bast shoes, and the pitiful groan of the old man as he muttered through his teeth: "Softly, motherkin, I have sores here."

Sémka needed mainly objective pictures: bast shoes, an overcoat, an old man, a woman, almost without any connection between them; but Fédka had to evoke the feeling of pity with which he himself was permeated. He ran ahead of the story, telling how he would feed the old man, how he would fall down at night, and how he would later teach a boy in the field to read, so that I was obliged to ask him not to be in such a hurry and not to forget what he had said. His eyes sparkled to the point of tears; his swarthy, thin little hands were cramped convulsively; he was angry with me, and kept urging me on: "Have you written it, have you written it?" he kept asking me.

He treated all the rest despotically; he wanted to talk all the time, not as a story is told, but as it is written, that is, artistically to clothe in words the sensuous pictures. Thus, for example, he would not allow words to be transposed; if he once said, "I have sores on my feet," he would not permit me to say, "On my feet I have sores." His soul, now softened and irritated by the sentiment of pity, that is, of love, clothed every image in an artistic form, and denied everything that did not correspond to the idea of eternal beauty and harmony.

The moment Sémka was carried away by the expression of disproportionable details about the lambs in the door-bench, and so forth, Fédka grew angry and said, "What a lot of bosh!" I only needed to suggest what the peasant was doing, while his wife went to the gossip, when in Fédka's imagination there would immediately arise a picture with lambs, bleating in the door-bench, with the sighs of the old man and the delirium of the boy Serézhka; I only needed to suggest an artificial and false picture, when he immediately would angrily remark that that was not necessary.

For example, I suggested the description of the peasant's looks, to which he agreed; but to my proposition to describe what the peasant was thinking while his wife had run over to the gossip, there immediately rose before him the very form of the thought: "If you got in the way of Savóska the corpse, he would pull all your locks out!" He said this in such a fatigued and calmly serious and habitual and, at the same time, good-natured voice, leaning his head on his hand, that the boys rolled in laughter.

The chief quality in every art, the feeling of measure, was developed in him to an extraordinary degree. He writhed at the suggestion of any superfluous feature, made by some one of the boys.

He directed the structure of the story so despotically, and with such right to this despotism, that the boys soon went home, and only he and Sémka, who would not give in to him, though working in another direction, were left. We worked from seven to eleven o'clock; they felt neither hunger nor fatigue, and even got angry at me when I stopped writing; they undertook to relieve me in writing, but they soon gave that up as matters would not go well.

It was then for the first time that Fédka asked my name. We laughed because he did not know.

"I know," he said, "how to call you; but how do they call you in the manor? We have such names as Fokanýchev, Zyábrev, Ermílin."

I told him.

"Are we going to print it?" he asked.

"Yes."

"Then we shall have to print: Work by Makárov, Morózov, and Tolstóy."

He was agitated for a long time and could not fall asleep, and I cannot express that feeling of agitation, joy, fear, and almost regret, which I experienced during that evening. I felt that with that day a new world of enjoyment and suffering was opened up to him— the world of art; I thought that I had received an insight in what no one has a right to see—the germination of the mysterious flower of poetry.

I felt both dread and joy, like the seeker after the treasure who suddenly sees the flower of the fern—I felt joy, because suddenly and quite unexpectedly there was revealed to me that stone of the philosophers, which I had vainly been trying to find for two years—the art of teaching the expression of thoughts; and dread, because this art called for new demands, a whole world of desires, which stood in no relation to the surroundings of the pupils, as I thought in the first moment. There was no mistaking. It was not an accident, but a conscious creation.

I beg the reader to read the first chapter of the story and to notice that wealth of features of true creative talent scattered through it; for example, the feature when the woman in anger complains about her husband to the gossip, and yet weeps, although the author has an apparent dislike for her, when the gossip reminds her of the ruin of her house. For the author, who writes by reasoning out and from memory, the cross woman represents only the opposite of the peasant—she had to invite the gossip for no other reason than the desire to annoy her husband; but with Fédka the artistic feeling extends also to the woman, and she, too, weeps, fears, and suffers—she is not guilty, to his manner of thinking. Then the accessory feature when the gossip puts on a woman's fur coat. I remember how struck I was by this and how I asked: "Why a woman's fur coat?" None of us had led Fédka up to the idea that the gossip had put on a fur coat.

He said: "It is more like it!"

When I asked him whether it would do to say that he put on a man's fur coat, he said:

"No, a woman's fur coat is better."

Indeed, this feature is extraordinary. At first it does not occur to one why it should be a woman's fur coat, and yet one feels that it is excellent and cannot be otherwise.

Every artistic word, whether it belongs to Göthe or to Fédka, differs from the inartistic in that it evokes an endless mass of thoughts, images, and explanations.

The gossip in a woman's fur coat involuntarily presents himself to us as a sickly, narrow-chested peasant, just such as he apparently ought to be. The woman's fur coat, carelessly thrown on the bench and the first to fall into his hands, in addition, presents to us a winter evening scene in the life of the peasant. The fur coat leads you to imagine the late evening, during which the peasant is sitting without his wraps near a torch, and the women, coming in and out to fetch water and attend to the cattle, and all that external disorder of the peasant life, where not a person has his clearly defined clothes, and no one thing a definite place. With this one sentence, "He put on a woman's fur coat," the whole character of the surroundings, in which the action takes place, is clearly outlined, and this phrase is not used by accident, but consciously.

I remember vividly how in his imagination arose the words used by the peasant when he found the paper which he could not read.

"Now, if my Serézhka knew how to read, he would have come running to me, and would have grabbed the paper out of my hands, and would have read it all, and would have told me who the old man is."

One almost can see the relation of the peasant to the book which he is holding in his sunburnt hands; the kind man with his patriarchal and pious inclinations rises before you in his whole stature. You feel that the author has taken a deep liking to him and, therefore, has fully comprehended him, so that soon after he lets him make a digression about there being such times nowadays that, before one knows it, one's soul is perished.

The idea about the dream was suggested by me, but it was Fédka's idea to let the goat have sores on its legs, and this conception gave him much pleasure. The reflection of the peasant, while his back is itching, and the picture of the nocturnal quiet—all that is far from being accidental, and in all these features one feels so strongly the conscious power of the artist!

I also remember how, when the peasant was to fall asleep, I proposed to make him reflect on the future of his son and on the future relations of his son with the old man, and to let the old man teach Serézhka reading, and so forth.

Fédka frowned and said: "Yes, yes, that is good," but it was obvious that he did not like that suggestion, and twice he forgot it.

His feeling of measure was stronger in him than in any of the authors I am acquainted with—the feeling of measure, which but few artists acquire at the cost of immense labour and study, lived in its primitive force in his uncorrupted childish soul.

I gave up the lesson, because I was too much agitated.

"What is the matter with you? You are so pale—are you ill?" my companion asked me. Indeed, only two or three times in my life have I experienced such a strong sensation as on that evening, and for a long time I was unable to render an account to myself of what I was experiencing. I dimly felt that I had criminally looked through a glass hive at the work of the bees, concealed from the gaze of mortal man; it seemed to me that I had debauched the pure, primitive soul of a peasant boy. I dimly felt something like repentance for an act of sacrilege. I thought of the children, whom idle and debauched old men allow to contort themselves and represent lascivious pictures in order to fan their wearied, worn-out imaginations, and, at the same time, I was happy, as must be happy the man who beholds that which no one beheld before.

For a long time I was unable to render an account to myself of the impression which it had produced on me, though I felt that this impression was one of those which at a mature age educate a man and lead him to a new stage of life, making him renounce the old and fully devote himself to the new. Even on the following day I could not make myself believe that which I had experienced the day before. It seemed so strange to me that a peasant boy, with the bare knowledge of reading, should suddenly manifest a conscious artistic power, such as Göthe, in all his immeasurable height of development, had been unable to equal. It seemed so strange and offensive to me that I, the author of "Childhood," who had had certain success and had earned recognition for artistic talent from a cultivated Russian public—that I, in the matter of art, not only should be unable to teach anything to eleven-year-old Sémka or Fédka or to help them, but that I only with difficulty and in a happy moment of excitement should be able to follow and understand them. All that seemed so strange to me that I could not believe that which had happened the day before.

The next day we took up the continuation of the story. When I asked Fédka whether he had thought out the continuation, he only swayed his hands and said: "I know, I know! Who will write?"

We went to work, and again the children displayed the same feeling of artistic truth, measure, and enthusiasm.

In the middle of the lesson I was obliged to leave them.

They continued to write without me and finished two pages just as well done, just as well felt, and just as correctly, as the first. The only thing about these pages was that they were paler in details, that these details were not aptly disposed, and that there were two or three repetitions. All that apparently was due to the fact that the mechanism of writing hampered them.

The same took place on the third day. During these lessons other boys frequently joined us, and, as they knew the tenor and the contents of the story, they often helped us out by adding their correct features. Sémka now kept up with us, and now stayed away. Fédka alone carried the story from beginning to end and passed upon all the proposed changes.

There could no longer be any doubt or thought that this success was a matter of accident: we had apparently struck the method which was more natural and a greater incentive than everything tried before. But it was all so unusual that I did not believe that which took place before our eyes. It looked as though a special incident were necessary in order to destroy all my doubts.

I had to leave for a few days, and the story remained unfinished. The manuscript, three large sheets, closely covered with writing, was left in the room of the teacher, to whom I had shown it.

Even before my departure, while I was busy composing, a newly entered pupil had shown our boys the art of making paper flaps, and, as is generally the case, the whole school entered upon a period of flaps, which had supplanted a period of snow-balls, as these again had supplanted a period of whittling sticks. The period of the flaps lasted during my absence.

Sémka and Fédka, who were among the singers, used to come to the teacher's room for singing exercises, and they remained there whole evenings, and even nights. Between the singing and during the singing, the flaps, of course, did their business, and all kinds of paper, which fell into their hands, was transformed into flaps.

The teacher went to get his supper, having forgotten to mention that the papers on the table were important, and so the work of Makárov, Morózov, and Tolstóy was changed into flaps. On the following day, before the lessons, the clacking of the flaps so very much annoyed the pupils that they themselves instituted a persecution against the flaps: they were confiscated with shouts and screams, and solemnly stuck into the fire of the oven.

The period of the flaps came to an end, but with it perished our manuscript. Never had any loss been so hard to bear as the loss of these three sheets of writing. I was in despair, I wanted to give it all up and begin a new story, but I could not forget the loss, and so involuntarily every minute kept nagging at the teacher and at the makers of the flaps.

(I must remark here, upon this occasion, that just by means of the external disorder and full freedom of the pupils, which Mr. Márkov takes so charmingly to task in the *Russian Messenger,* and Mr. Glyébov in No. 4 of the periodical *Education,* I, without the least trouble, threats, or cunning, learned all the details of the complicated story of the transformation of the manuscript into flaps, and of its consignment to the flames.)

Sémka and Fédka saw that I was aggrieved, not understanding by what, and they sympathized with me. Fédka finally timidly proposed to me to begin another such a story.

"By yourselves?" I asked. "I shall not help you now."

"Sémka and I will stay here overnight," said Fédka.

And so they did. At nine o'clock, when the lessons were over, they came to the house, locked themselves up in my cabinet, which afforded me much pleasure, laughed awhile, and grew quiet. Until midnight I could hear them, every time I came up to the door, talking with each other in low tones and scratching their pens. Once only they debated about what came first and what later, and they came to me to settle the dispute, whether he looked for the wallet before the woman went to the gossip, or after. I told them that it made no difference which.

At midnight I knocked and asked to be let in. Fédka in a new white fur coat, with black trimming, was sitting deep in the arm-chair, with one leg over the other, leaning his shaggy little head on his hand, and fumbling the scissors in the other hand. His large black eyes, gleaming with an unnatural, but serious sparkle, like that of a grown person, were looking somewhere into the distance; his irregular lips, compressed as though for a whistle, apparently held back the word which he, having coined it in his imagination, was about to express.

Sémka, standing at the large writing-table, with a large white patch of sheepskin over his back (the tailors had but lately been in the village), with ungirt belt, and dishevelled hair, was writing crooked lines, constantly sticking his pen into the inkstand.

I tossed Sémka's hair, and his fat face with protruding cheek-bones and matted hair, as he, with surprised and sleepy eyes, looked in fright at me, was so funny, that I burst out into a laugh, but the children did not laugh with me.

Without changing the expression of his face, Fédka touched Sémka's sleeve and told him to go on. "Thou must wait," he said, "we shall be through soon." (Fédka says "thou" to me whenever he is carried away by something and agitated.) He continued to dic-tate.

I took away their copy-book, and five minutes later, when they, seating themselves near a small safe, were getting away with pota-toes and kvas, and, looking at the silver spoons, which they thought so funny, laughing their sonorous, childish laugh, without any cause whatever—the old woman, hearing them up-stairs, also burst out laughing, without knowing why.

"Don't tip so!" said Sémka. "Sit straight, or you will eat on one side only."

They took off their fur coats, and, spreading them under the writing-table, lay down on them to sleep, all the time rolling out their healthy, charming, childish, peasant laugh.

I read over what they had written. It was a new variant of the same thing. A few things were left out, and a few new, artistic beau-ties were added. Again there was the same feeling of beauty, truth, and measure. Later on one sheet of the lost manuscript was found. In the printed story I combined both variants from memory, and from the sheet which was recovered.

The writing of this story took place early in spring, before the end of our scholastic year. For various reasons I was unable to make new experiments. On given proverbs only one story was written by two very mediocre and spoilt children, being the sons of manorial servants. "He who is fond of a holiday gets drunk before daybreak," was printed in the third number. The same phenomena were repeated with these boys and with this story as had been observed with Sémka and Fédka and the first story, only with a difference in the degree of talent and in the enthusiasm and the cooperation on my part.

In the summer we have never had school and never will have. We shall devote a separate article to the cause why teaching is impossible in the summer in our school.

One part of the summer Fédka and some other boys lived with me. Having had a swim, and being tired of playing, they took it into their heads to work. I proposed to them to write a composition, and so told them several themes. I told them a very entertaining story about the theft of some money, the story of a murder, the story of a marvellous conversion of a Milker to Orthodoxy, and I also proposed to them to write in the form of an autobiography the history of a boy whose poor and dissolute father is sent to the army, and to whom the father later returns a reformed, good man.

I said: "I should write it like this. I remember that when I was a child I had a father, a mother, and some other relatives, and who they were. Then I should write that I remember how my father was all the time out on sprees, while my mother wept, and he beat her; then, how he was sent to the army; how she wept; how our life grew harder; how father returned, and he did not seem to recognize me, but asked me whether Matréna—that is, his wife—was alive; and how all were happy, and we began to live well."

That was all which I said in the beginning. Fédka took a great liking to this theme. He immediately took the pen and paper, and began to write. During his writing, I only hinted to him about the sister and about the mother's death. The rest he wrote himself and did not even show it to me, except the first chapter, until it was all done.

When he showed me the first chapter, and I began to read, I felt that he was greatly agitated and that, holding his breath, he kept looking now at the manuscript and watching my reading, and now at my face, wishing to divine upon it an expression of approbation or disapproval.

When I told him that it was very good, he flamed up, without saying anything to me, with agitated, though slow, steps walked with the copy-book up to the table, put it down, and slowly walked out into the yard. Outside he was madly wanton with the boys during the day, and, whenever our eyes met, looked at me with a grateful and kindly glance. The next day he forgot entirely about what he had written.

I only wrote out the title, divided the story into chapters, and here and there corrected the mistakes, which were due to carelessness. This story, in its primitive form, is being printed in a book under the title of "A Soldier's Life."

I do not speak of the first chapter, although there are some inimitable beauties even there, and although heedless Gordyéy is there represented exceedingly true to life and vividly—Gordyéy, who seems to be ashamed to confess his repentance, and who regards it as proper to beg the meeting of the Commune only about his son; still, this chapter is incomparably weaker than all the following. The fault is all my own, for I could not keep, during the writing of this chapter, from suggesting to him and telling him how I should have written. If there is a certain triteness in the introduction, when describing persons and dwellings, I am exclusively to blame for it. If I had left him alone, I am sure he would have described the same in action, imperceptibly, much more artistically, without the accepted and really impossible manner of logically distributed descriptions, which consists in first describing the *dramatis personæ*, even their biographies, then the locality and the surroundings, and then only the action itself.

Strange to say, all these descriptions, sometimes on dozens of pages, acquaint the reader much less with the persons than a care-lessly dropped artistic feature during an action which has already begun among persons totally unfamiliar to the reader. Even thus in this first chapter, the one phrase of Gordyéy's, "That is all I need," when he, renouncing everything, acquiesces in his fate to become a soldier, and only asks the Commune not to abandon his son—this phrase acquaints the reader much better with the person than the description of his attire, his figure, and his habit of frequenting the tavern, several times repeated and urged upon him by me. The same effect is produced by the words of the old woman, who always scolded her son, when, during her grief, she enviously remarks to her daughter-in-law: "Stop, Matréna! What is to be done? Evi-dently God has willed it so! You are young yet—maybe God will grant you to see him again. But see how old I am—I am ill—before you know it, I shall be dead!"

In the second chapter there may still be noted my influence of triteness and tampering, but here again the profoundly artistic fea-tures in the description of pictures and of the boy's death redeem the whole matter. I suggested to him that the boy had thin legs, I also suggested the sentimental details about Uncle Nefédya, who digs the little grave; but the lamentation of the mother, expressed in one clause, "O Lord, when will this slavery end!" presents to the reader the whole essence of the situation; and thereupon that night, when the elder brother is wakened by his mother's tears, and her answer to the grandmother's inquiry what the matter was, with the simple words, "My son has died," and the grandmother, getting up and making a fire and washing the little body—all that is strictly his own; all this is so compressed, so simple, so strong—not one word may be omitted, not one word changed, nor added. There are in all five lines, and in these five lines there is painted for the reader the whole picture of that sad night—a picture reflected in the imagina-tion of a boy six or seven years old.

"At midnight the mother for some reason began to weep. Grand-mother arose and said: 'What is the matter? Christ be with you!' The mother said: 'My son has died.' Grandmother made a fire, washed the boy, put a shirt on him, girded him, and placed him beneath the images. When day broke—"

You see the boy himself, awakened by the familiar tears of his mother, half-sleepy, under a caftan somewhere on the hanging bed, with frightened and sparkling eyes watching the proceedings in the hut; you see the haggard soldier's widow, who but the day before had said, "How soon will this slavery come to an end?" repentant and crushed by the thought of the end of this slavery, to such an extent that she only says, "My son has died," and knows not what to do, and calls for the grandmother to help her; and you see the old woman, worn out by the sufferings of life, bent down, emaciated, with bony limbs, as she calmly takes hold of the work with her hands that are accustomed to labour; she lights a torch, brings the water, and washes the boy; she places everything in the right place, and sets the boy, washed and girt, under the images. And you see those images, and all that night without sleep, until daybreak, as though you yourself were living through it, as that boy lived through it, gazing at it from underneath the caftan; that night arises before you with all its details and remains in your imagination.

In the third chapter there is less of my influence. The whole personality of the nurse belongs to him. Even in the first chapter, he characterized the relations of the nurse with the family in one sentence: "She was working for her own dowry, to get ready for marriage."

This one feature paints the girl as she is: she cannot take part, and she really does not take part, in the joys and sorrows of her family. She has her lawful interests, her only aim, decreed by Providence—her future marriage, her future family.

An author of our kind, especially one who wants to instruct the people by presenting to them models of morality worthy of imitation, would certainly have treated the nurse with reference to the interest she took in the common want and sorrow of the family. He would have made her a disgraceful example of indifference, or a model of love and self-sacrifice, and there would have been an idea, but not a living person, the nurse. Only a man who has profoundly studied and learned life could understand that for the nurse the question of the family's bereavement, and of the father's military service, was lawfully a secondary question, for she has her marriage ahead.

This very thing, in the simplicity of his heart, sees the artist, though but a child. If we had described the nurse as a most sympathetic, self-sacrificing girl, we should not be able at all to present her to our imagination, and we should not love her, as we love her now. Now there stands before me the dear, living form of the fat-cheeked, ruddy-faced girl, running in the evening to take part in the round dance, in shoes and red cotton kerchief bought with the money earned by her, loving her family, though distressed by that poverty and gloom which form such a contrast to her own mood.

I feel that she is a good girl, if for no other reason than because her mother never complained about her nor was aggrieved by her. On the contrary, I feel that she, with the cares about her attire, with the snatches of tunable songs, with the village gossips, brought from the summer field work or from the wintry street, was the only representative of mirth, youth, and hope during the sad time of the soldier woman's loneliness. He says with good reason that the only joy there was, was when the nurse-girl was married. It is, therefore, with good reason that he describes the wedding-feast at such length and with so much love; it is with good reason that he makes the mother say after the wedding, "Now we are completely ruined." It is evident that, by giving up the nurse, they lost that joy and merriment which she had brought with her into the house.

All that description of the wedding is uncommonly good. There are some details there which simply stagger you, and, remembering that it is an eleven-year-old boy who wrote it, you ask yourself, "Is it possible it is not merest accident?" Back of this compressed and strong description you just see the eleven-year-old boy, not taller than the table, with his bright and intelligent eyes, to whom nobody pays any attention, but who remembers and notices everything.

When, for example, he wanted some bread, he did not say that he asked his mother for it, but that he bent his mother down. This is not said by accident, but because he remembers his relation to his mother at that stage of his growth, and because he remembers how timid that relation was in the presence of others, and how familiar in their absence. There is one other thing out of a mass of observations which he could have made during the wedding ceremony which seemed to have impressed him, and which he noted down, because to him and to each of us it pictures the whole character of these ceremonies. When they said that it was bitter, the nurse took Kondráshka by his ears, and they began to kiss each other. Then the death of the grandmother, her thought of her son before her death, and the peculiar character of the mother's grief—all that is so firm and so compressed, and all that is strictly his own.

I told him most about the father's return when I gave him the plot of the story. I liked that scene, and I told it to him with trite sentimentality. He, too, liked the scene, and he asked me: "Don't tell me anything! I know it all myself, I do," and sat down to write, after which he finished the story at one sitting.

It will be very interesting for me to know the opinion of other judges, but I consider it my duty frankly to express my opinion. I have not come across anything like these pages in Russian literature. In the whole meeting there is not one reference to its having been touching; all that there is told is how it happened, and only so much of what took place is told as is necessary for the reader to understand the situation of all the persons.

The soldier said only three sentences in his house. At first he braced himself and said, "Good morning!" When he began to forget the part he was to play, he said, "Is that all there is of your family?" And everything was said in the words, "Where is my mother?"

What simple and natural words they all are, and not one person is forgotten! The boy was happy, and even wept; but he was a child, and so he, in spite of his father's tears, kept examining his wallet and pockets. Nor is the nurse forgotten. You almost see that ruddy woman, who, in shoes and fine attire, timidly enters the room, and, without saying anything, kisses her father. You almost see the embarrassed and happy father, who kisses all in succession, without knowing whom, and who, upon learning that the young woman is his daughter, calls her up once more and now kisses her, not as any young woman, but as a daughter, whom he had once left behind, without taking any thought of her.

The father is reformed. How many false and inept phrases we should have used upon that occasion! But Fédka simply told how the nurse brought some liquor, and he did not drink it. You just seem to see the woman, who, taking out of her pouch the last twenty-three kopeks, breathing heavily, in a whisper orders the young woman in the vestibule to bring some liquor, and deposits the copper money in her open hand.

You see the young woman, who, raising her apron with her hand, with the bottle underneath it, thumping with her shoes and swinging her elbows, runs down to the tavern. You see her enter the room with flushed face, taking the bottle out from underneath the apron, and you see her mother place it on the table with an expression of self-contentment and joy, and how she feels both annoyed and happy because her husband has stopped drinking. And you see that if he has given up drinking at such an occasion, he certainly has reformed. You feel that the members of the family have become different people.

"My father said a prayer and sat down at the table. I sat down by his side; the nurse sat down on the door-bench, and mother stood at the table, and looked at him, and said: 'See how much younger you look! You have no beard now!' All laughed."

Only when all the others left, the real family conversation began. Only then it was revealed that the soldier had grown rich. He had become enriched in the simplest and most natural manner, as nearly all people in the world grow rich, that is, money which did not belong to him, the Crown's money, by a lucky accident came into his hands. Some of the readers of the story remarked that this detail was immoral, and that the conception of the Crown as a milch-cow ought to be eradicated, and not strengthened in the masses. But to me this feature, leaving alone its artistic truth, is particularly pleasing. The Crown's money always remains somewhere—why, then, is it not to remain in the hands of some homeless soldier Gordyéy?

We frequently meet with diametrically opposite conceptions of honesty in the masses and in the upper classes. The demands of the masses are peculiarly serious and severe in respect to honesty in the nearest relations, for example, in relation to the family, the village, the Commune. In relation to outsiders—the public, the government, especially the foreigner, the treasury—the application of the common rules of honesty presents itself but dimly. A peasant who will never tell a lie to his brother, who will endure all kinds of privations for his family, who will not take a superfluous or unearned kopek from his fellow villager or neighbour—the same peasant will strip a foreigner or townsman like a linden switch, and will at every word tell a man of the gentry or an official a lie; if he be a soldier, he will without the slightest compunction stab a captive Frenchman, and, if Crown money falls into his hands, he will not regard it a crime before his family to take advantage of it.

In the upper classes, on the contrary, the very opposite takes place. A man of our kind will much sooner deceive a wife, a brother, a merchant, with whom he has had dealings for dozens of years, his servants, his peasants, his neighbour—and this same man abroad is all the time consumed by fear lest he should cheat somebody, and begs all the time to have pointed out to him any one he may be owing money to. This same gentleman of our class will stint his company and regiment, to obtain money for his champagne and gloves, and will bubble up with civilities before a captive Frenchman. The same man regards it as the greatest crime to make use of the Crown's money, when he is penniless—he only regards it so, for generally he will not stand his ground when the opportunity offers itself, but will commit that which he himself regards as a piece of rascality.

I am not saying which is better—I am only telling what is, as it appears to me. I will, however, remark that honesty is not a conviction and that the expression "honest convictions" is nonsense. Honesty is a moral habit; in order to acquire it, it is impossible to go by any other part than to begin with the nearest relations. The expression "honest convictions" is, in my opinion, absolutely meaningless: there are honest habits, but not honest convictions.

The words "honest convictions" are an empty phrase; for this reason those reputed honest convictions, which refer to the most remote vital conditions, to the Crown's money, to the government, to Europe, to humanity, and which are not based on habits of honesty and not educated on the nearest vital relations—for this reason those honest convictions, or, more correctly, those empty phrases of honesty, prove inadequate in relation to life.

I return to the story. The mention of the money taken from the Crown, which in the first moment may appear immoral, in our opinion, on the contrary, is a charming, touching characteristic. How often a *littérateur* of our class, wishing, in the simplicity of his soul, to represent his hero as an ideal of honesty, shows us all the dirty and corrupt interior of his imagination! Here, on the contrary, the author must make his hero happy: for happiness, his return to his family would suffice, but he had to abolish the poverty which had been weighing so heavily on the family for so many years; where was he to get the wealth from? From the impersonal Crown. To give wealth, one has to get it first—and it could not have been got in a more lawful and clever manner.

In the very scene when the money is mentioned there is a tiny detail, one word, which seems to strike me anew, every time I read it. It illumines the whole picture, paints all the persons and their relations, and only one word, and an incorrectly, syntactically incorrectly, used word at that—the word "hastened." A teacher of syntax must say that it is irregular. Hastened demands some modification—hastened to do what? the teacher ought to ask. And here it is simply said: "Mother took the money and hastened and carried it away to bury it," and it is charming. I wish I myself had used such a word, and I wish that teachers, who teach language, might say or write such a sentence.

"When we had eaten, the nurse kissed father again and went home. Then father began to rummage through his wallet, and mother and I just looked on. Mother saw a little book there, so she says: 'Oh, you have learned to read?' Says father: 'I have.'

"Then father took out a kerchief tied in a large knot and gave it to mother.

"Says mother: 'What is this?'

"Says father: 'Money.'

"Mother was happy and hastened and carried it away to bury it. Then mother came back, and says she:

" 'Where did you get it?'

"Says father: 'I was an under-officer and had Crown money: I gave it to the soldiers, and what was left in my hands, I kept.'

"My mother was so happy and ran around like a mad person. The day had passed, and the evening came. They lighted a fire. My father took the book and began to read. I sat down near him and listened, and mother held the torch. Father read the book for a long time. Then we lay down to sleep. I lay down on the back bench with father, and mother lay down at our feet, and they talked for a long time, almost until midnight. Then we fell asleep."

Here again we have a scarcely perceptible detail, which does not startle us in the least, but which leaves a deep impression—the detail of their going to bed: the father lay down with his son, the mother lay at their feet, and they did not get tired talking for a long time. How tightly, I think, the son must have hugged to his father's breast, and what a joy and happiness it was for him, falling asleep and waking again, to hear the two voices, one of which he had not heard for so long a time.

One would think all is ended: the father has returned, and there is no more poverty. But Fédka was not satisfied with that (his imaginary people apparently made a deep impression upon his imagination); he had to form a picture of their changed life, to present to himself vividly that now the woman was no longer alone, a saddened soldier's wife with small babies, but that there was a strong man in the house, who would take off the wearied shoulders of his wife all the burden of the crushing sorrow and want, and would independently, firmly, and merrily begin a new life.

For this purpose he paints us only one scene: the powerful soldier with a notched axe chops some wood and brings it into the house. You see the keen-eyed boy, used to the groans of his feeble mother and grandmother, with wonderment, respect, and pride admiring the bared muscular arms of his father, the energetic swinging of the axe, coinciding with the pectoral sigh of masculine labour, and the block, which, like a piece of kindling-wood, is split under the notched axe. You look at it, and your mind is eased about the future life of the soldier's wife. Now she will not be lost, the dear one, I think.

"In the morning mother got up, walked over to father, and says she: 'Gordyéy, get up! I need some wood to make a fire in the oven.'

"Father got up, dressed himself, put on his cap, and says he: 'Have you an axe?'

"Says mother: 'I have—it is notched; maybe it won't cut.'

"My father took the axe firmly with both his hands, walked over to the block, put it up standing, swung the axe with all his might, and split the block; he chopped up some wood and brought it to the house. Mother made a fire in the oven, and it burned, and soon it grew daylight."

But the artist is not satisfied with that. He wants to show us another side of their lives, the poetry of the happy family life, and so he paints the following picture for us:

"When it was all daylight, my father said: 'Matréna!'

"My mother came up, and says she: 'Well, what?'

"Says father: 'I am thinking of buying a cow, five sheep, two little horses, and a hut—this one is falling to pieces—well, that will take about one hundred and fifty roubles.'

"Mother thought awhile, then says she: 'Well, we shall spend all the money.'

"Says father: 'We will begin to work.'

"Says mother: 'All right, we will buy it all, but where shall we get the timber?'

"Says father: 'Hasn't Kiryúkha any?'

"Says mother: 'That's where the trouble is: the Fokanýchevs have taken it away.'

"Father thought awhile, and says he: 'Well, we shall get it from Brántsev.'

"Says mother: 'I doubt whether he has any.'

"Says father: 'Why should he not have? He has a forest.'

"Says mother: 'I am afraid he will ask too much—he is such a beast.'

"Says father: 'I will take some brandy to him, and maybe we shall come to some understanding; and you bake an egg in the ashes for dinner.'

"Mother got the dinner ready—she borrowed from her friends. Then father took the brandy and went to Brántsev's, and we stayed at home, waiting for a long time. I felt lonely without father. I began to ask mother to let me go there where father was.

"Says mother: 'You will lose your way.'

"I began to cry and wanted to go, but mother slapped me, and I sat down on the oven and cried more than before. Then I saw father coming into the room. Says he: 'Why are you crying?'

"Says mother: 'Fédka wanted to run after you, and I gave him a beating.'

"Father walked over to me, and says he: 'What are you crying about?'

"I began to complain of mother. Father went up to mother and began to beat her, in jest, saying: 'Don't beat Fédka! Don't beat Fédka!'

"Mother pretended to be crying. I sat down on father's knees and was happy. Then father sat down at the table, and put me by his side, and shouted: 'Mother, give Fédka and me something to eat—we are hungry!'

"And mother gave us some beef, and we began to eat. When we were through dinner, says mother: 'What about the timber?'

"Says father: 'Fifty roubles in silver.'

"Says mother: 'That is not bad.'

"Says father: 'I must say, it is fine timber.' "

It seems so simple: so little is said, and you see the perspective of their whole domestic life. You see that the boy is still a child, who will cry and a minute later will be happy; you see that the boy is not able to appreciate his mother's love, and that he has exchanged her for the virile father who was chopping the block; you see that the mother knows that it must be so, and she is not jealous; you see that splendid Gordyéy, whose heart is brimful of happiness.

You notice that they ate beef, and that is a charming comedy, which they all play, and all know that it is a comedy, which they play from excess of happiness. "Don't beat Fédka! Don't beat Fédka!" says the father, raising his hand against her. And the mother, who is used to unfeigned tears, pretends to be crying, with a smile of happiness at the father and the son, and the boy, who climbed on his father's knees, was proud and happy, not knowing why—proud and happy, no doubt, because now they were all happy.

"Then father sat down at the table, and put me by his side, and shouted: 'Mother, give Fédka and me something to eat—we are hungry!'"

"We are hungry," and he placed him by his side. What love and happy pride of love breathes in these words! There is nothing more charming and heartfelt in the whole charming story than this last chapter.

But what do we mean to say by all that? What import does this story, written, probably, by an exceptional boy, have pedagogically? We shall be told: "You, the teacher, may unconsciously, to yourself, have helped in the composition of these stories, and it would be too difficult to find the limits of that which belongs to you, and of that which is original."

We shall be told: "We shall admit that the story is good, but that is only one kind of literature."

We shall be told: "Fédka and the other boys, whose compositions you have printed, are happy exceptions."

We shall be told: "You are yourself a writer, and, without knowing it, you have been helping the pupils along paths which cannot be prescribed as a rule to other teachers who are not authors themselves."

We shall be told: "From all that it is impossible to deduce a common rule or theory. It is partially an interesting phenomenon, and nothing else."

I shall try to give my deductions in such a manner as to serve as answers to all the retorts imagined by me.

The feelings of truth, beauty, and goodness are independent of the degree of development. Beauty, truth, and goodness are conceptions which express only the harmony of relations in the sense of truth, beauty, and goodness. Lie is only a non-correspondence of relations in the sense of truth; there is no absolute truth. I am not lying when I say that the tables whirl about under the touch of my fingers, if I believe it to be so, even though it is an untruth; but I am lying when I say that I have no money when, according to my ideas, I have money. No immense nose is monstrous, but it is monstrous on a small face. Monstrosity is only a disharmony in relation to beauty. To give away my dinner to a mendicant, or to eat it up myself has nothing of badness in it; but to give it away, or eat it up myself, while my mother is starving is a disharmony of relations in the sense of goodness.

In bringing up, educating, developing, or in any way you please influencing the child, we ought to have and unconsciously do have one aim in view—to attain the greatest harmony possible in the sense of truth, beauty, and goodness. If time did not run, if the child did not live with every side of himself, we should be able quietly to attain this harmony by supplementing there where there seems to be a lack, and by reducing where there seems to be a superfluity. But the child lives; every side of his existence strives after development, trying to outstrip every other side, and, for the most part, we mistake the progress of these sides of his being for the aim, and coöperate in this development only, instead of aiding the harmony of the development. In this lies the eternal mistake of all pedagogical theories.

We see our ideal before us, whereas it is behind us. The necessary development of man is far from being a means of attaining that ideal of harmony which we bear within us; it is, on the contrary, a hindrance, put in our way by the Creator, in the attainment of the highest ideal of harmony. In this necessary law of forward motion lies the meaning of that fruit of that tree of the knowledge of good and evil, which our first ancestor tasted.

A healthy child is born into the world, completely satisfying all the demands of unconditional harmony in relation to truth, beauty, and goodness, which we bear within us; he is near to inanimate beings—to the plant, to the animal, to Nature, which always represents to us that truth, beauty, and goodness, which we are seeking and wishing for. In all the ages and with all men, the child has been represented as a model of innocence, sinlessness, goodness, truth, and beauty. "Man is born perfect" is a great word enunciated by Rousseau, and this word will remain firm and true, like a rock. At birth man represents the prototype of harmony, truth, beauty, and goodness. But every hour in life, every minute of time increases the extent, the quantity, and the duration of those relations which during his birth were in full harmony, and every step and every hour threaten the impairment of that harmony, and every successive step and every successive hour threaten a new impairment and give no hope of the restitution of the impaired harmony.

For the most part educators forget that the child's age is the prototype of harmony, and they assume the development of the child, which goes on independently according to immutable laws, as the aim. The development is erroneously taken for the aim because to the educators happens that which takes place with poor sculptors.

Instead of trying to arrest a local exaggerated development or the general development, instead of waiting for a new incident to destroy the irregularity which has arisen, just as a poor sculptor, instead of eradicating that which is superfluous, keeps pasting on more and more—even thus educators seem to be concerned only about not interrupting the process of development, and if they ever think of the harmony, they try to attain it by approaching an unknown prototype in the future, by departing from the prototype in the present and in the past.

No matter how irregular the development of a child may be, there are always left in him the primitive features of harmony. By moderating, at least by not pushing, the development, we may hope to get a certain approach to regularity and harmony. But we are so sure of ourselves, we are so visionarily devoted to the false ideal of manhood perfection, we are so impatient with irregularities which are near to us and so firmly believe in our ability to correct them, we are so little able to comprehend and value the primitive beauty of a child, that we, as fast as we can, magnify and paste up the irregularities that strike our vision—we correct, we educate the child.

Now one side has to be equalized with the other, now the other has to be equalized with the first. The child is developed more and more, and all the time departs more and more from the former shattered prototype, and the attainment of the imaginary prototype of the perfection of manhood becomes ever more impossible. Our ideal is behind us, not before us. Education spoils, it does not correct men. The more a child is spoiled, the less he ought to be educated, the more liberty he needs.

It is impossible and absurd to teach and educate a child, for the simple reason that the child stands nearer than I do, than any grown-up man does, to that ideal of harmony, truth, beauty, and goodness, to which I, in my pride, wish to raise him. The consciousness of this ideal is more powerful in him than in me. All he needs of me is the material, in order to fill out harmoniously and on all sides. The moment I gave him full liberty and stopped teaching him, he wrote a poetical production, the like of which cannot be found in Russian literature. Therefore, it is my conviction that we cannot teach children in general, and peasant children in particular, to write and compose. All that we can do is to teach them how to go about writing.

If what I did in order to obtain this result may be called method, this method consisted in the following:

(1) Give a great variety of themes, not inventing them specially for the children, but propose such as appear most serious and interesting to the teacher himself.

(2) Give the children children's compositions to read, and give them only children's compositions as models, for children's compositions are always more correct, more artistic, and more moral than the compositions of grown people.

(3) (Most important.) When looking through a pupil's composition, never make any remarks to him about the cleanliness of the copy-book, nor about penmanship, nor orthography, nor, above all, about the structure of the sentences and about logic.

(4) Since the difficulty of composition does not lie in the volume, nor the contents, nor the artistic quality of the theme, the sequence of the themes is not to be based on volume, nor on the

contents, nor on the language, but in the mechanism of the work, which consists, first, in selecting one out of a large number of ideas and images presented; secondly, in choosing words for it and clothing it in words; thirdly, in remembering it and finding a place for it; fourthly, in not repeating nor leaving out anything, and in the ability of combining what follows with that which precedes, all the time keeping in mind what is already written down; fifthly, and finally, in thinking and writing at the same time, without having one of these acts interfere with the other. To obtain this end, I did as follows: A few of those sides of the labour I at first took upon myself, by degrees transferring them to their care. At first I chose from the ideas and images that presented themselves to them such as I considered best, and retained them, and pointed out the place, and consulted what had already been written, keeping them from repetitions, and myself wrote, leaving to them only the clothing of the images and ideas in words; then I allowed them to make their own choice, and later to consult that which had been written down, until, at last, as in the case of "A Soldier's Life," they took the whole matter into their own hands.

———

LEO TOLSTOY (1828–1910) wrote *War and Peace, Anna Karenina,* and *Resurrection,* but he also wrote social and political essays—his effort to reflect on the world as he saw it and came to understand it, even as he imagined and rendered his own fictional world.

September, the First Day of School

Howard Nemerov

I

My child and I hold hands on the way to school,
And when I leave him at the first-grade door
He cries a little but is brave; he does
Let go. My selfish tears remind me how
I cried before that door a life ago.
I may have had a hard time letting go.

Each fall the children must endure together
What every child also endures alone:
Learning the alphabet, the integers,
Three dozen bits and pieces of a stuff
So arbitrary, so peremptory,
That worlds invisible and visible

Bow down before it, as in Joseph's dream
The sheaves bowed down and then the stars bowed down
Before the dreaming of a little boy.
That dream got him such hatred of his brothers

As cost the greater part of life to mend,
And yet great kindness came of it in the end.

II

A school is where they grind the grain of thought,
And grind the children who must mind the thought.
It may be those two grindings are but one,
As from the alphabet come Shakespeare's Plays,
As from the integers comes Euler's Law,
As from the whole, inseparably, the lives,

The shrunken lives that have not been set free
By law or by poetic phantasy.
But may they be. My child has disappeared
Behind the schoolroom door. And should I live
To see his coming forth, a life away,
I know my hope, but do not know its form

Nor hope to know it. May the fathers he finds
Among his teachers have a care of him
More than his father could. How that will look
I do not know, I do not need to know.
Even our tears belong to ritual.
But may great kindness come of it in the end.

———

HOWARD NEMEROV (1920–1991) wrote poetry, novels, and short stories. He served as poet laureate of the United States from 1988 to 1990.

II

EVOCATION AND

OBSERVATION

"Human particularity above all" the physician and poet William Carlos Williams once urged on himself, as a storyteller, and on all of us as readers. His summons gets heeded in the stories that follow.

FROM *YO!*

THE STUDENT

VARIATION

Julia Alvarez

Lou Castellucci had made good. Tall, handsome with the winning smile of a pro whose team is headed for the championships, Lou had won almost every game he had played in his life. In high school he had been a star football player, taking his small town team to the State championship first time ever.

His high school prowess had won him a full scholarship at a small liberal arts college, where he played less impressively with each succeeding year. But then, football was no longer his game. His attention had been caught by other things. His senior year he became interested in writing and in a tall girl with a mess of pretty blond hair, Penny Ross.

He had not been able to attract Penny's attention although he had tried to put himself in her way. He had taken The Contemporary Novel on the off-chance that Penny, an English major, might be in the large, popular lecture course. She hadn't been, but the class had turned out to be Lou's favorite. He was sorry now that he had so doggedly pursued his computer science major. He envied the kids who were English majors and sat around in black turtlenecks, smoking, and intensely discussed the meaning of a book. They really got into it, and it made Lou feel, listening in on their conversations in the dining hall or lounges, as if he were, well, not that smart, not that sensitive, not that vital a human being.

Spring of his senior year, Lou signed up for a writing workshop. If he could write novels like the ones he had read, he could wow her and anyone else. But it wasn't just to wow her that he took the course. Writing was the new game he wanted to learn to play. When that guy Updike or that Mailer guy wrote a book, it was a touchdown at the end of each chapter. Sometimes as he read, Lou would catch himself, making a fist, pumping his arm forward as if to say, Go, Mailer, go!

The teacher was supposed to be a known writer but not one Lou had ever heard of. She was a Dominican-American-USA-Latina— or whatever she had explained she was during the first class. Her pretty olive color made Lou think of honey in a jar. Lou had never before known a Hispanic person without ten pounds of shoulder and chest pads on him and a teeth guard in his mouth and a helmet on his head. The couple of Hispanic guys here on the team had an attitude that Lou didn't like. Christ, it hadn't been him who made their daddies pick grapes or whatever.

Anyhow that first day, this lady was real friendly. Said she wanted you to call her Yolanda or Yo or whatever you liked and talked about writing as a game you played for the fun of it, not just for the deep meaning. It made Lou feel better sitting in that circle, his big hands sweating all over this poem Yolanda passed out. They were going around the circle, having to say what they thought of it. Skinny, brainy girls found things in that poem that made Lou feel like a whole different poem had been handed to him. His neck started to get hot, and he wished he'd taken a lecture class instead of putting himself out there this way.

When his turn came, Lou said that maybe he just didn't have the background, but this poem seemed, to him, a lot more simple than everyone else had said. Yolanda's eyes lit up, and she kept nodding her head like one of those little dogs with a spring in its neck. She asked him how did he read this line and that line, and Lou did the best he could with it. "Yeah-yeah, yeah-yeah," she kept saying, and flashing her eyes at him. The writer types looked at him as if he were some kind of authority. Everyone, even the deep-thought girls, began nodding. Lou wished he'd taken his baseball cap off.

He wrote a lot of stories for this class. First one, he got back all marked up in pencil to make him feel as if everything were just a suggestion, but he got the gist of it. Big note at the bottom said, *You expect me to believe this?* He read his story over about a spy caught in a war zone, and he had to agree with her. A bunch of crap. Some episode he'd seen on TV. He thought he could put a new twist on it by having the spy wake up at the end and the whole story be a dream. In the note she said he should write about what he knew, and so in the next story, he wrote about a big football hero who gets paralyzed from the waist down in an accident and, in order to free his girl from marrying him, he commits suicide. This time the note at the bottom read, *Please come see me.*

In conference she explained she meant writing stories out of his own life. He pushed his cap back and looked down at his palms as if to reassure himself of a lifeline. "That's kind of personal," he told her.

"Yeah-yeah," she nodded enthusiastically, "stories *are* personal." The way she said it was like he was Helen Keller and she'd finally gotten through to him that *water* meant water.

It was wild talking to her in that little office. Everything he said, she tied into something she'd read. She kept climbing up on her chair to pull down this book and that from her shelves. She read him long passages of something someone famous had said that was supposed to contradict what he'd said, and kept looking up at him so hopeful. He finally said, yes, he'd try writing like she said.

Later, a buddy told Lou the woman was on a seven-year tenure track. Lou didn't really understand how this tenure ring worked. All he could think of was the racetrack his stepfather Harvey had taken him to when he was still a kid. Hyper horses sprang out of their stalls when the gates lifted, giving it all they had, to the finish line. But seven years, Jesus! No wonder some of these profs were a little odd after going around in circles for so long.

Lou had a hard time writing his next story about his dad leaving.

He gave the kid in the story a different name and colored his hair yellow and his eyes blue. He told how his mom fell apart and had to be hospitalized, and how Uncle Harvey started coming around. Course, he changed Harvey's name to Henry. One day, the kid betrays Henry by telling some friends that Henry isn't his real father. Story ends with the little kid seeing the pain go through Henry's face like a crack in china.

That day in class when they got to his story, Lou felt woozier than a pregnant girl on a roller coaster. Everyone waited for Yolanda to say what she thought and then they all fell in with her that the story was really great. Of course, soon after the praise, the "suggestions" followed. "One little thing that did bother me," they always began, and then everyone tore Lou's story apart like it was now meat for the dogs. But at least when he got the story back from Yolanda the final note read, *You're onto rich material here!*

Lou had finally gotten the hang of this story game, and he was on a winning streak now. Story after story he wrote, this Yo lady was treating it like Hemingway in the rough or something. Kids in class returned his stories with smiley faces, going on and on about how this or that part was really awesome. Then, the last story he wrote for class, he just about put himself up on that computer screen like an X-ray of his chest with a dark shadow for his aching heart.

The story was about the only game Lou could ever remember losing. It happened when he was twelve. That Saturday afternoon, Harvey was right behind the team's bench, as always, rooting for him. Then suddenly, Lou's father had showed, first time Lou'd seen the old man in ages. He was loud and obnoxious up in the bleachers. "That's my kid!" he kept shouting at the crowd.

As Lou got more and more into the writing, he forgot his fears. It was the last quarter, score tied, and his team's turn to make a final touchdown. But as he ran towards the arc of the descending ball, he couldn't think straight, worrying about what would happen after the game, if he'd go up to his dad or Harvey to be congratulated. Losing his concentration, Lou tipped the ball into his opposing teammate's hands. The visitors scored the last touchdown. Afterwards, he sat with Harvey in the car and bawled like a baby. As he wrote the story, Lou realized he hadn't cried because he had lost the game for his team. His father had left without so much as saying hello to him.

Even now, Lou could feel his goddamn eyes tingling!

But the amazing thing was you could write a story about losing and feel like you'd won. And one other thing he had learned writing these stories. He had to put himself out there more. After all, he'd taken a chance with this course, and it had been pretty terrific. He would ask this Penny girl out to dinner, and if she was dating someone else, let her up and say so. He would take the job he'd been offered even if it wasn't a big-time company his friends had heard of. He had liked the people who interviewed him, low-key and real, and they made sports equipment he believed in.

In conference, over his final folder, Yolanda told him how much she liked his last story. She sure was glad he'd taken the course. She hinted at how she'd had a tough time herself. She'd been divorced (it sounded like more than once) and kicked around for a while. What saved her was she could write books, and she just kept writing them and writing them, until something inside settled down.

"Wow," he noted. He had really wanted to ask her if she was okay now. Some little thing she said hinted she was lonely. "I mean, it sounds like you've written a lot of books."

"Not enough," she said, twirling a strand of her hair like it wasn't curly enough already. "My first-year review board feels my publications aren't *substantial* enough. They want a major publisher." She said the word *major*, rolling her eyes, like Lou would understand.

"Well, I think you're terrific," he said, shifting in his chair. Now he was the one getting nervous. What if she thought, you know, like he was coming on? Quickly, he added, "A really terrific teacher."

She laughed. "Thanks," she said. "Anyhow, I've got six more years to prove myself in the major leagues. Tenure," she pronounced, in the solemn voice of a diagnosis of a terminal illness.

"Wow," Lou said to be encouraging.

"I'm doing short stories for now," she explained. "It's been hard to concentrate on something longer this year. There's a lot going on." Yolanda sighed, on the verge of saying more.

But Lou cut the talk short. His old habit of not getting in over his head was automatic by now. He put out his hand and shook Yolanda's and thanked her for everything. "Gotta go," he said as if he had something to do besides hang out this sunny spring afternoon drinking beers with his buddies in the cemetery behind the dorms.

That afternoon, he kept thinking about her, and during a lull in the yak, he asked if any of his buddies knew this Yo person in the English department. One know-it-all guy Lou didn't like much had the scoop. García had been living in a run-down old house that burned down. She was single but had some out-of-town, pothead boyfriend.

"So is she going to marry him or what?" Lou wanted to know.

"What am I? Her counselor or something?" The guy got a laugh from everyone. He was a guy who worked for laughs, so you could never trust what he said. He went on. "Someone told me she's been having some troubles, you know." He spun small circles by his forehead with his index finger. Some of the guys laughed.

Lou defended her. "She's not crazy, she's real fine."

"Man, I'm not saying she's not fine," the buddy returned, pumping his hips as if that was what Lou had meant. "I'm just telling you what I heard, okay?"

Lou's roommate intervened. "Speaking of what we've heard. Anybody know if the rumor on Ross is true?"

Lou didn't let his face show his interest. The guys knew about his crush on Penny Ross. They knew Lou hadn't asked her out, that he worried she'd be over his head, never sure of her dating status since she was always hanging out with Philip Ballinger of the Black Turtleneck, who co-edited the literary magazine with her.

Same guy who knew the dope on Yolanda had news to report here too. Goddamn guy should start a Dear Andy column or something. He held his thumb down. "Ballinger and Ross broke off," he announced. "Ballinger's balling the Contessa." He twirled his arm elaborately like someone greeting royalty. The Contessa was an Italian beauty whose Papa owned a line of spaghetti sauce and pasta products. She had a beautiful face with pouty lips and elaborate headbands that looked like tiaras in her dramatic auburn hair. The editor went in for hair, all right. And looks. But unlike Penny Ross, the Contessa seemed totally unapproachable. She dated only the richest, brainiest guys on campus, and them she treated with a dispassionate, affected air as if she were saving herself for something better, and these little American boys were her equivalent of sleeping with the gardener.

Later, his roommate prodded Lou about Penny. "This is your chance, Castellucci. We're almost out of here. It's now or the fifth reunion, and by then, she might be married with babies."

That night in the dining room, they were sitting at their usual tables, and Penny Ross walked in with a bunch of girlfriends. "Go for it," his roommate said. Before he knew it, Lou had left his own untouched tray behind, broken into the line, reached for Penny's tray in her hands, and offered, "Can I buy you a real dinner?" She gave him an assessing look as if she wasn't sure what to make of his invitation.

Briefly it flashed through Lou's head something he'd heard his buddies say after they'd seen Penny marching at some rally. She was a feminist. He thought of the word in the same tone as Yolanda had pronounced *tenure*. "Do I know you?" she finally said.

"This is a way to get to know me," he blurted. His goddamn hands were shaking like a goddamn car with a bad fan belt.

But then, fate or something was on his side because the Contessa walked in with the editor, and Lou could see by the tightening of the muscles on her face that Penny had seen them too. He didn't necessarily like being the spare, but, hey, when you had a flat, the spare became the regular, right? Sure enough, Penny slipped her hand in the crook of his elbow and gave her head a pretty toss. "Let's get to know each other," she said. As they passed by his table of buddies, Lou lifted up the tray in his hand and waved it like a trophy for a game he'd just won.

—

For their fifth reunion, Penny and Lou brought baby Louie, and a load like you wouldn't believe. Lou just about had a heart attack every time they packed to go somewhere. Seemed to him that the amount of luggage you brought should bear some direct proportion to your body size. This little tyke's Portacrib and playpen and box of Pampers and extra bag of clean clothes and handbag of rattles and stuffed animals with lullabies inside them just about took up the whole back of the car and some of the trunk. He had stopped saying anything, though, because every time he did, Penny would burst into tears and accuse him of not loving his own son.

As if anyone could love a kid more! Maybe he wouldn't have felt so attached to this kid if things had been going better with Penny. First two years had been like a corny movie. He'd find love notes in his briefcase, and when he'd go on business trips, there'd be chocolate kisses and once a package of ladyfingers in with his underwear. He'd risen quickly in the company he joined after graduation, SportsAMER! With his good looks—he still worked out at the gym and ran his daily five miles—and his personable, persistent, but non-pushy manners (the same three p's Lou plugged to his team of salesmen), Lou was everyone's winner. Recently, he had been promoted from regional sales manager in the northeast to Vice President of Marketing, with a relocation to Dayton, Ohio.

That's when the trouble started with Penny. He was doing a lot of traveling to coordinate nationwide markets. Penny was understanding at first, but with each lonely, unemployed month in Dayton, she became withdrawn and nagging. She changed her name back to Penny Ross Castellucci, even though he'd bought her a real nice luggage set with just PC on it. Nothing seemed to please her, least of all getting pregnant.

She had awful morning sickness, and then a hard, uncomfortable pregnancy. Lou had asked to stay put in the home office till the baby was born, but he couldn't be spared from minding the national accounts. In fact, Lou was busier than ever. The bad economy had hit the company hard. SportsAMER! just couldn't compete. With a kid coming, expensive house and car payments, Lou could not afford to lose his job. At the back of his mind, of course, was what he most dreaded losing—his marriage with Penny.

After she'd gotten pregnant, she stopped being interested in much of anything. She sat around, reading all the time, like that kid was going to be an Einstein and his brain cells had to be pumped full of info. Many nights arriving home to a darkened house, Lou would climb the stairs to their bedroom. There, in a warm circle of light from the bedside lamp Penny would be reading. "I'll be with you in a sec, honey, I only have a couple of pages left."

But then she'd read on and on, way past the end of the chapter.

Penny had nagged and nagged about going to their reunion. It'd give them their first vacation in almost two years, she'd see her native New England again, and they'd get a chance to connect with old friends. Lou cringed. He wouldn't have minded going when he was on top of the world, but now, he didn't want to feel like a loser among his old-time, successful buddies. On the other hand, this might be an opportunity to network with some of those guys, put out his feelers, who knows, maybe even land another job. And even if a job lead didn't come of it, the reunion would give Lou the chance to show off little Louie to the fellows. None of those guys had had the balls to get married yet, much less have a son. If nothing else, he had sure beat them all to fatherhood.

That Saturday afternoon of reunion weekend, Lou took Louie on a tour through his alma mater. Penny had gone off with her girlfriends to play tennis, and the buddies went golfing, a sport Lou only pretended to like because SportsAMER!'s golf line was a big seller. He begged off playing ("Gotta babysit, guys!"), and instead wandered the campus until he found the old bookstore, open for the alums and stocked with memorabilia, a rocking chair with the college's insignia, a mug with the college's insignia, pennants and even a yuppie espresso cup set with the college's insignia. He bought little Louie a college sweatshirt he'd take a few years growing into and a college bib he could dirty this very day. Then he moved on to the book section to get a present for Penny, and there it was on a shelf of books by faculty authors: *Return from Left Field,* by Yolanda García. So she was still here! He bought the book, and once outside, while Louie slept on his blanket in the shade under a tree where Lou and his pals had downed many a beer and exchanged many a leer at the young coeds passing by, he began to read.

The book was a collection of short stories. In a brief introduction she wrote pretty much what Lou remembered her saying during their last conference. How these stories had kept her going through some pretty dark days. How all these stories had been in one way or another gifts from her family and friends and students over the years. How she'd like to thank so and so, and so and so. Lou ran his eye over all the names hoping to find his own, but there was no mention of the young football player who'd learned to take risks in her class. Obviously, he hadn't made too much of an impression on her. And why should he? Hadn't he been the one to cut off their last meeting when he sensed she had needed to talk with him? And what would she have said? Maybe something not much different from what he would say now to her about his own loneliness and fears for this marriage.

He skimmed through the book, reading first paragraphs to see if he'd get hooked by any one story. It was a diverse bunch all right. In some of them, he thought he recognized a certain character or situation, probably because she'd told them some of these stories in class. Then he got to the title story, the one that began, *That morning, Tío Marcos was so nervous, he put juice in my cereal instead of milk, he boiled my egg soft instead of hard, he went out to get his paper and came back empty-handed saying, "Now what was it I was going to get?" It was the day of the Little League State Championship, and Tío Marcos had been training me since the day he walked into my life, six years before, and replaced my father.*

Lou's eye was caught like a fish in the hook of the print. This was *his* story, his goddamn story, right down to the kid at the end sitting in the car, his face in his hands, bawling. Only difference was this Yo-yo lady had made all his characters Hispanic, changed the sport to baseball, and written up the story nicer than Lou had been able to write it.

Lou combed through the rest of the book, reading the stories that sounded familiar. Maybe she'd lifted stories by other kids in the class? Jesus, maybe they could bring a class action suit together? He looked for her picture in the back, but there wasn't one. A brief biography mentioned that Yolanda García had written numerous works of fiction, that she taught at this college, that she was living on a farm in New Hampshire with her cats, Fidel and Jesús. Lou remembered the story he had heard from his buddy five years ago. Yolanda was having emotional problems. Well, she sounded settled down now, so he didn't have to feel protective of her. It crossed his mind that she must be on her next to last go-around on the tenure track.

He was re-reading the story so intently, Penny's voice made him start. "Looo-oo, Looo-oo!" She was calling him from the window of the dorm they were staying in, waving and laughing! Her pretty hair hung down like the girl in the fairytale they'd be reading little Louie in a few years.

She was waiting at the dorm room door, and her face lit up again when she saw Lou and the baby. "My two boys," she greeted them, taking the baby. Lou hadn't heard that lightness in her voice in a while. He put his arm around her shoulder. "You having a good time, sweetheart?"

She smiled warmly, her eye wandering by force of habit to his book. "What you reading?" She cocked her head to one side and read the name on the spine. "I remember her! Must be good. I called you five or six times before you heard me!"

He thought of telling Penny about the plagiarized story then, but watching her, happily nuzzling the baby, he held back. Years ago, when she had been co-editor of *Musings* along with—what was his name?—Lou had submitted a couple of the Henry stories to the magazine, including this one. He had been too afraid to do so under his own name, so his roommate had sent them in like they were his. A note had come back from *the editors*, saying that the stories did not quite work. They were a little too maudlin. *Maudlin?* Lou looked it up just to be sure. *Maudlin?* What the hell was wrong with being sentimental? That rejection note had made it even harder for Lou to ask Penny out.

So for now, he kept his secret to himself. He could feel a closeness growing between them, and he didn't feel like admitting this small failure to her. Instead, while the baby napped, they made sweet, silly love in one of the small twin beds like in the old days. From the room under them came the clowning thumps of one of the envious alums.

During the president's cocktail party, Lou kept an eye out for Yolanda. He had brought the book in Louie's diaper bag for her to autograph. He wouldn't say a thing to her about the title story and see if she acknowledged she had lifted it from him. He didn't know where he'd go from there. It was like he remembered when he was writing a story. You never really knew what the ending would be until you'd written yourself right up to it.

The chairman of the English department came up to Penny to meet her little boy. He was heavily freckled, and so his skin looked like a tweedy continuation of his jacket. "And this is my husband," Penny said, turning to Lou, who stood holding the diaper bag, plastic cradle seat, and Big Bird rattle, grinning at the chairman who didn't remember him. After some catch-up between Penny and the chairman, Lou asked after Yolanda García. "She's up for tenure in the fall," the chairman informed them. "We're very hopeful," he said confidentially. "She's published a new book with Norton, and she seems happy here now."

"She wasn't happy before?" Lou asked. Yolanda's little crime made him feel intimately tied to the secrets in her life.

"It's hard for our young women professors, a remote place like this, a good old boy network firmly entrenched—"

Penny was nodding away like the chair was talking about her. In fact, he sounded just like Penny when she complained about living in Dayton and wasting her life away. "Not to mention that being a minority in New Hampshire is no picnic—" The chair threw up his hands. "Anyhow, she has done well. Says her students have saved her—quite enthusiastic about her classes."

Lou felt like saying, Let me tell you just how *quite*.

Penny and the chair looked at him, sensing he was about to say something.

"Yolanda García is a plagiarist," he would start. He had a sudden picture of her standing on her desk the first time he had come to her office, reaching up for a book on her shelf. Her legs had surprised him, skinny like a schoolgirl's, a faint, white, endearing scar just below one knee. He remembered, too, her fingers, nervously tugging at her hair, the nails bitten back but still painted a bright red. That she should paint her nails red, and then, bite them off! And her lipstick, she never could get it on right, so she looked as if she'd just eaten something messy and red. Suddenly, Lou knew he wasn't going to tell on this Yolanda García he had pictured in his head. Details, she had always said, the goddamn details could break your heart.

And so he said, "As one of her ex-students, I can tell you she was terrific!" His marketing vice president voice put extra punch in his recommendation. The chairman lifted his pale eyebrows.

"I didn't know you'd taken a course from her," Penny said, looking at him with surprise. "You took a writing course?"

Lou nodded. "My favorite course, too. Made me wish I'd been an English major. Not to mention I would have met you a lot sooner!" Lou laughed, and the chair laughed. Everything had worked out so well for his star student.

———

Driving away the next day, they waved to their friends. Once on the highway, Lou looked over at the silent Penny. She was turned towards the window, one of her wistful moods that could so easily turn dark. It had been good for her to be with her friends, but she was readying herself for the long days with a little baby and no companionship but a pile of books. He thought of how Yolanda had said her students had saved her, and he wondered what he could do to make Penny happier.

"Baby asleep?" he asked, hoping to engage her in the one subject in which she was always interested.

Penny nodded. "Little guy's exhausted."

Lou looked in the rearview mirror, and sure enough, baby Louie lay pooped out in the car seat. "Tell you what, why don't you read us one of those stories? Get our minds off leaving."

"You're really turning into a reader." Penny picked Yolanda's book out of the carry-on bag beside the baby and opened to the table of contents. "Why don't I read all the titles, and you tell me which one sounds like a story you want to hear."

It was not hard for him to decide, of course, and Penny began the story, *Return from Left Field*. Her tense voice relaxed as she read paragraph after paragraph. She turned pages eagerly, smiled and sometimes chuckled. *"That was the first failure in my life, and I can't say it prepared me for the rest."* She read the last sentences. *"But whenever they've come, I've thought of sitting in that car, looking out at that deserted diamond, thinking, I'll never get over this. And Tio Marcos leaning over and saying, Don't worry, Miguelito. You'll return from left field."*

Penny closed the book and stroked the cover with her open hand. "That was a sweet story," she said. There was no irony in her voice.

"Really?" he said. "You didn't think it was just a little sentimental?"

Penny shook her head. "It took risks, if that's what you mean. That's what I loved about it." She was defending that story as if it were little Louie or something.

His heart was making such a racket in his chest, he was sure she would hear it and tell him to quiet down, he was going to wake up the baby. But instead she reached over and squeezed his hand. "Funny, but that story reminded me—" she began.

"Yeah?" he said, grinning, on the verge of telling her.

As Lou listened, her voice opened up into a story of a remembered childhood loss. Out the window, the landscape blurred into the emerald green of a playing field. "Wow," he kept saying.

—

JULIA ALVAREZ was born on March 27, 1950, in New York City. Her family moved to the Dominican Republic shortly after her birth, and returned to the United States when she was ten. It was in high school in New York that Alvarez decided to become a writer. She received her Bachelor of Arts from Middlebury College, and followed it with an M.F.A. from Syracuse University in 1975.

Alvarez has been a professor of creative writing and English at Phillips Andover Academy in Massachusetts, the University of Vermont, the University of Illinois, and Middlebury College. She now lives in the Champlain Valley in Vermont.

THE BUS TO ST. JAMES'S

John Cheever

The bus to St. James's—a Protestant Episcopal school for boys and girls—started its round at eight o'clock in the morning, from a corner of Park Avenue in the Sixties. The earliness of the hour meant that some of the parents who took their children there were sleepy and still without coffee, but with a clear sky the light struck the city at an extreme angle, the air was fresh, and it was an exceptionally cheerful time of day. It was the hour when cooks and doormen walk dogs, and when porters scrub the lobby floor mats with soap and water. Traces of the night—the parents and children once watched a man whose tuxedo was covered with sawdust wander home— were scarce.

When the fall semester began, five children waited for the school bus at this stop, and they all came from the limestone apartment houses of the neighborhood. Two of the children, Louise and Emily Sheridan, were newcomers. The others—the Pruitt boy, Katherine Bruce, and the little Armstrong girl—had met the bus for St. James's the year before.

Mr. Pruitt brought his son to the corner each morning. They had the same tailor and they both tipped their hats to the ladies. Although Katherine Bruce was old enough to walk to the bus stop by herself, she was nearsighted and her father made the trip with her unless he was out of town on business, in which case a maid brought her. Stephen Bruce's first wife, Katherine's mother, had died, and he was more painstakingly attentive to his daughter than fathers usually are. She was a large girl, but he took her hand tenderly and led her across the street and sometimes stood on the corner with his arm around her shoulders. The second Mrs. Bruce had no children. Mrs. Armstrong took her daughter to the bus stop only when her maid or her cook refused. Like Mrs. Armstrong, Mrs. Sheridan shared this chore with a maid, but she was more constant. At least three mornings a week she came to the corner with her daughters and with an old Scotch terrier on a leash.

St. James's was a small school, and the parents, waiting on the street corner until the bus arrived, spoke confidently to one another. Mr. Bruce knew Mr. Pruitt's brother-in-law and was the second cousin of a woman who had roomed with Mrs. Armstrong in boarding school. Mrs. Sheridan and Mr. Pruitt had friends in common. "We saw some friends of yours last night," Mr. Pruitt said one morning. "The Murchisons?" "Oh yes," Mrs. Sheridan said, *"yes."* She never gave a simple affirmative; she always said, "Oh yes, *yes,"* or "Oh yes, *yes,* yes."

Mrs. Sheridan dressed plainly and her hair was marked with gray. She was not pretty or provocative, and compared to Mrs. Armstrong, whose hair was golden, she seemed plain; but her features were fine and her body was graceful and slender. She was a well-mannered woman of perhaps thirty-five, Mr. Bruce decided, with a well-ordered house and a perfect emotional digestion—one of those women who, through their goodness, can absorb anything. A great deal of authority seemed to underlie her mild manner. She would have been raised by solid people, Mr. Bruce thought, and would respect all the boarding-school virtues: courage, good sportsmanship, chastity, and honor. When he heard her say in the morning, "Oh yes, *yes!*" it seemed to him like a happy combination of manners and spirit.

Mr. Pruitt continued to tell Mrs. Sheridan that he had met her friends, but their paths never seemed to cross directly. Mr. Bruce, eavesdropping on their conversation, behind his newspaper, was gratified by this because he disliked Mr. Pruitt and respected Mrs. Sheridan; but he knew they were bound to meet somewhere other than on the street, and one day Mr. Pruitt took his hat off to Mrs. Sheridan and said, "Wasn't it a delightful party?" "Oh, yes," Mrs. Sheridan said, "yes." Then Mr. Pruitt asked Mrs. Sheridan when she and her husband had left, and she said they had left at midnight. She did not seem anxious to talk about the party, but she answered all of Mr. Pruitt's questions politely.

Mr. Bruce told himself that Mrs. Sheridan was wasting her time; Pruitt was a fool and she deserved better. His dislike of Pruitt and his respect for Mrs. Sheridan seemed idle, but he was pleased, one morning, to get to the corner and find that Mrs. Sheridan was there with her two daughters and the dog, and that Pruitt wasn't. He wished her a good morning.

"Good morning," she said. "We seem to be early."

Katherine and the older Sheridan girl began to talk together.

"I think I knew Katherine's mother," Mrs. Sheridan said politely. "Wasn't your first wife Martha Chase?"

"Yes."

"I knew her in college. I didn't know her well. She was in the class ahead of me. How old is Katherine now?"

"She was eight last summer," Mr. Bruce said.

"We have a brother," the younger Sheridan girl said, standing beside her mother. "He's eight."

"Yes, dear," Mrs. Sheridan said.

"He was drowned," the little girl said.

"Oh, I'm sorry," Mr. Bruce said.

"He was quite a good swimmer," the little girl went on, "but we think that he must have gotten a cramp. You see, there was a thunderstorm, and we all went into the boathouse and we weren't looking and—"

"That was a long time ago, dear," Mrs. Sheridan said gently.

"It wasn't so long ago," the little girl said. "It was only last summer."

"Yes, dear," her mother said. "Yes, yes."

Mr. Bruce noticed that there was no trace of pain, or of the effort to conceal it, on her face, and her composure seemed to him a feat of intelligence and grace. They continued to stand together, without talking, until the other parents arrived with their children, just as the bus came up the street. Mrs. Sheridan called to the old dog and went down Park Avenue, and Mr. Bruce got into a taxi and went to work.

Toward the end of October, on a rainy Friday night, Mr. and Mrs. Bruce took a taxi to St. James's School. It was Parents' Night. One of the senior boys ushered them into a pew at the rear of the chapel. The altar was stripped of its mysteries, and the rector stood on the raised floor between the choir stalls, waiting for the laggard parents to be seated. He tucked and pulled nervously at his clericals, and then signaled for silence by clearing his throat.

"On behalf of the faculty and the board of trustees," he said, "I welcome the parents of St. James's here this evening. I regret that we have such inclement weather, but it doesn't seem to have kept any of you at home." This was said archly, as if the full attendance reflected his powers of intimidation. "Let us begin," he said, "with a prayer for the welfare of our school: Almighty Father, Creator of Heaven and earth!..." Kneeling, and with their heads bowed, the congregation looked indestructible and as if the permanence of society depended and could always depend on them. And when the prayer ended, the rector spoke to them about their durability. "I have some very interesting statistics for you all tonight," he said. "This year we have sixteen children enrolled in the school whose parents *and* whose grandparents were St. James's children. I think that's a very impressive number. I doubt that any other day school in the city could equal it."

During the brief speech in defense of conservative education that followed, Mr. Bruce noticed that Mrs. Sheridan was seated a few pews in front of him. With her was a tall man—her husband, presumably—with a straight back and black hair. When the talk ended, the meeting was opened for questions. The first question was from a mother who wanted advice on how to restrict her children's use of television. While the rector was answering this question, Mr. Bruce noticed that the Sheridans were having an argument. They were whispering, and their disagreement seemed intense. Suddenly, Mrs. Sheridan separated herself from the argument. She had nothing further to say. Mr. Sheridan's neck got red. He continued, in a whisper, to press his case, bending toward his wife, and shaking his head. Mrs. Sheridan raised her hand.

"Yes, Mrs. Sheridan," the rector said.

Mr. Sheridan picked up his coat and his derby, and, saying "Excuse me, please," "Thank you," "Excuse me," passed in front of the other people in the pew, and left the chapel.

"Yes, Mrs. Sheridan?" the rector repeated.

"I wonder, Dr. Frisbee," Mrs. Sheridan said, "if you and the board of trustees have ever thought of enrolling Negro children in St. James's?"

"That question came up three years ago," the rector said impatiently, "and a report was submitted to the board of trustees on the question. There have been very few requests for it, but if you would like a copy, I will have one sent to you."

"Yes," Mrs. Sheridan said, "I would like to read it."

The rector nodded and Mrs. Sheridan sat down.

"Mrs. Townsend?" the rector asked.

"I have a question about science and religion," Mrs. Townsend said. "It seems to me that the science faculty stresses science to the detriment of religious sentiment, especially concerning the Creation. It seems to me..."

Mrs. Sheridan picked up her gloves and, smiling politely and saying "Excuse me," "Thank you," "Please excuse me," she brushed past the others in the pew. Mr. Bruce heard her heels on the paved floor of the hall and, by craning his neck, was able to see her. The noise of traffic and of the rain grew louder as she pushed open one of the heavy doors, and faded as the door swung to.

—

Late one afternoon the following week, Mr. Bruce was called out of a stockholders' meeting to take a telephone call from his wife. She wanted him to stop at the stable where Katherine took riding lessons and bring her home. It exasperated him to have been called from the meeting to take this message, and when he returned, the meeting itself had fallen into the hands of an old man who had brought with him Robert's Rules of Order. Business that should have been handled directly and simply dragged, and the meeting ended in a tedious and heated argument. Immediately afterward, he took a taxi up to the Nineties, and went through the tack room of the riding stable into the ring. Katherine and some other girls, wearing hunting bowlers and dark clothes, were riding. The ring was cold and damp, its overhead lights burned whitely, the mirrors along the wall were fogged and streaked with moisture, and the riding mistress spoke to her pupils with an elaborate courteousness. Mr. Bruce watched his daughter. Katherine wore glasses, her face was plain, and her light hair was long and stringy. She was a receptive and obedient girl, and her exposure to St. James's had begun faintly to show in her face. When the lesson ended, he went back into the tack room. Mrs. Sheridan was there, waiting for her daughters.

"Can I give you a lift home?" Mr. Bruce said.

"You most certainly can," Mrs. Sheridan said. "We were going to take a bus."

The children joined them and they all went out and waited for a cab. It was dark.

"I was interested in the question you asked at the parents' meeting," Mr. Bruce said. This was untrue. He was not interested in the question, and if Negroes had been enrolled in St. James's, he would have removed Katherine.

"I'm glad someone was interested," she said. "The Rector was wild."

"That's principally what interested me," Mr. Bruce said, trying to approach the truth.

A cab came along, and they got into it. He let Mrs. Sheridan off at the door of her apartment house, and watched her walk with her two daughters into the lighted lobby.

Mrs. Sheridan had forgotten her key and a maid let her in. It was late and she had asked people for dinner. The door to her husband's room was shut, and she bathed and dressed without seeing him. While she was combing her hair, she heard him go into the living room and turn on the television set. In company, Charles Sheridan always spoke contemptuously of television. "By Jove," he would say, "I don't see how anyone can look at that trash. It must be a year since I've turned our set on." Now his wife could hear him laughing uproariously.

She left her room and went down the hall to the dining room to check on everything there. Then she went through the pantry into the kitchen. She sensed trouble as soon as the door closed after her. Helen, the waitress, was sitting at a table near the sink. She had been crying. Anna, the cook, put down the pan she had been washing, to be sure of hearing everything that was said.

"What's the matter, Helen?" Mrs. Sheridan asked.

"From my pie he took twelff dollars, Mrs. Seridan," Helen said. She was Austrian.

"What for, Helen?"

"The day I burn myself. You told me to go to the doctor?"

"Yes."

"For that he took from my pie twelff dollars."

"I'll give you a check tomorrow, Helen," Mrs. Sheridan said. "Don't worry."

"Yes, ma'am," Helen said. "Thank you."

Mr. Sheridan came through the pantry into the kitchen. He looked handsome in his dark clothes. "Oh, here you are," he said to his wife. "Let's have a drink before they come." Then, turning to the waitress, he asked, "Have you heard from your family recently?"

"No, Mr. Seridan," Helen said.

"Where is it your family lives?" he asked.

"In Missigan, Mr. Seridan." She giggled, but this joke had been made innumerable times in the past few years and she was tired of it.

"Where?" Mr. Sheridan asked.

"In Missigan, Mr. Seridan," she repeated.

He burst out laughing. "By Jove, I think that's funny!" he said. He put his arm around his wife's waist and they went in to have a drink.

Mr. Bruce returned to a much pleasanter home. His wife, Lois, was a pretty woman, and she greeted him affectionately. He sat down with her for a cocktail. "Marguerite called me this morning," she said, "and told me that Charlie's lost his job. When I heard the phone ring, I sensed trouble; I *sensed* it. Even before I picked up the receiver, I knew that something was wrong. At first, I thought it was going to be poor Helen Luckman. She's had so many misfortunes recently that she's been on my mind a lot of the time. Then I heard Marguerite's voice. She said that poor Charlie had been a wonderful sport about the whole thing and that he was determined to get an even better job. He's traveled all over the United States for that firm and now they're just letting him go. *She* called while I was in bed, and the reason I stayed in bed this morning is because my back's been giving me a little trouble again. It's nothing serious—it's nothing serious at all—but the pain's excruciating and I'm going to Dr. Parminter tomorrow and see if he can help me."

Lois had been frail when Mr. Bruce first met her. It had been one of her great charms. The extreme pallor and delicacy of her skin could be accounted for partly by a year of her life when, as she said, the doctors had given her up for dead. Her frailness was a fact, a mixture of chance and inheritance, and she could not be blamed for her susceptibility to poison oak, cold germs, and fatigue.

"I'm very sorry to hear about your back, dear," Mr. Bruce said.

"Well, I didn't spend the whole day in bed," she said. "I got up around eleven and had lunch with Betty and then went shopping."

Lois Bruce, like a great many women in New York, spent a formidable amount of time shopping along Fifth Avenue. She read the advertisements in the newspapers more intently than her husband read the financial section. Shopping was her principal occupation. She would get up from a sickbed to go shopping. The atmosphere of the department stores had a restorative effect on her disposition. She would begin her afternoon at Altman's—buy a pair of gloves on the first floor, and then travel up on the escalator and look at andirons. She would buy a purse and some face cream at Lord & Taylor's, and price coffee tables, upholstery fabrics, and cocktail glasses. "Down?" she would ask the elevator operator when the doors rolled open, and if the operator said "Up," Lois would board the car anyhow, deciding suddenly that whatever it was that she wanted might be in the furniture or the linen department. She would buy a pair of shoes and a slip at Saks, send her mother some napkins from Mosse's, buy a bunch of cloth flowers at De Pinna's, some hand lotion at Bonwit's, and a dress at Bendel's. By then, her feet and her head would be pleasantly tired, the porter at Tiffany's would be taking in the flag, the lamps on the carriages by the Plaza would be lighted. She would buy a cake at Dean's, her last stop, and walk home through the early dark like an honest workman, contented and weary.

When they sat down to dinner, Lois watched her husband taste his soup and smiled when she saw that he was pleased. "It is good, isn't it?" she said. "I can't taste it myself—I haven't been able to taste anything for a week—but I don't want to tell Katie, bless her, because it would hurt her feelings, and I didn't want to compliment her if it wasn't right. Katie," she called, through the pantry, "your soup is delicious."

———

Mrs. Sheridan did not come to the corner all the next week. On Wednesday afternoon, Mr. Bruce stopped by for Katherine at her dancing class, on the way home from his office. The Sheridan girls were in the same class, and he looked for Mrs. Sheridan in the lobby of the Chardin Club, but she wasn't there. He didn't see her again, actually, until he went, on Sunday afternoon, to bring Katherine home from a birthday party.

Because Lois sometimes played cards until seven o'clock, it often fell to Mr. Bruce to call for Katherine at some address at the end of the day, to see her through the stiff thanks and goodbyes that end a children's party. The streets were cold and dark; the hot rooms where the parties were smelled of candy and flowers. Among the friends and relatives there he was often pleased to meet people with whom he had summered or been to school. Some of these parties were elaborate, and he had once gone to get Katherine at an apartment in the Waldorf Towers where six little girls were being entertained by a glass blower.

In the hallway that Sunday afternoon, an Irish maid was taking up peanut shells with a carpet sweeper, lost balloons were bunched on the ceiling above her white head, and Mr. Bruce met a dwarf, dressed as a clown, who had entertained at parties in his own childhood. The old man had not changed his stock of tricks or his patter, and he was proud that he was able to remember the names and faces of most of the generations of children he had entertained. He held Mr. Bruce in the hall until, after several wrong guesses, he came up with his name. In the living room a dozen friends and relatives were drinking cocktails. Now and then, a weary child, holding a candy basket or a balloon, would wander through the crowd of grown people. At the end of the living room, a couple who worked a marionette show were dismantling their stage. The woman's hair was dyed, and she smiled and gesticulated broadly while she worked, like a circus performer, though no one was watching her.

While Mr. Bruce was waiting for Katherine to put her coat on, Mrs. Sheridan came in from the foyer. They shook hands. "Can I take you home?" he asked.

She said, "Yes, *yes*," and went in search of her older daughter.

Katherine went up to her hostess and dropped a curtsy. "It was nice of you to ask me to your party, Mrs. Howells," she said, without mumbling. "And thank you very much."

"She's such a dear. It's such a joy to have her!" Mrs. Howells said to Mr. Bruce, and laid a hand absent-mindedly on Katherine's head.

Mrs. Sheridan reappeared with her daughter. Louise Sheridan curtsied and recited her thanks, but Mrs. Howells was thinking about something else and did not hear. The little girl repeated her thanks, in a louder voice.

"Why, thank you for coming!" Mrs. Howells exclaimed abruptly.

Mr. Bruce and Mrs. Sheridan and the two children went down in the elevator. It was still light when they came out of the building onto Fifth Avenue.

"Let's walk," Mrs. Sheridan said. "It's only a few blocks."

The children went on ahead. They were in the lower Eighties and their view was broad; it took in the avenue, the Museum, and the Park. As they walked, the double track of lights along the avenue went on with a faint click. There was a haze in the air that made the lamps give off a yellow light, and the colonnades of the Museum, the mansard roof of the Plaza above the trees, and the multitude of yellow lights reminded Stephen Bruce of many pictures of Paris and London ("Winter Afternoon") that had been painted at the turn of the century. This deceptive resemblance pleased him, and his pleasure in what he could see was heightened by the woman he was with. He felt that she saw it all very clearly. They walked along without speaking most of the way. A block or two from the building where she lived, she took her arm out of his.

"I'd like to talk with you someday about St. James's School," Mr. Bruce said. "Won't you have lunch with me? Could you have lunch with me on Tuesday?"

"I'd love to have lunch with you," Mrs. Sheridan said.

———

The restaurant where Mrs. Sheridan and Mr. Bruce met for lunch on Tuesday was the kind of place where they were not likely to see anyone they knew. The menu was soiled, and so was the waiter's tuxedo. There are a thousand places like it in the city. When they greeted one another, they could have passed for a couple that had been married fifteen years. She was carrying bundles and an umbrella. She might have come in from the suburbs to get some clothes for the children. She said she had been shopping, she had taken a taxi, she had been rushed, she was hungry. She took off her gloves, rattled the menu, and looked around. He had a whiskey and she asked for a glass of sherry.

"I want to know what you really think about St. James's School," he said, and she began, animatedly, to talk.

They had moved a year earlier from New York to Long Island, she said, because she wanted to send her children to a country school. She had been to country schools herself. The Long Island school had been unsatisfactory, and they had moved back to New York in September. Her husband had gone to St. James's, and that had determined their choice. She spoke excitedly, as Mr. Bruce had known she would, about the education of her daughters, and he guessed that this was something she couldn't discuss with the same satisfaction with her husband. She was excited at finding someone who seemed interested in her opinions, and she put herself at a disadvantage, as he intended she should, by talking too much. The deep joy we take in the company of people with whom we have just recently fallen in love is undisguisable, even to a purblind waiter, and they both looked wonderful. He got her a taxi at the corner. They said goodbye.

"You'll have lunch with me again?"

"Of course," she said, "of course."

She met him for lunch again. Then she met him for dinner—her husband was away. He kissed her in the taxi, and they said good night in front of her apartment house. When he called her a few days later, a nurse or a maid answered the telephone and said that Mrs. Sheridan was ill and could not be disturbed. He was frantic. He called several times during the afternoon, and finally Mrs. Sheridan answered. Her illness was not serious, she said. She would be up in a day or two and she would call him when she was well. She called him early the next week, and they met for lunch at a restaurant in an uptown apartment house. She had been shopping. She took off her gloves, rattled the menu, and looked around another failing restaurant, poorly lighted and with only a few customers. One of her daughters had a mild case of measles, she said, and Mr. Bruce was interested in the symptoms. But he looked, for a man who claimed to be interested in childhood diseases, bilious and vulpine. His color was bad. He scowled and rubbed his forehead as if he suffered from a headache. He repeatedly wet his lips and crossed and recrossed his legs. Presently, his uneasiness seemed to cross the table. During the rest of the time they sat there, the conversation was about commonplace subjects, but an emotion for which they seemed to have no words colored the talk and darkened and enlarged its shapes. She did not finish her dessert. She let her coffee get cold. For a while, neither of them spoke. A stranger, noticing them in the restaurant, might have thought that they were a pair of old friends who had met to discuss a misfortune. His face was gray. Her hands were trembling. Leaning toward her, he said, finally, "The reason I asked you to come here is because the firm I work for has an apartment upstairs."

"Yes," she said. *"Yes."*

For lovers, touch is metamorphosis. All the parts of their bodies seem to change, and they seem to become something different and better. That part of their experience that is distinct and separate, the totality of the years before they met, is changed, is redirected toward this moment. They feel they have reached an identical point of intensity, an ecstasy of rightness that they command in every part, and any recollection that occurs to them takes on this final clarity, whether it be a sweep hand on an airport clock, a snow owl, a Chicago railroad station on Christmas Eve, or anchoring a yawl in a strange harbor while all along the stormy coast strangers are blowing their horns for the yacht-club tender, or running a ski trail at that hour when, although the sun is still in the sky, the north face of every mountain lies in the dark.

———

"Do you want to go downstairs alone? The elevator men in these buildings—" Stephen Bruce said when they had dressed.

"I don't care about the elevator men in these buildings," she said lightly.

She took his arm, and they went down in the elevator together. When they left the building, they were unwilling to part, and they decided on the Metropolitan Museum as a place where they were not likely to be seen by anyone they knew. The nearly empty rotunda looked, at that hour of the afternoon, like a railroad station past train time. It smelled of burning coal. They looked at stone horses and pieces of cloth. In a dark passage, they found a prodigal representation of the Feast of Love. The god—disguised now as a woodcutter, now as a cowherd, a sailor, a prince—came through every open door. Three spirits waited by a holly grove to lift the armor from his shoulders and undo his buckler. A large company encouraged his paramour. The whole creation was in accord—the civet and the bear, the lion and the unicorn, fire and water.

Coming back through the rotunda, Mr. Bruce and Mrs. Sheridan met a friend of Lois's mother. It was impossible to avoid her and they said How-do-you-do and I'm-happy-to-meet-you, and Stephen promised to remember the friend to his mother-in-law. Mr. Bruce and Mrs. Sheridan walked over to Lexington and said goodbye. He returned to his office and went home at six. Mrs. Bruce had not come in, the maid told him. Katherine was at a party, and he was supposed to bring her home. The maid gave him the address and he went out again without taking off his coat. It was raining. The doorman, in a white raincoat, went out into the storm, and returned riding on the running board of a taxi. The taxi had orange seats, and as it drove uptown, he heard the car radio playing a tango. Another doorman let him out and he went into a lobby that, like the one in the building where he lived, was meant to resemble the hall of a manor house. Upstairs, there were peanut shells on the rug, balloons on the ceiling; friends and relatives were drinking cocktails in the living room, and at the end of the room, the marionette stage was again being dismantled. He drank a Martini and talked with a friend while he waited for Katherine to put her coat on. "Oh yes, *yes*!" he heard Mrs. Sheridan say, and then he saw her come into the room with her daughters.

Katherine came between them before they spoke, and he went, with his daughter, over to the hostess. Katherine dropped her curtsy and said brightly, "It was very nice of you to ask me to your party, Mrs. Bremont, and thank you very much." As Mr. Bruce started for the elevator, the younger Sheridan girl dropped her curtsy and said, "It was a very nice party, Mrs. Bremont. . . ."

He waited downstairs, with Katherine, for Mrs. Sheridan, but something or someone delayed her, and when the elevator had come down twice without bringing her, he left.

Mr. Bruce and Mrs. Sheridan met at the apartment a few days later. Then he saw her in a crowd at the Rockefeller Center skating rink, waiting for her children. He saw her again in the lobby of the Chardin Club, among the other parents, nursemaids, and chauffeurs who were waiting for the dancing class to end. He didn't speak to her, but he heard her at his back, saying to someone, "Yes, Mother's very well, thank you. Yes, I will give her your love." Then he heard her speaking to someone farther away from him and then her voice fell below the music. That night, he left the city on business and did not return until Sunday, and he went Sunday afternoon to a football game with a friend. The game was slow and the last quarter was played under lights. When he got home, Lois met him at the door of the apartment. The fire in the living room was lighted. She fixed their drinks and then sat across the room from him in a chair near the fire. "I forgot to tell you that Aunt Helen called on Wednesday. She's moving from Gray's Hill to a house nearer the shore."

He tried to find something to say to this item of news and couldn't. After five years of marriage he seemed to have been left with nothing to say. It was like being embarrassed by a shortage of money. He looked desperately back to the football game and the trip to Chicago for something that might please her, and couldn't find a word. Lois felt his struggle and his failure. She stopped talking herself. I haven't had anyone to talk to since Wednesday, she thought, and now he has nothing to say. "While you were away, I strained my back again, reaching for a hatbox," she said. "The pain is excruciating, and Dr. Parminter doesn't seem able to help me, so I'm going to another doctor, named Walsh, who—"

"I'm terribly sorry your back is bothering you," he said. "I hope Dr. Walsh will be able to help."

The lack of genuine concern in his voice hurt her feelings. "Oh, and I forgot to tell you—there's been some *trouble*," she said crossly. "Katherine spent the afternoon with Helen Woodruff and some other children. There were some boys. When the maid went into the playroom to call them for supper, she found them all undressed. Mrs. Woodruff was very upset and I told her you'd call."

"Where is Katherine?"

"She's in her room. She won't speak to me. I don't like to be the one to say it, but I think you ought to get a psychiatrist for that girl."

"I'll go and speak to her," Mr. Bruce said.

"Well, will you want any supper?" Lois asked.

"Yes," he said, "I would like some supper."

Katherine had a large room on the side of the building. Her furniture had never filled it. When Mr. Bruce went in, he saw her sitting on the edge of her bed, in the dark. The room smelled of a pair of rats that she had in a cage. He turned on the light and gave her a charm bracelet that he had bought at the airport, and she thanked him politely. He did not mention the trouble at the Woodruffs', but when he put his arm around her shoulders, she began to cry bitterly.

"I didn't want to do it this afternoon," she said, "but *she* made me, and she was the hostess, and we always have to do what the hostess says."

"It doesn't matter if you wanted to or not," he said. "You haven't done anything terribly wrong."

He held her until she was quiet, and then left her and went into his bedroom and telephoned Mrs. Woodruff. "This is Katherine Bruce's father," he said. "I understand that there was some difficulty there this afternoon. I just wanted to say that Katherine has been given her lecture, and as far as Mrs. Bruce and I are concerned, the incident has been forgotten."

"Well, it hasn't been forgotten over here," Mrs. Woodruff said. "I don't know who started it, but I've put Helen to bed without any supper. Mr. Woodruff and I haven't decided how we're going to punish her yet, but we're going to punish her severely." He heard Lois calling to him from the living room that his supper was ready. "I suppose you know that immorality is sweeping this country," Mrs. Woodruff went on. "Our child has never heard a dirty word spoken in her life in this household. There is no room for filth here. If it takes fire to fight fire, that's what I'm going to do!"

The ignorant and ill-tempered woman angered him, but he listened helplessly to her until she had finished, and then went back to Katherine.

Lois looked at the clock on the mantelpiece and called to her husband sharply, a second time. She had not felt at all like making his supper. His lack of concern for her feelings and then her having to slave for him in the kitchen had seemed like an eternal human condition. The ghosts of her injured sex thronged to her side when she slammed open the silver drawer and again when she poured his beer. She set the tray elaborately, in order to deepen her displeasure in doing it at all. She heaped cold meat and salad on her husband's plate as if they were poisoned. Then she fixed her lipstick and carried the heavy tray into the dining room herself, in spite of her lame back.

Now, smoking a cigarette and walking around the room, she let five minutes pass. Then she carried the tray back to the kitchen, dumped the beer and coffee down the drain, and put the meat and salad in the icebox. When Mr. Bruce came back from Katherine's room he found her sobbing with anger—not at him but at her own foolishness. "Lois?" he asked, and she ran out of the room and into her bedroom and slammed the door.

———

During the next two months, Lois Bruce heard from a number of sources that her husband had been seen with a Mrs. Sheridan. She confided to her mother that she was losing him and, at her mother's insistence, employed a private detective. Lois was not vindictive; she didn't want to trap or intimidate her husband; she had, actually, a feeling that this maneuver would somehow be his salvation.

The detective telephoned her one day when she was having lunch at home, and told her that her husband and Mrs. Sheridan had just gone upstairs in a certain hotel. He was telephoning from the lobby, he said. Lois left her lunch unfinished but changed her clothes. She put on a hat with a veil, because her face was strained, and she was able because of the veil to talk calmly with the doorman, who got her a taxi. The detective met her on the sidewalk. He told her the floor and the number of the apartment, and offered to go upstairs with her. She dismissed him officiously then, as if his offer was a reflection on her ability to handle the situation competently. She had never been in the building before, but the feeling that she was acting on her rights kept her from being impressed at all with the building's strangeness.

The elevator man closed the door after her when she got off at the tenth floor, and she found herself alone in a long, windowless hall. The twelve identical doors painted dark red to match the dusty carpet, the dim ceiling lights, and the perfect stillness of the hall made her hesitate for a second, and then she went directly to the door of the apartment, and rang the bell. There was no sound, no answer. She rang the bell several times. Then she spoke to the shut door. "Let me in, Stephen. It's Lois. Let me in. I know you're in there. Let me in."

She waited. She took off her gloves. She put her thumb on the bell and held it there. Then she listened. There was still no sound. She looked at the shut red doors around her. She jabbed the bell. "Stephen!" she called. "Stephen. Let me in there. Let me in. I know you're in there. I saw you go in there. I can hear you. I can hear you moving around. I can hear you whispering. Let me in, Stephen. Let me in. If you don't let me in, I'll tell her husband."

She waited again. The silence of the early afternoon filled the interval. Then she attacked the door handle. She pounded on the door with the frame of her purse. She kicked it. "You let me in there, Stephen Bruce!" she screamed. "You let me in there, do you hear! Let me in, let me in, let me in!"

Another door into the hallway opened, and she turned and saw a man in his shirtsleeves, shaking his head. She ran into the back hall and, crying, started down the fire stairs. Like the stairs in a monument, they seemed to have no beginning and no end, but at last she came down into a dark hall where tricycles and perambulators were stored, and found her way into the lobby.

When Mr. Bruce and Mrs. Sheridan left the hotel, they walked through the Park, which, in the late-winter sunshine, smelled faintly like a wood. Crossing a bridle path, they saw Miss Prince, the children's riding mistress. She was giving a lesson to a fat little girl whose horse was on a lead. "Mrs. Sheridan!" she said. "Mr. Bruce! Isn't this fortunate!" She stopped the horses. "I wanted to speak to both of you," she said. "I'm having a little gymkhana next month, and I want your children to ride in it. I want them all three to ride in the good-hands class.... And perhaps the next year," she said, turning to the fat little girl, "you too may ride in the good-hands class."

They promised to allow their children to take part in the gymkhana, and Miss Prince said goodbye and resumed her riding lesson. In the Seventies they heard the roaring of a lion. They walked to the southern edge of the Park. It was then late in the afternoon. From the Plaza he telephoned his office. Among the messages was one from the maid; he was to stop at the Chardin Club and bring Katherine home.

From the sidewalk in front of the dancing school they could hear the clatter of the piano. The Grand March had begun. They moved through the crowd in the vestibule and stood in the door of the ballroom, looking for their children. Through the open door they could see Mrs. Bailey, the dancing teacher, and her two matrons curtsying stiffly as the children came to them in couples. The boys wore white gloves. The girls were simply dressed. Two by two the children bowed, or curtsied, and joined the grown people at the door. Then Mr. Bruce saw Katherine. As he watched his daughter doing obediently what was expected of her, it struck him that he and the company that crowded around him were all cut out of the same cloth. They were bewildered and confused in principle, too selfish or too unlucky to abide by the forms that guarantee the permanence of a society, as their fathers and mothers had done. Instead, they put the burden of order onto their children and filled their days with specious rites and ceremonies.

One of the dancing teachers came up to them and said, "Oh, I'm so glad to see you, Mrs. Sheridan. We were afraid that you'd been taken sick. Very soon after the class began this afternoon, Mr. Sheridan came and got the two girls. He said he was going to take them out to the country, and we wondered if you were ill. He seemed very upset."

The assistant smiled and wandered off.

Mrs. Sheridan's face lost its color and got dark. She looked very old. It was hot in the ballroom, and Mr. Bruce led her out the door into the freshness of a winter evening, holding her, supporting her really, for she might have fallen. "It will be all right," he kept saying, "it will be all right, my darling, it will be all right."

―――

JOHN CHEEVER (1912–1982) was born in Quincy, Massachusetts. For a time, he was a student at Thayer Academy. Cheever settled in New York, where in 1935 he began to write for *The New Yorker*. His first collection of stories, titled *The Way Some People Live*, appeared in 1943. *The Stories of John Cheever*, from which this story is taken, was published in 1978 and won the Pulitzer Prize for fiction.

A Classical Student

Anton Chekhov

Before setting off for his examination in Greek, Vanya kissed all the holy images. His stomach felt as though it were upside down; there was a chill at his heart, while the heart itself throbbed and stood still with terror before the unknown. What would he get that day? A three or a two? Six times he went to his mother for her blessing, and, as he went out, asked his aunt to pray for him. On the way to school he gave a beggar two kopecks, in the hope that those two kopecks would atone for his ignorance, and that, please God, he would not get the numerals with those awful forties and eighties.

He came back from the high school late, between four and five. He came in, and noiselessly lay down on his bed. His thin face was pale. There were dark rings round his red eyes.

"Well, how did you get on? How were you marked?" asked his mother, going to his bedside.

Vanya blinked, twisted his mouth, and burst into tears. His mother turned pale, let her mouth fall open, and clasped her hands. The breeches she was mending dropped out of her hands.

"What are you crying for? You've failed, then?" she asked.

"I am plucked.... I got a two."

"I knew it would be so! I had a presentiment of it," said his mother. "Merciful God! How is it you have not passed? What is the reason of it? What subject have you failed in?"

"In Greek.... Mother, I ... They asked me the future of *phero,* and I ... instead of saying *oisomai* said *opsomai.* Then ... then there isn't an accent, if the last syllable is long, and I ... I got flustered.... I forgot that the alpha was long in it.... I went and put in the accent. Then Artaxerxov told me to give the list of the enclitic particles.... I did, and I accidentally mixed in a pronoun ... and made a mistake ... and so he gave me a two.... I am a miserable ... person.... I was working all night.... I've been getting up at four o'clock all this week ..."

"No, it's not you but I who am miserable, you wretched boy! It's I that am miserable! You've worn me to a threadpaper, you Herod, you torment, you bane of my life! I pay for you, you good-for-nothing rubbish; I've bent my back toiling for you, I'm worried to death, and, I may say, I am unhappy, and what do you care? How do you work?"

"I ... I do work. All night.... You've seen it yourself."

"I prayed to God to take me, but He won't take me, a sinful woman.... You torment! Other people have children like everyone else, and I've one only and no sense, no comfort out of him. Beat you? I'd beat you, but where am I to find the strength? Mother of God, where am I to find the strength?"

The mamma hid her face in the folds of her blouse and broke into sobs. Vanya wriggled with anguish and pressed his forehead against the wall. The aunt came in.

"So that's how it is. ... Just what I expected," she said, at once guessing what was wrong, turning pale and clasping her hands. "I've been depressed all the morning.... There's trouble coming, I thought ... and here it's come...."

"The villain, the torment!"

"Why are you swearing at him?" cried the aunt, nervously pulling her coffee-coloured kerchief off her head and turning upon the mother. "It's not his fault! It's your fault! You are to blame! Why did you send him to that high school? You are a fine lady! You want to be a lady? A-a-ah! I dare say, as though you'll turn into gentry! But if you had sent him, as I told you, into business...to an office, like my Kuzya...here is Kuzya getting five hundred a year....Five hundred roubles is worth having, isn't it? And you are wearing yourself out, and wearing the boy out with this studying, plague take it! He is thin, he coughs...just look at him! He's thirteen, and he looks no more than ten."

"No, Nastenka, no, my dear! I haven't thrashed him enough, the torment! He ought to have been thrashed, that's what it is! Ugh ... Jesuit, Mahomet, torment!" she shook her fist at her son. "You want a flogging, but I haven't the strength. They told me years ago when he was little, 'Whip him, whip him!' I didn't heed them, sinful woman as I am. And now I am suffering for it. You wait a bit! I'll flay you! Wait a bit..."

The mamma shook her wet fist, and went weeping into her lodger's room. The lodger, Yevtihy Kuzmitch Kuporossov, was sitting at his table, reading "Dancing Self-taught." Yevtihy Kuzmitch was a man of intelligence and education. He spoke through his nose, washed with a soap the smell of which made everyone in the house sneeze, ate meat on fast days, and was on the look-out for a bride of refined education, and so was considered the cleverest of the lodgers. He sang tenor.

"My good friend," began the mamma, dissolving into tears. "If you would have the generosity—thrash my boy for me....Do me the favour! He's failed in his examination, the nuisance of a boy! Would you believe it, he's failed! I can't punish him, through the weakness of my ill-health....Thrash him for me, if you would be so obliging and considerate, Yevtihy Kuzmitch! Have regard for a sick woman!"

Kuporossov frowned and heaved a deep sigh through his nose. He thought a little, drummed on the table with his fingers, and sighing once more, went to Vanya.

"You are being taught, so to say," he began, "being educated, being given a chance, you revolting young person! Why have you done it?"

He talked for a long time, made a regular speech. He alluded to science, to light, and to darkness.

"Yes, young person."

When he had finished his speech, he took off his belt and took Vanya by the hand.

"It's the only way to deal with you," he said. Vanya knelt down submissively and thrust his head between the lodger's knees. His prominent pink ears moved up and down against the lodger's new serge trousers, with brown stripes on the outer seams.

Vanya did not utter a single sound. At the family council in the evening, it was decided to send him into business.

—

ANTON CHEKHOV (1860–1904) continues to inspire readers a century after his death with his keen sense of life's complexities and his ability to render them accurately, tellingly.

I Stand Here Ironing

Tillie Olsen

I stand here ironing, and what you asked me moves tormented back and forth with the iron.

"I wish you would manage the time to come in and talk with me about your daughter. I'm sure you can help me understand her. She's a youngster who needs help and whom I'm deeply interested in helping."

"Who needs help." ... Even if I came, what good would it do? You think because I am her mother I have a key, or that in some way you could use me as a key? She has lived for nineteen years. There is all that life that has happened outside of me, beyond me.

And when is there time to remember, to sift, to weigh, to estimate, to total? I will start and there will be an interruption and I will have to gather it all together again. Or I will become engulfed with all I did or did not do, with what should have been and what cannot be helped.

She was a beautiful baby. The first and only one of our five that was beautiful at birth. You do not guess how new and uneasy her tenancy in her now-loveliness. You did not know her all those years she was thought homely, or see her poring over her baby pictures, making me tell her over and over how beautiful she had been—and would be, I would tell her—and was now, to the seeing eye. But the seeing eyes were few or nonexistent. Including mine.

I nursed her. They feel that's important nowadays. I nursed all the children, but with her, with all the fierce rigidity of first motherhood, I did like the books then said. Though her cries battered me to trembling and my breasts ached with swollenness, I waited till the clock decreed.

Why do I put that first? I do not even know if it matters, or if it explains anything.

She was a beautiful baby. She blew shining bubbles of sound. She loved motion, loved light, loved color and music and textures. She would lie on the floor in her blue overalls patting the surface so hard in ecstasy her hands and feet would blur. She was a miracle to me, but when she was eight months old I had to leave her daytimes with the woman downstairs to whom she was no miracle at all, for I worked or looked for work and for Emily's father, who "could no longer endure" (he wrote in his good-bye note) "sharing want with us."

I was nineteen. It was the pre-relief, pre-WPA world of the depression. I would start running as soon as I got off the streetcar, running up the stairs, the place smelling sour, and awake or asleep to startle awake, when she saw me she would break into a clogged weeping that could not be comforted, a weeping I can hear yet.

After a while I found a job hashing at night so I could be with her days, and it was better. But it came to where I had to bring her to his family and leave her.

It took a long time to raise the money for her fare back. Then she got chicken pox and I had to wait longer. When she finally came, I hardly knew her, walking quick and nervous like her father, looking like her father, thin, and dressed in a shoddy red that yellowed her skin and glared at the pockmarks. All the baby loveliness gone.

She was two. Old enough for nursery school they said, and I did not know then what I know now—the fatigue of the long day, and the lacerations of group life in the kinds of nurseries that are only parking places for children.

Except that it would have made no difference if I had known. It was the only place there was. It was the only way we could be together, the only way I could hold a job.

And even without knowing, I knew. I knew that the teacher was evil because all these years it has curdled into my memory, the little boy hunched in the corner, her rasp, "why aren't you outside, because Alvin hits you? that's no reason, go out, scaredy." I knew Emily hated it even if she did not clutch and implore "don't go Mommy" like the other children, mornings.

She always had a reason why we should stay home. Momma, you look sick. Momma, I feel sick. Momma, the teachers aren't there today, they're sick. Momma, we can't go, there was a fire there last night. Momma, it's a holiday today, no school, they told me.

But never a direct protest, never rebellion. I think of our others in their three-, four-year-oldness—the explosions, the tempers, the denunciations, the demands—and I feel suddenly ill. I put the iron down. What in me demanded that goodness in her? And what was the cost, the cost to her of such goodness?

The old man living in the back once said in his gentle way: "You should smile at Emily more when you look at her." What *was* in my face when I looked at her? I loved her. There were all the acts of love.

It was only with the others I remembered what he said, and it was the face of joy, and not of care or tightness or worry I turned to them—too late for Emily. She does not smile easily, let alone almost always as her brothers and sisters do. Her face is closed and sombre, but when she wants, how fluid. You must have seen it in her pantomimes, you spoke of her rare gift for comedy on the stage that rouses a laughter out of the audience so dear they applaud and applaud and do not want to let her go.

Where does it come from, that comedy? There was none of it in her when she came back to me that second time, after I had had to send her away again. She had a new daddy now to learn to love, and I think perhaps it was a better time.

Except when we left her alone nights, telling ourselves she was old enough.

"Can't you go some other time, Mommy, like tomorrow?" she would ask. "Will it be just a little while you'll be gone? Do you promise?"

The time we came back, the front door open, the clock on the floor in the hall. She rigid awake. "It wasn't just a little while. I didn't cry. Three times I called you, just three times, and then I ran downstairs to open the door so you could come faster. The clock talked loud. I threw it away, it scared me what it talked."

She said the clock talked loud again that night I went to the hospital to have Susan. She was delirious with the fever that comes before red measles, but she was fully conscious all the week I was gone and the week after we were home when she could not come near the new baby or me.

She did not get well. She stayed skeleton thin, not wanting to eat, and night after night she had nightmares. She would call for me, and I would rouse from exhaustion to sleepily call back: "You're all right, darling, go to sleep, it's just a dream," and if she still called, in a sterner voice, "now go to sleep, Emily, there's nothing to hurt you." Twice, only twice, when I had to get up for Susan anyhow, I went in to sit with her.

Now when it is too late (as if she would let me hold and comfort her like I do the others) I get up and go to her at once at her moan or restless stirring. "Are you awake, Emily? Can I get you something?" And the answer is always the same: "No, I'm all right, go back to sleep, Mother."

They persuaded me at the clinic to send her away to a convalescent home in the country where "she can have the kind of food and care you can't manage for her, and you'll be free to concentrate on the new baby." They still send children to that place. I see pictures on the society page of sleek young women planning affairs to raise money for it, or dancing at the affairs, or decorating Easter eggs or filling Christmas stockings for the children.

They never have a picture of the children so I do not know if the girls still wear those gigantic red bows and the ravaged looks on the every other Sunday when parents can come to visit "unless other-wise notified"—as we were notified the first six weeks.

Oh it is a handsome place, green lawns and tall trees and fluted flower beds. High up on the balconies of each cottage the children stand, the girls in their red bows and white dresses, the boys in white suits and giant red ties. The parents stand below shrieking up to be heard and the children shriek down to be heard, and between them the invisible wall "Not To Be Contaminated by Parental Germs or Physical Affection."

There was a tiny girl who always stood hand in hand with Emily. Her parents never came. One visit she was gone. "They moved her to Rose Cottage," Emily shouted in explanation. "They don't like you to love anybody here."

She wrote once a week, the labored writing of a seven-year-old. "I am fine. How is the baby. If I write my leter nicly I will have a star. Love." There never was a star. We wrote every other day, letters she could never hold or keep but only hear read—once. "We simply do not have room for children to keep any personal possessions," they patiently explained when we pieced one Sun-day's shrieking together to plead how much it would mean to Emily, who loved so to keep things, to be allowed to keep her letters and cards.

Each visit she looked frailer. "She isn't eating," they told us.

(They had runny eggs for breakfast or mush with lumps, Emily said later, I'd hold it in my mouth and not swallow. Nothing ever tasted good, just when they had chicken.)

It took us eight months to get her released home, and only the fact that she gained back so little of her seven lost pounds con-vinced the social worker.

I used to try to hold and love her after she came back, but her body would stay stiff, and after a while she'd push away. She ate little. Food sickened her, and I think much of life too. Oh she had physical lightness and brightness, twinkling by on skates, bouncing like a ball up and down up and down over the jump rope, skimming over the hill; but these were momentary.

She fretted about her appearance, thin and dark and foreign-looking at a time when every little girl was supposed to look or thought she should look a chubby blonde replica of Shirley Temple. The doorbell sometimes rang for her, but no one seemed to come and play in the house or be a best friend. Maybe because we moved so much.

There was a boy she loved painfully through two school semesters. Months later she told me how she had taken pennies from my purse to buy him candy. "Licorice was his favorite and I brought him some every day, but he still liked Jennifer better'n me. Why, Mommy?" The kind of question for which there is no answer.

School was a worry to her. She was not glib or quick in a world where glibness and quickness were easily confused with ability to learn. To her overworked and exasperated teachers she was an over-conscientious "slow learner" who kept trying to catch up and was absent entirely too often.

I let her be absent, though sometimes the illness was imaginary. How different from my now-strictness about attendance with the others. I wasn't working. We had a new baby, I was home anyhow. Sometimes, after Susan grew old enough, I would keep her home from school, too, to have them all together.

Mostly Emily had asthma, and her breathing, harsh and labored, would fill the house with a curiously tranquil sound. I would bring the two old dresser mirrors and her boxes of collections to her bed. She would select beads and single earrings, bottle tops and shells, dried flowers and pebbles, old postcards and scraps, all sorts of oddments; then she and Susan would play Kingdom, setting up landscapes and furniture, peopling them with action.

Those were the only times of peaceful companionship between her and Susan. I have edged away from it, that poisonous feeling between them, that terrible balancing of hurts and needs I had to do between the two, and did so badly, those earlier years.

Oh there are conflicts between the others too, each one human, needing, demanding, hurting, taking—but only between Emily and Susan, no, Emily toward Susan that corroding resentment. It seems so obvious on the surface, yet it is not obvious. Susan, the second child, Susan, golden- and curly-haired and chubby, quick and articulate and assured, everything in appearance and manner Emily was not; Susan, not able to resist Emily's precious things, losing or sometimes clumsily breaking them; Susan telling jokes and riddles to company for applause while Emily sat silent (to say to me later: that was *my* riddle, Mother, I told it to Susan); Susan, who for all the five years' difference in age was just a year behind Emily in developing physically.

I am glad for that slow physical development that widened the difference between her and her contemporaries, though she suffered over it. She was too vulnerable for that terrible world of youthful competition, of preening and parading, of constant measuring of yourself against every other, of envy, "If I had that copper hair," "If I had that skin...." She tormented herself enough about not looking like the others, there was enough of the unsureness, the having to be conscious of words before you speak, the constant caring—what are they thinking of me? without having it all magnified by the merciless physical drives.

Ronnie is calling. He is wet and I change him. It is rare there is such a cry now. That time of motherhood is almost behind me when the ear is not one's own but must always be racked and listening for the child cry, the child call. We sit for a while and I hold him, looking out over the city spread in charcoal with its soft aisles of light. *"Shoogily,"* he breathes and curls closer. I carry him back to bed, asleep. *Shoogily.* A funny word, a family word, inherited from Emily, invented by her to say: *comfort.*

In this and other ways she leaves her seal, I say aloud. And startle at my saying it. What do I mean? What did I start to gather together, to try and make coherent? I was at the terrible, growing years. War years. I do not remember them well. I was working, there were four smaller ones now, there was not time for her. She had to help be a mother, and housekeeper, and shopper. She had to set her seal. Mornings of crisis and near hysteria trying to get lunches packed, hair combed, coats and shoes found, everyone to school or Child

Care on time, the baby ready for transportation. And always the paper scribbled on by a smaller one, the book looked at by Susan then mislaid, the homework not done. Running out to that huge school where she was one, she was lost, she was a drop; suffering over her unpreparedness, stammering and unsure in her classes.

There was so little time left at night after the kids were bedded down. She would struggle over books, always eating (it was in those years she developed her enormous appetite that is legendary in our family) and I would be ironing, or preparing food for the next day, or writing V-mail to Bill, or tending the baby. Sometimes, to make me laugh, or out of her despair, she would imitate happenings or types at school.

I think I said once: "Why don't you do something like this in the school amateur show?" One morning she phoned me at work, hardly understandable through the weeping: "Mother, I did it. I won, I won; they gave me first prize; they clapped and clapped and wouldn't let me go."

Now suddenly she was Somebody, and as imprisoned in her difference as she had been in her anonymity.

She began to be asked to perform at other high schools, even in colleges, then at city and statewide affairs. The first one we went to, I only recognized her that first moment when thin, shy, she almost drowned herself into the curtains. Then: Was this Emily? The control, the command, the convulsing and deadly clowning, the spell, then the roaring, stamping audience, unwilling to let this rare and precious laughter out of their lives.

Afterwards: You ought to do something about her with a gift like that—but without money or knowing how, what does one do? We have left it all to her, and the gift has as often eddied inside, clogged and clotted, as been used and growing.

She is coming. She runs up the stairs two at a time with her light graceful step, and I know she is happy tonight. Whatever it was that occasioned your call did not happen today.

"Aren't you ever going to finish the ironing, Mother? Whistler painted his mother in a rocker. I'd have to paint mine standing over an ironing board." This is one of her communicative nights and she tells me everything and nothing as she fixes herself a plate of food out of the icebox.

She is so lovely. Why did you want me to come in at all? Why were you concerned? She will find her way.

She starts up the stairs to bed. "Don't get *me* up with the rest in the morning." "But I thought you were having midterms." "Oh, those," she comes back in, kisses me, and says quite lightly, "in a couple of years when we'll all be atom-dead they won't matter a bit."

She has said it before. She *believes* it. But because I have been dredging the past, and all that compounds a human being is so heavy and meaningful in me, I cannot endure it tonight.

I will never total it all. I will never come in to say: She was a child seldom smiled at. Her father left me before she was a year old. I had to work away from her her first six years when there was work, or I sent her home and to his relatives. There were years she had care she hated.

She was dark and thin and foreign-looking in a world where the prestige went to blondeness and curly hair and dimples, she was slow where glibness was prized. She was a child of anxious, not proud, love. We were poor and could not afford for her the soil of easy growth. I was a young mother, I was a distracted mother. There were the other children pushing up, demanding. Her younger sister seemed all that she was not. There were years she did not let me touch her. She kept too much in herself, her life was such she had to keep too much in herself. My wisdom came too late. She has much to her and probably little will come of it. She is a child of her age, of depression, of war, of fear.

Let her be. So all that is in her will not bloom—but in how many does it? There is still enough left to live by. Only help her to know—help make it so there is cause for her to know—that she is more than this dress on the ironing board, helpless before the iron.

—

TILLIE OLSEN was born in Nebraska in 1912, and for many years has written trenchant, affecting fiction and essays. Her book of stories, *Tell Me a Riddle*, from which this piece is taken, continues to have a strong hold on readers who, through the author's probing attention to ordinary life, become her companions in psychological and social exploration.

CATHEDRAL

Raymond Carver

This blind man, an old friend of my wife's, he was on his way to spend the night. His wife had died. So he was visiting the dead wife's relatives in Connecticut. He called my wife from his in-laws'. Arrangements were made. He would come by train, a five-hour trip, and my wife would meet him at the station. She hadn't seen him since she worked for him one summer in Seattle ten years ago. But she and the blind man had kept in touch. They made tapes and mailed them back and forth. I wasn't enthusiastic about his visit. He was no one I knew. And his being blind bothered me. My idea of blindness came from the movies. In the movies, the blind moved slowly and never laughed. Sometimes they were led by seeing-eye dogs. A blind man in my house was not something I looked forward to.

That summer in Seattle she had needed a job. She didn't have any money. The man she was going to marry at the end of the summer was in officers' training school. He didn't have any money, either. But she was in love with the guy, and he was in love with her, etc. She'd seen something in the paper: HELP WANTED—*Reading to*

Blind Man, and a telephone number. She phoned and went over, was hired on the spot. She'd worked with this blind man all summer. She read stuff to him, case studies, reports, that sort of thing. She helped him organize his little office in the county social-service department. They'd become good friends, my wife and the blind man. How do I know these things? She told me. And she told me something else. On her last day in the office, the blind man asked if he could touch her face. She agreed to this. She told me he touched his fingers to every part of her face, her nose—even her neck! She never forgot it. She even tried to write a poem about it. She was always trying to write a poem. She wrote a poem or two every year, usually after something really important had happened to her.

When we first started going out together, she showed me the poem. In the poem, she recalled his fingers and the way they had moved around over her face. In the poem, she talked about what she had felt at the time, about what went through her mind when the blind man touched her nose and lips. I can remember I didn't think much of the poem. Of course, I didn't tell her that. Maybe I just don't understand poetry. I admit it's not the first thing I reach for when I pick up something to read.

Anyway, this man who'd first enjoyed her favors, the officer-to-be, he'd been her childhood sweetheart. So okay. I'm saying that at the end of the summer she let the blind man run his hands over her face, said goodbye to him, married her childhood etc., who was now a commissioned officer, and she moved away from Seattle. But they'd kept in touch, she and the blind man. She made the first contact after a year or so. She called him up one night from an Air Force base in Alabama. She wanted to talk. They talked. He asked her to send him a tape and tell him about her life. She did this. She sent the tape. On the tape, she told the blind man about her husband and about their life together in the military. She told the blind man she loved her husband but she didn't like it where they lived and she didn't like it that he was a part of the military-industrial thing. She told the blind man she'd written a poem and he was in it. She told him that she was writing a poem about what it was like to be an Air Force officer's wife. The poem wasn't finished yet. She was still writing it. The blind man made a tape. He sent her the tape. She made a tape. This went on for years. My wife's officer was posted to one base and then another. She sent tapes from Moody AFB, McGuire, McConnell, and finally Travis, near Sacramento, where one night she got to feeling lonely and cut off from people she kept losing in that moving-around life. She got to feeling she couldn't go it another step. She went in and swallowed all the pills and capsules in the medicine chest and washed them down with a bottle of gin. Then she got into a hot bath and passed out.

But instead of dying, she got sick. She threw up. Her officer—why should he have a name? he was the childhood sweetheart, and what more does he want?—came home from somewhere, found her, and called the ambulance. In time, she put it all on a tape and sent the tape to the blind man. Over the years, she put all kinds of stuff on tapes and sent the tapes off lickety-split. Next to writing a poem every year, I think it was her chief means of recreation. On one tape, she told the blind man she'd decided to live away from her officer for a time. On another tape, she told him about her divorce. She and I began going out, and of course she told her blind man about it. She told him everything, or so it seemed to me. Once she asked me if I'd like to hear the latest tape from the blind man. This was a year ago. I was on the tape, she said. So I said okay, I'd listen to it. I got us drinks and we settled down in the living room. We made ready to listen. First she inserted the tape into the player and adjusted a couple of dials. Then she pushed a lever. The tape squeaked and someone began to talk in this loud voice. She lowered the volume. After a few minutes of harmless chitchat, I heard my own name in the mouth of this stranger, this blind man I didn't even know! And then this: "From all you've said about him, I can only conclude—" But we were interrupted, a knock at the door, something, and we didn't ever get back to the tape. Maybe it was just as well. I'd heard all I wanted to.

Now this same blind man was coming to sleep in my house.

"Maybe I could take him bowling," I said to my wife. She was at the draining board doing scalloped potatoes. She put down the knife she was using and turned around.

"If you love me," she said, "you can do this for me. If you don't love me, okay. But if you had a friend, any friend, and the friend came to visit, I'd make him feel comfortable." She wiped her hands with the dish towel.

"I don't have any blind friends," I said.

"You don't have *any* friends," she said. "Period. Besides," she said, "goddamn it, his wife's just died! Don't you understand that? The man's lost his wife!"

I didn't answer. She'd told me a little about the blind man's wife. Her name was Beulah. Beulah! That's a name for a colored woman.

"Was his wife a Negro?" I asked.

"Are you crazy?" my wife said. "Have you just flipped or something?" She picked up a potato. I saw it hit the floor, then roll under the stove. "What's wrong with you?" she said. "Are you drunk?"

"I'm just asking," I said.

Right then my wife filled me in with more detail than I cared to know. I made a drink and sat at the kitchen table to listen. Pieces of the story began to fall into place.

Beulah had gone to work for the blind man the summer after my wife had stopped working for him. Pretty soon Beulah and the blind man had themselves a church wedding. It was a little wedding—who'd want to go to such a wedding in the first place?—just the two of them, plus the minister and the minister's wife. But it was a church wedding just the same. It was what Beulah had wanted, he'd said. But even then Beulah must have been carrying the cancer in her glands. After they had been inseparable for eight years—my wife's word, *inseparable*—Beulah's health went into a rapid decline. She died in a Seattle hospital room, the blind man sitting beside the bed and holding on to her hand. They'd married, lived and worked together, slept together—had sex, sure—and then the blind man had to bury her. All this without his having ever seen what the goddamned woman looked like. It was beyond my understanding. Hearing this, I felt sorry for the blind man for a little bit. And then I found myself thinking what a pitiful life this woman must have led. Imagine a woman who could never see herself as she was seen in the eyes of her loved one. A woman who could go on day after day and never receive the smallest compliment from her beloved. A woman whose husband could never read the expression on her face, be it misery or something better. Someone who could wear makeup or not—what difference to him? She could, if she wanted, wear green eye-shadow around one eye, a straight pin in her nostril, yellow slacks and purple shoes, no matter. And then to slip off into death, the blind man's hand on her hand, his blind eyes streaming tears—I'm imagining now—her last thought maybe this: that he never even knew what she looked like, and she on an express to the grave. Robert was left with a small insurance policy and half of a twenty-peso Mexican coin. The other half of the coin went into the box with her. Pathetic.

So when the time rolled around, my wife went to the depot to pick him up. With nothing to do but wait—sure, I blamed him for that—I was having a drink and watching the TV when I heard the car pull into the drive. I got up from the sofa with my drink and went to the window to have a look.

I saw my wife laughing as she parked the car. I saw her get out of the car and shut the door. She was still wearing a smile. Just amazing. She went around to the other side of the car to where the blind man was already starting to get out. This blind man, feature this, he was wearing a full beard! A beard on a blind man! Too much, I say. The blind man reached into the back seat and dragged out a suitcase. My wife took his arm, shut the car door, and, talking all the way, moved him down the drive and then up the steps to the front porch. I turned off the TV. I finished my drink, rinsed the glass, dried my hands. Then I went to the door.

My wife said, "I want you to meet Robert. Robert, this is my husband. I've told you all about him." She was beaming. She had this blind man by his coat sleeve.

The blind man let go of his suitcase and up came his hand.

I took it. He squeezed hard, held my hand, and then he let it go.

"I feel like we've already met," he boomed.

"Likewise," I said. I didn't know what else to say. Then I said, "Welcome. I've heard a lot about you." We began to move then, a little group, from the porch into the living room, my wife guiding him by the arm. The blind man was carrying his suitcase in his other hand. My wife said things like, "To your left here, Robert. That's right. Now watch it, there's a chair. That's it. Sit down right here. This is the sofa. We just bought this sofa two weeks ago."

I started to say something about the old sofa. I'd liked that old sofa. But I didn't say anything. Then I wanted to say something else, small-talk, about the scenic ride along the Hudson. How going *to* New York, you should sit on the right-hand side of the train, and coming *from* New York, the left-hand side.

"Did you have a good train ride?" I said. "Which side of the train did you sit on, by the way?"

"What a question, which side!" my wife said. "What's it matter which side?" she said.

"I just asked," I said.

"Right side," the blind man said. "I hadn't been on a train in nearly forty years. Not since I was a kid. With my folks. That's been a long time. I'd nearly forgotten the sensation. I have winter in my beard now," he said. "So I've been told, anyway. Do I look distinguished, my dear?" the blind man said to my wife.

"You look distinguished, Robert," she said. "Robert," she said. "Robert, it's just so good to see you."

My wife finally took her eyes off the blind man and looked at me. I had the feeling she didn't like what she saw. I shrugged.

I've never met, or personally known, anyone who was blind. This blind man was late forties, a heavy-set, balding man with stooped shoulders, as if he carried a great weight there. He wore brown slacks, brown shoes, a light-brown shirt, a tie, a sports coat. Spiffy. He also had this full beard. But he didn't use a cane and he didn't wear dark glasses. I'd always thought dark glasses were a must for the blind. Fact was, I wished he had a pair. At first glance, his eyes looked like anyone else's eyes. But if you looked close, there was something different about them. Too much white in the iris, for one thing, and the pupils seemed to move around in the sockets without his knowing it or being able to stop it. Creepy. As I stared at his face,

I saw the left pupil turn in toward his nose while the other made an effort to keep in one place. But it was only an effort, for that eye was on the roam without his knowing it or wanting it to be.

I said, "Let me get you a drink. What's your pleasure? We have a little of everything. It's one of our pastimes."

"Bub, I'm a Scotch man myself," he said fast enough in this big voice.

"Right," I said. Bub! "Sure you are. I knew it."

He let his fingers touch his suitcase, which was sitting alongside the sofa. He was taking his bearings. I didn't blame him for that.

"I'll move that up to your room," my wife said.

"No, that's fine," the blind man said loudly. "It can go up when I go up."

"A little water with the Scotch?" I said.

"Very little," he said.

"I knew it," I said.

He said, "Just a tad. The Irish actor, Barry Fitzgerald? I'm like that fellow. When I drink water, Fitzgerald said, I drink water. When I drink whiskey, I drink whiskey." My wife laughed. The blind man brought his hand up under his beard. He lifted his beard slowly and let it drop.

I did the drinks, three big glasses of Scotch with a splash of water in each. Then we made ourselves comfortable and talked about Robert's travels. First the long flight from the West Coast to Connecticut, we covered that. Then from Connecticut up here by train. We had another drink concerning that leg of the trip.

I remembered having read somewhere that the blind didn't smoke because, as speculation had it, they couldn't see the smoke they exhaled. I thought I knew that much and that much only about blind people. But this blind man smoked his cigarette down to the nubbin and then lit another one. This blind man filled his ashtray and my wife emptied it.

When we sat down at the table for dinner, we had another drink. My wife heaped Robert's plate with cube steak, scalloped potatoes, green beans. I buttered him up two slices of bread. I said, "Here's bread and butter for you." I swallowed some of my drink. "Now let us pray," I said, and the blind man lowered his head. My wife looked at me, her mouth agape. "Pray the phone won't ring and the food doesn't get cold," I said.

We dug in. We ate everything there was to eat on the table. We ate like there was no tomorrow. We didn't talk. We ate. We scarfed. We grazed that table. We were into serious eating. The blind man had right away located his foods, he knew just where everything was on his plate. I watched with admiration as he used his knife and fork on the meat. He'd cut two pieces of meat, fork the meat into his mouth, and then go all out for the scalloped potatoes, the beans next, and then he'd tear off a hunk of buttered bread and eat that. He'd follow this up with a big drink of milk. It didn't seem to bother him to use his fingers once in a while, either.

We finished everything, including half a strawberry pie. For a few moments, we sat as if stunned. Sweat beaded on our faces. Finally, we got up from the table and left the dirty plates. We didn't look back. We took ourselves into the living room and sank into our places again. Robert and my wife sat on the sofa. I took the big chair. We had us two or three more drinks while they talked about the major things that had come to pass for them in the past ten years. For the most part, I just listened. Now and then I joined in. I didn't want him to think I'd left the room, and I didn't want her to think I was feeling left out. They talked of things that had happened to them—to them!—these past ten years. I waited in vain to hear my name on my wife's sweet lips: "And then my dear husband came into my life"—something like that. But I heard nothing of the sort. More talk of Robert. Robert had done a little of everything, it seemed, a regular blind jack-of-all-trades. But most recently he and his wife had had an Amway distributorship, from which, I gathered, they'd earned their living, such as it was. The blind man was also a ham radio operator. He talked in his loud voice about conversations he'd had with fellow operators in Guam, in the Philippines, in Alaska, and even in Tahiti. He said he'd have a lot of friends there if he ever wanted to go visit those places. From time to time, he'd turn his blind face toward me, put his hand under his beard, ask me something. How long had I been in my present position? (Three years.) Did I like my work? (I didn't.) Was I going to stay with it? (What were the options?) Finally, when I thought he was beginning to run down, I got up and turned on the TV.

My wife looked at me with irritation. She was heading toward a boil. Then she looked at the blind man and said, "Robert, do you have a TV?"

The blind man said, "My dear, I have two TVs. I have a color set and a black-and-white thing, an old relic. It's funny, but if I turn the TV on, and I'm always turning it on, I turn on the color set. It's funny, don't you think?"

I didn't know what to say to that. I had absolutely nothing to say to that. No opinion. So I watched the news program and tried to listen to what the announcer was saying.

"This is a color TV," the blind man said. "Don't ask me how, but I can tell."

"We traded up a while ago," I said.

The blind man had another taste of his drink. He lifted his beard, sniffed it, and let it fall. He leaned forward on the sofa. He positioned his ashtray on the coffee table, then put the lighter to his cigarette. He leaned back on the sofa and crossed his legs at the ankles.

My wife covered her mouth, and then she yawned. She stretched. She said, "I think I'll go upstairs and put on my robe. I think I'll change into something else. Robert, you make yourself comfortable," she said.

"I'm comfortable," the blind man said.

"I want you to feel comfortable in this house," she said.

"I am comfortable," the blind man said.

After she'd left the room, he and I listened to the weather report and then to the sports roundup. By that time, she'd been gone so long I didn't know if she was going to come back. I thought she might have gone to bed. I wished she'd come back downstairs. I didn't want to be left alone with a blind man. I asked him if he wanted another drink, and he said sure. Then I asked if he wanted to smoke some dope with me. I said I'd just rolled a number. I hadn't, but I planned to do so in about two shakes.

"I'll try some with you," he said.

"Damn right," I said. "That's the stuff."

I got our drinks and sat down on the sofa with him. Then I rolled us two fat numbers. I lit one and passed it. I brought it to his fingers. He took it and inhaled.

"Hold it as long as you can," I said. I could tell he didn't know the first thing.

My wife came back downstairs wearing her pink robe and her pink slippers.

"What do I smell?" she said.

"We thought we'd have us some cannabis," I said.

My wife gave me a savage look. Then she looked at the blind man and said, "Robert, I didn't know you smoked."

He said, "I do now, my dear. There's a first time for everything. But I don't feel anything yet."

"This stuff is pretty mellow," I said. "This stuff is mild. It's dope you can reason with," I said. "It doesn't mess you up."

"Not much it doesn't, bub," he said, and laughed.

My wife sat on the sofa between the blind man and me. I passed her the number. She took it and toked and then passed it back to me. "Which way is this going?" she said. Then she said, "I shouldn't be smoking this. I can hardly keep my eyes open as it is. That dinner did me in. I shouldn't have eaten so much."

"It was the strawberry pie," the blind man said. "That's what did it," he said, and he laughed his big laugh. Then he shook his head.

"There's more strawberry pie," I said.

"Do you want some more, Robert?" my wife said.

"Maybe in a little while," he said.

We gave our attention to the TV. My wife yawned again. She said, "Your bed is made up when you feel like going to bed, Robert. I know you must have had a long day. When you're ready to go to bed, say so." She pulled his arm. "Robert?"

He came to and said, "I've had a real nice time. This beats tapes, doesn't it?"

I said, "Coming at you," and I put the number between his fingers. He inhaled, held the smoke, and then let it go. It was like he'd been doing it since he was nine years old.

"Thanks, bub," he said. "But I think this is all for me. I think I'm beginning to feel it," he said. He held the burning roach out for my wife.

"Same here," she said. "Ditto. Me, too." She took the roach and passed it to me. "I may just sit here for a while between you two guys with my eyes closed. But don't let me bother you, okay? Either one of you. If it bothers you, say so. Otherwise, I may just sit here with my eyes closed until you're ready to go to bed," she said. "Your bed's made up, Robert, when you're ready. It's right next to our room at the top of the stairs. We'll show you up when you're ready. You wake me up now, you guys, if I fall asleep." She said that and then she closed her eyes and went to sleep.

The news program ended. I got up and changed the channel. I sat back down on the sofa. I wished my wife hadn't pooped out. Her head lay across the back of the sofa, her mouth open. She'd turned so that her robe had slipped away from her legs, exposing a juicy thigh. I reached to draw her robe back over her, and it was then that I glanced at the blind man. What the hell! I flipped the robe open again.

"You say when you want some strawberry pie," I said.

"I will," he said.

I said, "Are you tired? Do you want me to take you up to your bed? Are you ready to hit the hay?"

"Not yet," he said. "No, I'll stay up with you, bub. If that's all right. I'll stay up until you're ready to turn in. We haven't had a chance to talk. Know what I mean? I feel like me and her monopolized the evening." He lifted his beard and he let it fall. He picked up his cigarettes and his lighter.

"That's all right," I said. Then I said, "I'm glad for the company."

And I guess I was. Every night I smoked dope and stayed up as long as I could before I fell asleep. My wife and I hardly ever went to bed at the same time. When I did go to sleep, I had these dreams. Sometimes I'd wake up from one of them, my heart going crazy.

Something about the church and the Middle Ages was on the TV. Not your run-of-the-mill TV fare. I wanted to watch something else. I turned to the other channels. But there was nothing on them, either. So I turned back to the first channel and apologized.

"Bub, it's all right," the blind man said. "It's fine with me. Whatever you want to watch is okay. I'm always learning something. Learning never ends. It won't hurt me to learn something tonight. I got ears," he said.

We didn't say anything for a time. He was leaning forward with his head turned at me, his right ear aimed in the direction of the set. Very disconcerting. Now and then his eyelids drooped and then they snapped open again. Now and then he put his fingers into his beard and tugged, like he was thinking about something he was hearing on the television.

On the screen, a group of men wearing cowls was being set upon and tormented by men dressed in skeleton costumes and men dressed as devils. The men dressed as devils wore devil masks, horns, and long tails. This pageant was part of a procession. The Englishman who was narrating the thing said it took place in Spain once a year. I tried to explain to the blind man what was happening.

"Skeletons," he said. "I know about skeletons," he said, and he nodded.

The TV showed this one cathedral. Then there was a long, slow look at another one. Finally, the picture switched to the famous one in Paris, with its flying buttresses and its spires reaching up to the clouds. The camera pulled away to show the whole of the cathedral rising above the skyline.

There were times when the Englishman who was telling the thing would shut up, would simply let the camera move around over the cathedrals. Or else the camera would tour the countryside, men in fields walking behind oxen. I waited as long as I could. Then I felt I had to say something. I said, "They're showing the outside of this cathedral now. Gargoyles. Little statues carved to look like monsters. Now I guess they're in Italy. Yeah, they're in Italy. There's paintings on the walls of this one church."

"Are those fresco paintings, bub?" he asked, and he sipped from his drink.

I reached for my glass. But it was empty. I tried to remember what I could remember. "You're asking me are those frescoes?" I said. "That's a good question. I don't know."

The camera moved to a cathedral outside Lisbon. The differences in the Portuguese cathedral compared with the French and Italian were not that great. But they were there. Mostly the interior stuff. Then something occurred to me, and I said, "Something has occurred to me. Do you have any idea what a cathedral is? What they look like, that is? Do you follow me? If somebody says cathedral to you, do you have any notion what they're talking about? Do you know the difference between that and a Baptist church, say?"

He let the smoke dribble from his mouth. "I know they took hundreds of workers fifty or a hundred years to build," he said. "I just heard the man say that, of course. I know generations of the same families worked on a cathedral. I heard him say that, too. The men who began their life's work on them, they never lived to see the completion of their work. In that wise, bub, they're no different from the rest of us, right?" He laughed. Then his eyelids drooped again. His head nodded. He seemed to be snoozing. Maybe he was imagining himself in Portugal. The TV was showing another cathedral now. This one was in Germany. The Englishman's voice droned on. "Cathedrals," the blind man said. He sat up and rolled his head back and forth. "If you want the truth, bub, that's about all I know. What I just said. What I heard him say. But maybe you could describe one to me? I wish you'd do it. I'd like that. If you want to know, I really don't have a good idea."

I stared hard at the shot of the cathedral on the TV. How could I even begin to describe it? But say my life depended on it. Say my life was being threatened by an insane guy who said I had to do it or else.

I stared some more at the cathedral before the picture flipped off into the countryside. There was no use. I turned to the blind man and said, "To begin with, they're very tall." I was looking around the room for clues. "They reach way up. Up and up. Toward the sky. They're so big, some of them, they have to have these supports. To help hold them up, so to speak. These supports are called buttresses. They remind me of viaducts, for some reason. But maybe you don't know viaducts, either? Sometimes the cathedrals have devils and such carved into the front. Sometimes lords and ladies. Don't ask me why this is," I said.

He was nodding. The whole upper part of his body seemed to be moving back and forth.

"I'm not doing so good, am I?" I said.

He stopped nodding and leaned forward on the edge of the sofa. As he listened to me, he was running his fingers through his beard. I wasn't getting through to him, I could see that. But he waited for me to go on just the same. He nodded, like he was trying to encourage me. I tried to think what else to say. "They're really big," I said. "They're massive. They're built of stone. Marble, too, sometimes. In those olden days, when they built cathedrals, men wanted to be close to God. In those olden days, God was an important part of everyone's life. You could tell this from their cathedral-building. I'm sorry," I said, "but it looks like that's the best I can do for you. I'm just no good at it."

"That's all right, bub," the blind man said. "Hey, listen. I hope you don't mind my asking you. Can I ask you something? Let me ask you a simple question, yes or no. I'm just curious and there's no offense. You're my host. But let me ask if you are in any way religious? You don't mind my asking?"

I shook my head. He couldn't see that, though. A wink is the same as a nod to a blind man. "I guess I don't believe in it. In anything. Sometimes it's hard. You know what I'm saying?"

"Sure, I do," he said.

"Right," I said.

The Englishman was still holding forth. My wife sighed in her sleep. She drew a long breath and went on with her sleeping.

"You'll have to forgive me," I said. "But I can't tell you what a cathedral looks like. It just isn't in me to do it. I can't do any more than I've done."

The blind man sat very still, his head down, as he listened to me.

I said, "The truth is, cathedrals don't mean anything special to me. Nothing. Cathedrals. They're something to look at on late-night TV. That's all they are."

It was then that the blind man cleared his throat. He brought something up. He took a handkerchief from his back pocket. Then he said, "I get it, bub. It's okay. It happens. Don't worry about it," he said. "Hey, listen to me. Will you do me a favor? I got an idea. Why don't you find us some heavy paper? And a pen. We'll do something. We'll draw one together. Get us a pen and some heavy paper. Go on, bub, get the stuff," he said.

So I went upstairs. My legs felt like they didn't have any strength in them. They felt like they did after I'd done some running. In my wife's room, I looked around. I found some ballpoints in a little basket on her table. And then I tried to think where to look for the kind of paper he was talking about.

Downstairs, in the kitchen, I found a shopping bag with onion skins in the bottom of the bag. I emptied the bag and shook it. I brought it into the living room and sat down with it near his legs. I moved some things, smoothed the wrinkles from the bag, spread it out on the coffee table.

The blind man got down from the sofa and sat next to me on the carpet.

He ran his fingers over the paper. He went up and down the sides of the paper. The edges, even the edges. He fingered the corners.

"All right," he said. "All right, let's do her."

He found my hand, the hand with the pen. He closed his hand over my hand. "Go ahead, bub, draw," he said. "Draw. You'll see. I'll follow along with you. It'll be okay. Just begin now like I'm telling you. You'll see. Draw," the blind man said.

So I began. First I drew a box that looked like a house. It could have been the house I lived in. Then I put a roof on it. At either end of the roof, I drew spires. Crazy.

"Swell," he said. "Terrific. You're doing fine," he said. "Never thought anything like this could happen in your lifetime, did you, bub? Well, it's a strange life, we all know that. Go on now. Keep it up."

I put in windows with arches. I drew flying buttresses. I hung great doors. I couldn't stop. The TV station went off the air. I put down the pen and closed and opened my fingers. The blind man felt around over the paper. He moved the tips of his fingers over the paper, all over what I had drawn, and he nodded.

"Doing fine," the blind man said.

I took up the pen again, and he found my hand. I kept at it. I'm no artist. But I kept drawing just the same.

My wife opened up her eyes and gazed at us. She sat up on the sofa, her robe hanging open. She said, "What are you doing? Tell me, I want to know."

I didn't answer her.

The blind man said, "We're drawing a cathedral. Me and him are working on it. Press hard," he said to me. "That's right. That's good," he said. "Sure. You got it, bub. I can tell. You didn't think you could. But you can, can't you? You're cooking with gas now. You know what I'm saying? We're going to really have us something here in a minute. How's the old arm?" he said. "Put some people in there now. What's a cathedral without people?"

My wife said, "What's going on? Robert, what are you doing? What's going on?"

"It's all right," he said to her. "Close your eyes now," the blind man said to me.

I did it. I closed them just like he said.

"Are they closed?" he said. "Don't fudge."

"They're closed," I said.

"Keep them that way," he said. He said, "Don't stop now. Draw."

So we kept on with it. His fingers rode my fingers as my hand went over the paper. It was like nothing else in my life up to now.

Then he said, "I think that's it. I think you got it," he said. "Take a look. What do you think?"

But I had my eyes closed. I thought I'd keep them that way for a little longer. I thought it was something I ought to do.

"Well?" he said. "Are you looking?"

My eyes were still closed. I was in my house. I knew that. But I didn't feel like I was inside anything.

"It's really something," I said.

———

RAYMOND CARVER (1938–1988) was born in Clatskanie, Oregon. His parents were working people, struggling to get by, and their life is echoed in much of his fiction. He has been widely read and applauded—sometimes called "the American Chekhov." His poems and short stories have been translated into more than twenty languages.

The Lame Shall Enter First

Flannery O'Connor

Sheppard sat on a stool at the bar that divided the kitchen in half, eating his cereal out of the individual pasteboard box it came in. He ate mechanically, his eyes on the child, who was wandering from cabinet to cabinet in the panelled kitchen, collecting the ingredients for his breakfast. He was a stocky blond boy of ten. Sheppard kept his intense blue eyes fixed on him. The boy's future was written in his face. He would be a banker. No, worse. He would operate a small loan company. All he wanted for the child was that he be good and unselfish and neither seemed likely. Sheppard was a young man whose hair was already white. It stood up like a narrow brush halo over his pink sensitive face.

The boy approached the bar with the jar of peanut butter under his arm, a plate with a quarter of a small chocolate cake on it in one hand and the ketchup bottle in the other. He did not appear to notice his father. He climbed up on the stool and began to spread peanut butter on the cake. He had very large round ears that leaned away from his head and seemed to pull his eyes slightly too far apart. His shirt was green but so faded that the cowboy charging across the front of it was only a shadow.

"Norton," Sheppard said, "I saw Rufus Johnson yesterday. Do you know what he was doing?"

The child looked at him with a kind of half attention, his eyes forward but not yet engaged. They were a paler blue than his father's as if they might have faded like the shirt; one of them listed, almost imperceptibly, toward the outer rim.

"He was in an alley," Sheppard said, "and he had his hand in a garbage can. He was trying to get something to eat out of it." He paused to let this soak in. "He was hungry," he finished, and tried to pierce the child's conscience with his gaze.

The boy picked up the piece of chocolate cake and began to gnaw it from one corner.

"Norton," Sheppard said, "do you have any idea what it means to share?"

A flicker of attention. "Some of it's yours," Norton said.

"Some of it's *his,*" Sheppard said heavily. It was hopeless. Almost any fault would have been preferable to selfishness—a violent temper, even a tendency to lie.

The child turned the bottle of ketchup upside down and began thumping ketchup onto the cake.

Sheppard's look of pain increased. "You are ten and Rufus Johnson is fourteen," he said. "Yet I'm sure your shirts would fit Rufus." Rufus Johnson was a boy he had been trying to help at the reformatory for the past year. He had been released two months ago. "When he was in the reformatory, he looked pretty good, but when I saw him yesterday, he was skin and bones. He hasn't been eating cake with peanut butter on it for breakfast."

The child paused. "It's stale," he said. "That's why I have to put stuff on it."

Sheppard turned his face to the window at the end of the bar. The side lawn, green and even, sloped fifty feet or so down to a small suburban wood. When his wife was living, they had often eaten outside, even breakfast, on the grass. He had never noticed then that the child was selfish. "Listen to me," he said, turning back to him, "look at me and listen."

The boy looked at him. At least his eyes were forward.

"I gave Rufus a key to this house when he left the reformatory—to show my confidence in him and so he would have a place he could come to and feel welcome any time. He didn't use it, but I think he'll use it now because he's seen me and he's hungry. And if he doesn't use it, I'm going out and find him and bring him here. I can't see a child eating out of garbage cans."

The boy frowned. It was dawning upon him that something of his was threatened.

Sheppard's mouth stretched in disgust. "Rufus's father died before he was born," he said. "His mother is in the state penitentiary. He was raised by his grandfather in a shack without water or electricity and the old man beat him every day. How would you like to belong to a family like that?"

"I don't know," the child said lamely.

"Well, you might think about it sometime," Sheppard said.

Sheppard was City Recreational Director. On Saturdays he worked at the reformatory as a counselor, receiving nothing for it but the satisfaction of knowing he was helping boys no one else cared about. Johnson was the most intelligent boy he had worked with and the most deprived.

Norton turned what was left of the cake over as if he no longer wanted it.

"Maybe he won't come," the child said and his eyes brightened slightly.

"Think of everything you have that he doesn't!" Sheppard said. "Suppose you had to root in garbage cans for food? Suppose you had a huge swollen foot and one side of you dropped lower than the other when you walked?"

The boy looked blank, obviously unable to imagine such a thing.

"You have a healthy body," Sheppard said, "a good home. You've never been taught anything but the truth. Your daddy gives you everything you need and want. You don't have a grandfather who beats you. And your mother is not in the state penitentiary."

The child pushed his plate away. Sheppard groaned aloud.

A knot of flesh appeared below the boy's suddenly distorted mouth. His face became a mass of lumps with slits for eyes. "If she was in the penitentiary," he began in a kind of racking bellow, "I could go to seeeeee her." Tears rolled down his face and the ketchup dribbled on his chin. He looked as if he had been hit in the mouth. He abandoned himself and howled.

Sheppard sat helpless and miserable, like a man lashed by some elemental force of nature. This was not a normal grief. It was all part of his selfishness. She had been dead for over a year and a child's grief should not last so long. "You're going on eleven years old," he said reproachfully.

The child began an agonizing high-pitched heaving noise.

"If you stop thinking about yourself and think what you can do for somebody else," Sheppard said, "then you'll stop missing your mother."

The boy was silent but his shoulders continued to shake. Then his face collapsed and he began to howl again.

"Don't you think I'm lonely without her too?" Sheppard said. "Don't you think I miss her at all? I do, but I'm not sitting around moping. I'm busy helping other people. When do you see me just sitting around thinking about my troubles?"

The boy slumped as if he were exhausted but fresh tears streaked his face.

"What are you going to do today?" Sheppard asked, to get his mind on something else.

The child ran his arm across his eyes. "Sell seeds," he mumbled.

Always selling something. He had four quart jars full of nickels and dimes he had saved and he took them out of his closet every few days and counted them. "What are you selling seeds for?"

"To win a prize."

"What's the prize?"

"A thousand dollars."

"And what would you do if you had a thousand dollars?"

"Keep it," the child said and wiped his nose on his shoulder.

"I feel sure you would," Sheppard said. "Listen," he said and lowered his voice to an almost pleading tone, "suppose by some chance you did win a thousand dollars. Wouldn't you like to spend it on children less fortunate than yourself? Wouldn't you like to give some swings and trapezes to the orphanage? Wouldn't you like to buy poor Rufus Johnson a new shoe?"

The boy began to back away from the bar. Then suddenly he leaned forward and hung with his mouth open over his plate. Sheppard groaned again. Everything came up, the cake, the peanut butter, the ketchup—a limp sweet batter. He hung over it gagging, more came, and he waited with his mouth open over the plate as if he expected his heart to come up next.

"It's all right," Sheppard said, "it's all right. You couldn't help it. Wipe your mouth and go lie down."

The child hung there a moment longer. Then he raised his face and looked blindly at his father.

"Go on," Sheppard said. "Go on and lie down."

The boy pulled up the end of his t-shirt and smeared his mouth with it. Then he climbed down off the stool and wandered out of the kitchen.

Sheppard sat there staring at the puddle of half-digested food. The sour odor reached him and he drew back. His gorge rose. He got up and carried the plate to the sink and turned the water on it and watched grimly as the mess ran down the drain. Johnson's sad thin hand rooted in garbage cans for food while his own child, selfish, unresponsive, greedy, had so much that he threw it up. He cut off the faucet with a thrust of his fist. Johnson had a capacity for real response and had been deprived of everything from birth; Norton was average or below and had had every advantage.

He went back to the bar to finish his breakfast. The cereal was soggy in the cardboard box but he paid no attention to what he was eating. Johnson was worth any amount of effort because he had the potential. He had seen it from the time the boy had limped in for his first interview.

Sheppard's office at the reformatory was a narrow closet with one window and a small table and two chairs in it. He had never been inside a confessional but he thought it must be the same kind of operation he had here, except that he explained, he did not absolve. His credentials were less dubious than a priest's; he had been trained for what he was doing.

When Johnson came in for his first interview, he had been reading over the boy's record—senseless destruction, windows smashed, city trash boxes set afire, tires slashed—the kind of thing he found where boys had been transplanted abruptly from the county to the city as this one had. He came to Johnson's I.Q. score. It was 140. He raised his eyes eagerly.

The boy sat slumped on the edge of his chair, his arms hanging between his thighs. The light from the window fell on his face. His eyes, steel-colored and very still, were trained narrowly forward. His thin dark hair hung in a flat forelock acoss the side of his forehead, not carelessly like a boy's, but fiercely like an old man's. A kind of fanatic intelligence was palpable in his face.

Sheppard smiled to diminish the distance between them.

The boy's expression did not soften. He leaned back in his chair and lifted a monstrous club foot to his knee. The foot was in a heavy black battered shoe with a sole four or five inches thick. The leather parted from it in one place and the end of an empty sock protruded like a gray tongue from a severed head. The case was clear to Sheppard instantly. His mischief was compensation for the foot.

"Well Rufus," he said, "I see by the record here that you don't have but a year to serve. What do you plan to do when you get out?"

"I don't make no plans," the boy said. His eyes shifted indifferently to something outside the window behind Sheppard in the far distance.

"Maybe you ought to," Sheppard said and smiled.

Johnson continued to gaze beyond him.

"I want to see you make the most of your intelligence," Sheppard said. "What's most important to you? Let's talk about what's important to *you*." His eyes dropped involuntarily to the foot.

"Study it and git your fill," the boy drawled.

Sheppard reddened. The black deformed mass swelled before his eyes. He ignored the remark and the leer the boy was giving him. "Rufus," he said, "you've got into a lot of senseless trouble but

I think when you understand why you do these things, you'll be less inclined to do them." He smiled. They had so few friends, saw so few pleasant faces, that half his effectiveness came from nothing more than smiling at them. "There are a lot of things about yourself that I think I can explain to you," he said.

Johnson looked at him stonily. "I ain't asked for no explanation," he said. "I already know why I do what I do."

"Well good!" Sheppard said. "Suppose you tell me what's made you do the things you've done?"

A black sheen appeared in the boy's eyes. "Satan," he said. "He has me in his power."

Sheppard looked at him steadily. There was no indication on the boy's face that he had said this to be funny. The line of his thin mouth was set with pride. Sheppard's eyes hardened. He felt a momentary dull despair as if he were faced with some elemental warping of nature that had happened too long ago to be corrected now. This boy's questions about life had been answered by signs nailed on the pine trees: DOES SATAN HAVE YOU IN HIS POWER? REPENT OR BURN IN HELL. JESUS SAVES. He would know the Bible with or without reading it. His despair gave way to outrage. "Rubbish!" he snorted. "We're living in the space age! You're too smart to give me an answer like that."

Johnson's mouth twisted slightly. His look was contemptuous but amused. There was a glint of challenge in his eyes.

Sheppard scrutinized his face. Where there was intelligence anything was possible. He smiled again, a smile that was like an invitation to the boy to come into a school room with all its windows thrown open to the light. "Rufus," he said, "I'm going to arrange for you to have a conference with me once a week. Maybe there's an explanation for your explanation. Maybe I can explain your devil to you."

After that he had talked to Johnson every Saturday for the rest of the year. He talked at random, the kind of talk the boy would never have heard before. He talked a little above him to give him something to reach for. He roamed from simple psychology and the dodges of the human mind to astronomy and the space capsules that were whirling around the earth faster than the speed of sound and would soon encircle the stars. Instinctively he concentrated on the stars. He wanted to give the boy something to reach for besides his neighbor's goods. He wanted to stretch his horizons. He wanted him to *see* the universe, to see that the darkest parts of it could be penetrated. He would have given anything to be able to put a telescope in Johnson's hands.

Johnson said little and what he did say, for the sake of his pride, was in dissent or senseless contradiction, with the clubfoot raised always to his knee like a weapon ready for use, but Sheppard was not deceived. He watched his eyes and every week he saw something in them crumble. From the boy's face, hard but shocked, braced against the light that was ravaging him, he could see that he was hitting dead center.

Johnson was free now to live out of garbage cans and rediscover his old ignorance. The injustice of it was infuriating. He had been sent back to the grandfather; the old man's imbecility could only be imagined. Perhaps the boy had by now run away from him. The idea of getting custody of Johnson had occurred to Sheppard before, but the fact of the grandfather had stood in the way. Nothing excited him so much as thinking what he could do for such a boy. First he would have him fitted for a new orthopedic shoe. His back was thrown out of line every time he took a step. Then he would encourage him in some particular intellectual interest. He thought of the telescope. He could buy a second-hand one and they could set it up in the attic window. He sat for almost ten minutes thinking what he could do if he had Johnson here with him. What was wasted on Norton would cause Johnson to flourish. Yesterday when he had seen him with his hand in the garbage can, he had waved and started forward. Johnson had seen him, paused a split-second, then vanished with the swiftness of a rat, but not before Sheppard had seen his expression change. Something had kindled in the boy's eyes, he was sure of it, some memory of the lost light.

He got up and threw the cereal box in the garbage. Before he left the house, he looked into Norton's room to be sure he was not still sick. The child was sitting cross-legged on his bed. He had emptied the quart jars of change into one large pile in front of him, and was sorting it out by nickels and dimes and quarters.

———

That afternoon Norton was alone in the house, squatting on the floor of his room arranging packages of flower seeds in rows around himself. Rain slashed against the window panes and rattled in the gutters. The room had grown dark but every few minutes it was lit by silent lightning and the seed packages showed up gaily on the floor. He squatted motionless like a large pale frog in the midst of this potential garden. All at once his eyes became alert. Without warning the rain had stopped. The silence was heavy as if the downpour had been hushed by violence. He remained motionless, only his eyes turning.

Into the silence came the distinct click of a key turning in the front door lock. The sound was a very deliberate one. It drew attention to itself and held it as if it were controlled more by a mind than by a hand. The child leapt up and got into the closet.

The footsteps began to move in the hall. They were deliberate and irregular, a light and then a heavy one, then a silence as if the visitor had paused to listen himself or to examine something. In a minute the kitchen door screeked. The footsteps crossed the kitchen to the refrigerator. The closet wall and the kitchen wall were the same. Norton stood with his ear pressed against it. The refrigerator door opened. There was a prolonged silence.

He took off his shoes and then tiptoed out of the closet and stepped over the seed packages. In the middle of the room, he stopped and remained where he was, rigid. A thin bony-face boy in a wet black suit stood in his door, blocking his escape. His hair was flattened to his skull by the rain. He stood there like an irate drenched crow. His look went through the child like a pin and paralyzed him. Then his eyes began to move over everything in the room—the unmade bed, the dirty curtains on the one large window, a photograph of a wide-faced young woman that stood up in the clutter on top of the dresser.

The child's tongue suddenly went wild. "He's been expecting

you, he's going to give you a new shoe because you have to eat out of garbage cans!" he said in a kind of mouse-like shriek.

"I eat out of garbage cans," the boy said slowly with a beady stare, "because I like to eat out of garbage cans. See?"

The child nodded.

"And I got ways of getting my own shoe. See?"

The child nodded, mesmerized.

The boy limped in and sat down on the bed. He arranged a pillow behind him and stretched his short leg out so that the big black shoe rested conspicuously on a fold of the sheet.

Norton's gaze settled on it and remained immobile. The sole was as thick as a brick.

Johnson wiggled it slightly and smiled. "If I kick somebody *once* with this," he said, "it learns them not to mess with me."

The child nodded.

"Go in the kitchen," Johnson said, "and make me a sandwich with some of that rye bread and ham and bring me a glass of milk."

Norton went off like a mechanical toy, pushed in the right direction. He made a large greasy sandwich with ham hanging out the sides of it and poured out a glass of milk. Then he returned to the room with the glass of milk in one hand and the sandwich in the other.

Johnson was leaning back regally against the pillow. "Thanks, waiter," he said and took the sandwich.

Norton stood by the side of the bed, holding the glass.

The boy tore into the sandwich and ate steadily until he finished it. Then he took the glass of milk. He held it with both hands like a child and when he lowered it for breath, there was a rim of milk around his mouth. He handed Norton the empty glass. "Go get me one of them oranges in there, waiter," he said hoarsely.

Norton went to the kitchen and returned with the orange. Johnson peeled it with his fingers and let the peeling drop in the bed. He ate it slowly, spitting the seeds out in front of him. When he finished, he wiped his hands on the sheet and gave Norton a long appraising stare. He appeared to have been softened by the service. "You're his kid all right," he said. "You got the same stupid face."

The child stood there stolidly as if he had not heard.

"He don't know his left hand from his right," Johnson said with a hoarse pleasure in his voice.

The child cast his eyes a little to the side of the boy's face and looked fixedly at the wall.

"Yaketty yaketty yak," Johnson said, "and never says a thing."

The child's upper lip lifted slightly but he didn't say anything.

"Gas," Johnson said. "Gas."

The child's face began to have a wary look of belligerence. He backed away slightly as if he were prepared to retreat instantly. "He's good," he mumbled. "He helps people."

"Good!" Johnson said savagely. He thrust his head forward. "Listen here," he hissed, "I don't care if he's good or not. He ain't *right*!"

Norton looked stunned.

The screen door in the kitchen banged and someone entered. Johnson sat forward instantly. "Is that him?" he said.

"It's the cook," Norton said. "She comes in the afternoon."

Johnson got up and limped into the hall and stood in the kitchen door and Norton followed him.

The colored girl was at the closet taking off a bright red raincoat. She was a tall light-yellow girl with a mouth like a large rose that had darkened and wilted. Her hair was dressed in tiers on top of her head and leaned to the side like the Tower of Pisa.

Johnson made a noise through his teeth. "Well look at Aunt Jemima," he said.

The girl paused and trained an insolent gaze on them. They might have been dust on the floor.

"Come on," Johnson said, "let's see what all you got besides a nigger." He opened the first door to his right in the hall and looked into a pink-tiled bathroom. "A pink can!" he murmured.

He turned a comical face to the child. "Does he sit on that?"

"It's for company," Norton said, "but he sits on it sometimes."

"He ought to empty his head in it," Johnson said.

The door was open to the next room. It was the room Sheppard had slept in since his wife died. An ascetic-looking iron bed stood on the bare floor. A heap of Little League baseball uniforms was piled in one corner. Papers were scattered over a large roll-top desk and held down in various places by his pipes. Johnson stood looking into the room silently. He wrinkled his nose. "Guess who?" he said.

The door to the next room was closed but Johnson opened it and thrust his head into the semi-darkness within. The shades were down and the air was close with a faint scent of perfume in it. There was a wide antique bed and a mammoth dresser whose mirror glinted in the half light. Johnson snapped the light switch by the door and crossed the room to the mirror and peered into it. A silver comb and brush lay on the linen runner. He picked up the comb and began to run it through his hair. He combed it straight down on his forehead. Then he swept it to the side, Hitler fashion.

"Leave her comb alone!" the child said. He stood in the door, pale and breathing heavily as if he were watching sacrilege in a holy place.

Johnson put the comb down and picked up the brush and gave his hair a swipe with it.

"She's dead," the child said.

"I ain't afraid of dead people's things," Johnson said. He opened the top drawer and slid his hand in.

"Take your big fat dirty hands off my mother's clothes!" the child said in a high suffocated voice.

"Keep your shirt on, sweetheart," Johnson murmured. He pulled up a wrinkled red polka dot blouse and dropped it back. Then he pulled out a green silk kerchief and whirled it over his head and let it float to the floor. His hand continued to plow deep into the drawer. After a moment it came up gripping a faded corset with four dangling metal supporters. "Thisyer must be her saddle," he observed.

He lifted it gingerly and shook it. Then he fastened it around his waist and jumped up and down, making the metal supporters dance. He began to snap his fingers and turn his hips from side to side. "Gonter rock, rattle and roll," he sang. "Gonter rock, rattle and roll. Can't please that woman, to save my doggone soul." He began to move around, stamping the good foot down and slinging the heavy one to the side. He danced out the door, past the stricken child and down the hall toward the kitchen.

———

A half hour later Sheppard came home. He dropped his raincoat on a chair in the hall and came as far as the parlor door and stopped. His face was suddenly transformed. It shone with pleasure. Johnson sat, a dark figure, in a high-backed pink upholstered chair. The wall behind him was lined with books from floor to ceiling. He was reading one. Sheppard's eyes narrowed. It was a volume of the Encyclopedia Britannica. He was so engrossed in it that he did not look up. Sheppard held his breath. This was the perfect setting for the boy. He had to keep him here. He had to manage it somehow.

"Rufus!" he said, "it's good to see you boy!" and he bounded forward with his arm oustretched.

Johnson looked up, his face blank. "Oh hello," he said. He ignored the hand as long as he was able but when Sheppard did not withdraw it, he grudgingly shook it.

Sheppard was prepared for this kind of reaction. It was part of Johnson's make-up never to show enthusiasm.

"How are things?" he said. "How's your grandfather treating you?" He sat down on the edge of the sofa.

"He dropped dead," the boy said indifferently.

"You don't mean it!" Sheppard cried. He got up and sat down on the coffee table nearer the boy.

"Naw," Johnson said, "he ain't dropped dead. I wisht he had."

"Well where is he?" Sheppard muttered.

"He's gone with a remnant to the hills," Johnson said. "Him and some others. They're going to bury some Bibles in a cave and take two of different kinds of animals and all like that. Like Noah. Only this time it's going to be fire, not flood."

Sheppard's mouth stretched wryly. "I see," he said. Then he said, "In other words the old fool has abandoned you?"

"He ain't no fool," the boy said in an indignant tone.

"Has he abandoned you or not?" Sheppard asked impatiently.

The boy shrugged.

"Where's your probation officer?"

"I ain't supposed to keep up with him," Johnson said. "He's supposed to keep up with me."

Sheppard laughed. "Wait a minute," he said. He got up and went into the hall and got his raincoat off the chair and took it to the hall closet to hang it up. He had to give himself time to think, to decide how he could ask the boy so that he would stay. He couldn't force him to stay. It would have to be voluntary. Johnson pretended not to like him. That was only to uphold his pride, but he would have to ask him in such a way that his pride could still be upheld. He opened the closet door and took out a hanger. An old gray winter coat of his wife's still hung there. He pushed it aside but it didn't move. He pulled it open roughly and winced as if he had seen the larva inside a cocoon. Norton stood in it, his face swollen and pale, with a drugged look of misery on it. Sheppard stared at him. Suddenly he was confronted with a possibility. "Get out of there," he said. He caught him by the shoulder and propelled him firmly into the parlor and over to the pink chair where Johnson was sitting with the encyclopedia in his lap. He was going to risk everything in one blow.

"Rufus," he said, "I've got a problem. I need your help."

Johnson looked up suspiciously.

"Listen," Sheppard said, "we need another boy in the house." There was a genuine desperation in his voice. "Norton here has never had to divide anything in his life. He doesn't know what it means to share. And I need somebody to teach him. How about helping me out? Stay here for a while with us, Rufus. I need your help." The excitement in his voice made it thin.

The child suddenly came to life. His face swelled with fury. "He went in her room and used her comb!" he screamed, yanking Sheppard's arm. "He put on her corset and danced with Leola, he ..."

"Stop this!" Sheppard said sharply. "Is tattling all you're capable of? I'm not asking you for a report on Rufus's conduct. I'm asking you to make him welcome here. Do you understand?"

"You see how it is?" he asked, turning to Johnson.

Norton kicked the leg of the pink chair viciously, just missing Johnson's swollen foot. Sheppard yanked him back.

"He said you weren't nothing but gas!" the child shrieked.

A sly look of pleasure crossed Johnson's face.

Sheppard was not put back. These insults were part of the boy's defensive mechanism. "What about it, Rufus?" he said. "Will you stay with us for a while?"

Johnson looked straight in front of him and said nothing. He smiled slightly and appeared to gaze upon some vision of the future that pleased him.

"I don't care," he said and turned a page of the encyclopedia. "I can stand anywhere."

"Wonderful," Sheppard said. "Wonderful."

"He said," the child said in a throaty whisper, "you didn't know your left hand from your right."

There was a silence.

Johnson wet his finger and turned another page of the encyclopedia.

"I have something to say to both of you," Sheppard said in a voice without inflection. His eyes moved from one to the other of them and he spoke slowly as if what he was saying he would say only once and it behooved them to listen. "If it made any difference to me what Rufus thinks of me," he said, "then I wouldn't be asking him here. Rufus is going to help me out and I'm going to help him out and we're both going to help you out. I'd simply be selfish if I let what Rufus thinks of me interfere with what I can do for Rufus. If I can help a person, all I want is to do it. I'm above and beyond simple pettiness."

Neither of them made a sound. Norton stared at the chair cushion. Johnson peered closer at some fine print in the encyclopedia. Sheppard was looking at the tops of their heads. He smiled. After all, he had won. The boy was staying. He reached out and ruffled Norton's hair and slapped Johnson on the shoulder. "Now you fellows sit here and get acquainted," he said gaily and started toward the door. "I'm going to see what Leola left us for supper."

When he was gone, Johnson raised his head and looked at Norton. The child looked back at him bleakly. "God, kid," Johnson said in a cracked voice, "how do you stand it?" His face was stiff with outrage. "He thinks he's Jesus Christ!"

II

Sheppard's attic was a large unfinished room with exposed beams and no electric light. They had set the telescope up on a tripod in one of the dormer windows. It pointed now toward the dark sky where a sliver of moon, as fragile as an egg shell, had just emerged from behind a cloud with a brilliant silver edge. Inside, a kerosene lantern set on a trunk cast their shadows upward and tangled them, wavering slightly, in the joints overhead. Sheppard was sitting on a packing box, looking through the telescope, and Johnson was at his elbow, waiting to get at it. Sheppard had bought it for fifteen dollars two days before at a pawn shop.

"Quit hoggin it," Johnson said.

Sheppard got up and Johnson slid onto the box and put his eye to the instrument.

Sheppard sat down on a straight chair a few feet away. His face was flushed with pleasure. This much of his dream was a reality. Within a week he had made it possible for this boy's vision to pass through a slender channel to the stars. He looked at Johnson's bent back with complete satisfaction. The boy had on one of Norton's plaid shirts and some new khaki trousers he had bought him. The shoe would be ready next week. He had taken him to the brace shop the day after he came and had him fitted for a new shoe. Johnson was as touchy about the foot as if it were a sacred object. His face had been glum while the clerk, a young man with a bright pink bald head, measured the foot with his profane hands. The shoe was going to make the greatest difference in the boy's attitude. Even a child with normal feet was in love with the world after he had got a new pair of shoes. When Norton got a new pair, he walked around for days with his eyes on his feet.

Sheppard glanced across the room at the child. He was sitting on the floor against a trunk, trussed up in a rope he had found and wound around his legs from his ankles to his knees. He appeared so far away that Sheppard might have been looking at him through the wrong end of the telescope. He had had to whip him only once since Johnson had been with them—the first night when Norton had realized that Johnson was going to sleep in his mother's bed. He did not believe in whipping children, particularly in anger. In this case, he had done both and with good results. He had had no more trouble with Norton.

The child hadn't shown any positive generosity toward Johnson but what he couldn't help, he appeared to be resigned to. In the mornings Sheppard sent the two of them to the Y swimming pool, gave them money to get their lunch at the cafeteria and instructed them to meet him in the park in the afternoon to watch his Little League baseball practice. Every afternoon they had arrived at the park, shambling, silent, their faces closed each on his own thoughts as if neither were aware of the other's existence. At least he could be thankful there were no fights.

Norton showed no interest in the telescope. "Don't you want to get up and look through the telescope, Norton?" he said. It irritated him that the child showed no intellectual curiosity whatsoever. "Rufus is going to be way ahead of you."

Norton leaned forward absently and looked at Johnson's back.

Johnson turned around from the instrument. His face had begun to fill out again. The look of outrage had retreated from his hollow cheeks and was shored up now in the caves of his eyes, like a fugitive from Sheppard's kindness. "Don't waste your valuable time, kid," he said. "You seen the moon once, you seen it."

Sheppard was amused by these sudden turns of perversity. The boy resisted whatever he suspected was meant for his improvement and contrived when he was vitally interested in something to leave the impression he was bored. Sheppard was not deceived. Secretly Johnson was learning what he wanted him to learn—that his benefactor was impervious to insult and that there were no cracks in his armor of kindness and patience where a successful shaft could be driven. "Some day you may go to the moon," he said. "In ten years men will probably be making round trips there on schedule. Why you boys may be spacemen. Astronauts!"

"Astro-nuts," Johnson said.

"Nuts or nauts," Sheppard said, "it's perfectly possible that you, Rufus Johnson, will go to the moon."

Something in the depths of Johnson's eyes stirred. All day his humor had been glum. "I ain't going to the moon and get there alive," he said, "and when I die I'm going to hell."

"It's at least possible to get to the moon," Sheppard said dryly. The best way to handle this kind of thing was with gentle ridicule. "We can see it. We know it's there. Nobody has given any reliable evidence there's a hell."

"The Bible has give the evidence," Johnson said darkly, "and if you die and go there you burn forever."

The child leaned forward.

"Whoever says it ain't a hell," Johnson said, "is contradicting Jesus. The dead are judged and the wicked are damned. They weep and gnash their teeth while they burn," he continued, "and it's everlasting darkness."

The child's mouth opened. His eyes appeared to grow hollow.

"Satan runs it," Johnson said.

Norton lurched up and took a hobbled step toward Sheppard. "Is she there?" he said in a loud voice. "Is she there burning up?" He kicked the rope off his feet. "Is she on fire?"

"Oh my God," Sheppard muttered. "No no," he said, "of course she isn't. Rufus is mistaken. Your mother isn't anywhere. She's not unhappy. She just isn't." His lot would have been easier if when his wife died he had told Norton she had gone to heaven and that some day he would see her again, but he could not allow himself to bring him up on a lie.

Norton's face began to twist. A knot formed in his chin.

"Listen," Sheppard said quickly and pulled the child to him, "your mother's spirit lives on in other people and it'll live on in you if you're good and generous like she was."

The child's pale eyes hardened in disbelief.

Sheppard's pity turned to revulsion. The boy would rather she be in hell than nowhere. "Do you understand?" he said. "She doesn't exist." He put his hand on the child's shoulder. "That's all I have to give you," he said in a softer, exasperated tone, "the truth."

Instead of howling, the boy wrenched himself away and caught Johnson by the sleeve. "Is she there, Rufus?" he said "Is she there, burning up?"

Johnson's eyes glittered. "Well," he said, "she is if she was evil. Was she a whore?"

"Your mother was not a whore," Sheppard said sharply. He had the sensation of driving a car without brakes. "Now let's have no more of this foolishness. We were talking about the moon."

"Did she believe in Jesus?" Johnson asked.

Norton looked blank. After a second he said, "Yes," as if he saw that this was necessary. "She did," he said. "All the time."

"She did not," Sheppard muttered.

"She did all the time," Norton said. "I heard her say she did all the time."

"She's saved," Johnson said.

The child still looked puzzled. "Where?" he said. "Where is she at?"

"On high," Johnson said.

"Where's that?" Norton gasped.

"It's in the sky somewhere," Johnson said, "but you got to be dead to get there. You can't go in no space ship." There was a narrow gleam in his eyes now like a beam holding steady on its target.

"Man's going to the moon," Sheppard said grimly, "is very much like the first fish crawling out of the water onto land billions and billions of years ago. He didn't have an earth suit. He had to grow his adjustments inside. He developed lungs."

"When I'm dead will I go to hell or where she is?" Norton asked.

"Right now you'd go where she is," Johnson said, "but if you live long enough, you'll go to hell."

Sheppard rose abruptly and picked up the lantern. "Close the window, Rufus," he said. "It's time we went to bed."

On the way down the attic stairs he heard Johnson say in a loud whisper behind him, "I'll tell you all about it tomorrow, kid, when Himself has cleared out."

———

The next day when the boys came to the ball park, he watched them as they came from behind the bleachers and around the edge of the field. Johnson's hand was on Norton's shoulder, his head bent toward the younger boy's ear, and on the child's face there was a look of complete confidence, of dawning light. Sheppard's grimace hardened. This would be Johnson's way of trying to annoy him. But he would not be annoyed. Norton was not bright enough to be damaged much. He gazed at the child's dull absorbed little face. Why try to make him superior? Heaven and hell were for the mediocre, and he was that if he was anything.

The two boys came into the bleachers and sat down about ten feet away, facing him, but neither gave him any sign of recognition. He cast a glance behind him where the Little Leaguers were spread out in the field. Then he started for the bleachers. The hiss of Johnson's voice stopped as he approached.

"What have you fellows been doing today?" he asked genially.

"He's been telling me…" Norton started.

Johnson pushed the child in the ribs with his elbow. "We ain't been doing nothing," he said. His face appeared to be covered with a blank glaze but through it a look of complicity was blazoned forth insolently.

Sheppard felt his face grow warm, but he said nothing. A child in a Little League uniform had followed him and was nudging him in the back of the leg with a bat. He turned and put his arm around the boy's neck and went with him back to the game.

That night when he went to the attic to join the boys at the telescope, he found Norton there alone. He was sitting on the packing box, hunched over, looking intently through the instrument. Johnson was not there.

"Where's Rufus?" Sheppard asked.

"I said where's Rufus?" he said louder.

"Gone somewhere," the child said without turning around.

"Gone where?" Sheppard asked.

"He just said he was going somewhere. He said he was fed up looking at stars."

"I see," Sheppard said glumly. He turned and went back down the stairs. He searched the house without finding Johnson. Then he went to the living room and sat down. Yesterday he had been convinced of his success with the boy. Today he faced the possibility that he was failing with him. He had been over-lenient, too concerned to have Johnson like him. He felt a twinge of guilt. What difference did it make if Johnson liked him or not? What was that to him? When the boy came in, they would have a few things understood. As long as you stay here there'll be no going out at night by yourself, do you understand?

I don't have to stay here. It ain't nothing to me staying here.

Oh my God, he thought. He could not bring it to that. He would have to be firm but not make an issue of it. He picked up the evening paper. Kindness and patience were always called for but he had not been firm enough. He sat holding the paper but not reading it. The boy would not respect him unless he showed firmness. The doorbell rang and he went to answer it. He opened it and stepped back, with a pained disappointed face.

A large dour policeman stood on the stoop, holding Johnson by the elbow. At the curb a patrol car waited. Johnson looked very white. His jaw was thrust forward as if to keep from trembling.

"We brought him here first because he raised such a fit," the policeman said, "but now that you've seen him, we're going to take him to the station and ask him a few questions."

"What happened?" Sheppard muttered.

"A house around the corner from here," the policeman said. "A real smash job, dishes broken all over the floor, furniture turned upside down..."

"I didn't have a thing to do with it!" Johnson said. "I was walking along minding my own bidnis when this cop came up and grabbed me."

Sheppard looked at the boy grimly. He made no effort to soften his expression.

Johnson flushed. "I was just walking along," he muttered, but with no conviction in his voice.

"Come on, bud," the policeman said.

"You ain't going to let him take me, are you?" Johnson said. "You believe me, don't you?" There was an appeal in his voice that Sheppard had not heard there before.

This was crucial. The boy would have to learn that he could not be protected when he was guilty. "You'll have to go with him, Rufus," he said.

"You're going to let him take me and I tell you I ain't done a thing?" Johnson said shrilly.

Sheppard's face became harder as his sense of injury grew. The boy had failed him even before he had had a chance to give him the shoe. They were to have got it tomorrow. All his regret turned suddenly on the shoe; his irritation at the sight of Johnson doubled.

"You made out like you had all this confidence in me," the boy mumbled.

"I did have," Sheppard said. His face was wooden.

Johnson turned away with the policeman but before he moved, a gleam of pure hatred flashed toward Sheppard from the pits of his eyes.

Sheppard stood in the door and watched them get into the patrol car and drive away. He summoned his compassion. He would go to the station tomorrow and see what he could do about getting him out of trouble. The night in jail would not hurt him and the experience would teach him that he could not treat with impunity someone who had shown him nothing but kindness. Then they would go get the shoe and perhaps after a night in jail it would mean even more to the boy.

———

The next morning at eight o'clock the police sergeant called and told him he could come pick Johnson up. "We booked a nigger on that charge," he said. "Your boy didn't have nothing to do with it."

Sheppard was at the station in ten minutes, his face hot with shame. Johnson sat slouched on a bench in a drab outer office, reading a police magazine. There was no one else in the room. Sheppard sat down beside him and put his hand tentatively on his shoulder.

The boy glanced up—his lip curled—and back to the magazine.

Sheppard felt physically sick. The ugliness of what he had done bore in upon him with a sudden dull intensity. He had failed him at just the point where he might have turned him once and for all in the right direction. "Rufus," he said, "I apologize. I was wrong and you were right. I misjudged you."

The boy continued to read.

"I'm sorry."

The boy wet his finger and turned a page.

Sheppard braced himself. "I was a fool, Rufus," he said.

Johnson's mouth slid slightly to the side. He shrugged without raising his head from the magazine.

"Will you forget it, this time?" Sheppard said. "It won't happen again."

The boy looked up. His eyes were bright and unfriendly. "I'll forget it," he said, "but you better remember it." He got up and stalked toward the door. In the middle of the room he turned and jerked his arm at Sheppard and Sheppard jumped up and followed him as if the boy had yanked an invisible leash.

"Your shoe," he said eagerly, "today is the day to get your shoe!" Thank God for the shoe!

But when they went to the brace shop, they found that the shoe had been made two sizes too small and a new one would not be ready for another ten days. Johnson's temper improved at once. The clerk had obviously made a mistake in the measurements but the boy insisted the foot had grown. He left the shop with a pleased expression, as if, in expanding, the foot had acted on some inspiration of its own. Sheppard's face was haggard.

After this he redoubled his efforts. Since Johnson had lost interest in the telescope, he bought a microscope and a box of prepared slides. If he couldn't impress the boy with immensity, he would try the infinitesimal. For two nights Johnson appeared absorbed in the new instrument, then he abruptly lost interest in it, but he seemed

content to sit in the living room in the evening and read the encyclopedia. He devoured the encyclopedia as he devoured his dinner,
steadily and without dint to his appetite. Each subject appeared to
enter his head, be ravaged, and thrown out. Nothing pleased Sheppard more than to see the boy slouched on the sofa, his mouth shut,
reading. After they had spent two or three evenings like this, he
began to recover his vision. His confidence returned. He knew that
some day he would be proud of Johnson.

On Thursday night Sheppard attended a city council meeting.
He dropped the boys off at a movie on his way and picked them
up on his way back. When they reached home, an automobile with
a single red eye above its windshield was waiting in front of the
house. Sheppard's lights as he turned into the driveway illuminated
two dour faces in the car.

"The cops!" Johnson said. "Some nigger has broke in somewhere
and they've come for me again."

"We'll see about that," Sheppard muttered. He stopped the car
in the driveway and switched off the lights. "You boys go in the
house and go to bed," he said. "I'll handle this."

He got out and strode toward the squad car. He thrust his head in
the window. The two policemen were looking at him with silent
knowledgeable faces. "A house on the corner of Shelton and Mills,"
the one in the driver's seat said. "It looks like a train run through it."

"He was in the picture show downtown," Sheppard said. "My
boy was with him. He had nothing to do with the other one and he
had nothing to do with this one. I'll be responsible."

"If I was you," the one nearest him said, "I wouldn't be responsible for any little bastard like him."

"I said I'd be responsible," Sheppard repeated coldly. "You
people made a mistake the last time. Don't make another."

The policemen looked at each other. "It ain't our funeral," the
one in the driver's seat said, and turned the key in the ignition.

Sheppard went in the house and sat down in the living room in
the dark. He did not suspect Johnson and he did not want the boy to
think he did. If Johnson thought he suspected him again, he would
lose everything. But he wanted to know if his alibi was airtight. He

thought of going to Norton's room and asking him if Johnson had left the movie. But that would be worse. Johnson would know what he was doing and would be incensed. He decided to ask Johnson himself. He would be direct. He went over in his mind what he was going to say and then he got up and went to the boy's door.

It was open as if he had been expected but Johnson was in bed. Just enough light came in from the hall for Sheppard to see his shape under the sheet. He came in and stood at the foot of the bed. "They've gone," he said. "I told them you had nothing to do with it and that I'd be responsible."

There was a muttered "Yeah," from the pillow.

Sheppard hesitated. "Rufus," he said, "you didn't leave the movie for anything at all, did you?"

"You make out like you got all this confidence in me!" a sudden outraged voice cried, "and you ain't got any! You don't trust me no more now than you did then!" The voice, disembodied, seemed to come more surely from the depths of Johnson than when his face was visible. It was a cry of reproach, edged slightly with contempt.

"I do have confidence in you," Sheppard said intensely. "I have every confidence in you. I believe in you and I trust you completely."

"You got your eye on me all the time," the voice said sullenly. "When you get through asking me a bunch of questions, you're going across the hall and ask Norton a bunch of them."

"I have no intention of asking Norton anything and never did," Sheppard said gently. "And I don't suspect you at all. You could hardly have got from the picture show downtown and out here to break in a house and back to the picture show in the time you had."

"That's why you believe me!" the boy cried, "—because you think I couldn't have done it."

"No, no!" Sheppard said. "I believe you because I believe you've got the brains and the guts not to get in trouble again. I believe you know yourself well enough now to know that you don't have to do such things. I believe that you can make anything of yourself that you set your mind to."

Johnson sat up. A faint light shone on his forehead but the rest of his face was invisible. "And I could have broke in there if I'd wanted to in the time I had," he said.

"But I know you didn't," Sheppard said. "There's not the least trace of doubt in my mind."

There was a silence. Johnson lay back down. Then the voice, low and hoarse, as if it were being forced out with difficulty, said, "You don't want to steal and smash up things when you've got everything you want already."

Sheppard caught his breath. The boy was thanking him! He was thanking him! There was gratitude in his voice. There was appreciation. He stood there, smiling foolishly in the dark, trying to hold the moment in suspension. Involuntarily he took a step toward the pillow and stretched out his hand and touched Johnson's forehead. It was cold and dry like rusty iron.

"I understand. Good night, son," he said and turned quickly and left the room. He closed the door behind him and stood there, overcome with emotion.

Across the hall Norton's door was open. The child lay on the bed on his side, looking into the light from the hall.

After this, the road with Johnson would be smooth.

Norton sat up and beckoned to him.

He saw the child but after the first instant, he did not let his eyes focus directly on him. He could not go in and talk to Norton without breaking Johnson's trust. He hesitated, but remained where he was a moment as if he saw nothing. Tomorrow was the day they were to go back for the shoe. It would be a climax to the good feeling between them. He turned quickly and went back into his own room.

The child sat for some time looking at the spot where his father had stood. Finally his gaze became aimless and he lay back down.

The next day Johnson was glum and silent as if he were ashamed that he had revealed himself. His eyes had a hooded look. He seemed to have retired within himself and there to be going through some crisis of determination. Sheppard could not get to the brace shop quickly enough. He left Norton at home because he did not want his attention divided. He wanted to be free to observe

Johnson's reaction minutely. The boy did not seem pleased or even interested in the prospect of the shoe, but when it became an actuality, certainly then he would be moved.

The brace shop was a small concrete warehouse lined and stacked with the equipment of affliction. Wheel chairs and walkers covered most of the floor. The walls were hung with every kind of crutch and brace. Artificial limbs were stacked on the shelves, legs and arms and hands, claws and hooks, straps and human harnesses and unidentifiable instruments for unnamed deformities. In a small clearing in the middle of the room there was a row of yellow plastic-cushioned chairs and a shoe-fitting stool. Johnson slouched down in one of the chairs and set his foot up on the stool and sat with his eyes on it moodily. What was roughly the toe had broken open again and he had patched it with a piece of canvas; another place he had patched with what appeared to be the tongue of the original shoe. The two sides were laced with twine.

There was an excited flush on Sheppard's face; his heart was beating unnaturally fast.

The clerk appeared from the back of the shop with the new shoe under his arm. "Got her right this time!" he said. He straddled the shoe-fitting stool and held the shoe up, smiling as if he had produced it by magic.

It was a black slick shapeless object, shining hideously. It looked like a blunt weapon, highly polished.

Johnson gazed at it darkly.

"With this shoe," the clerk said, "you won't know you're walking. You'll think you're riding!" He bent his bright pink bald head and began gingerly to unlace the twine. He removed the old shoe as if he were skinning an animal still half alive. His expression was strained. The unsheathed mass of foot in the dirty sock made Sheppard feel queasy. He turned his eyes away until the new shoe was on. The clerk laced it up rapidly. "Now stand up and walk around," he said, "and see if that ain't power glide." He winked at Sheppard. "In that shoe," he said, "he won't know he don't have a normal foot."

Sheppard's face was bright with pleasure.

Johnson stood up and walked a few yards away. He walked stiffly with almost no dip in his short side. He stood for a moment, rigid, with his back to them.

"Wonderful!" Sheppard said. "Wonderful." It was as if he had given the boy a new spine.

Johnson turned around. His mouth was set in a thin icy line. He came back to the seat and removed the shoe. He put his foot in the old one and began lacing it up.

"You want to take it home and see if it suits you first?" the clerk murmured.

"No," Johnson said. "I ain't going to wear it at all."

"What's wrong with it?" Sheppard said, his voice rising.

"I don't need no new shoe," Johnson said. "And when I do, I got ways of getting my own." His face was stony but there was a glint of triumph in his eyes.

"Boy," the clerk said, "is your trouble in your foot or in your head?"

"Go soak your skull," Johnson said. "Your brains are on fire."

The clerk rose glumly but with dignity and asked Sheppard what he wanted done with the shoe, which he dangled dispiritedly by the lace.

Sheppard's face was a dark angry red. He was staring straight in front of him at a leather corset with an artificial arm attached.

The clerk asked him again.

"Wrap it up," Sheppard muttered. He turned his eyes to Johnson. "He's not mature enough for it yet," he said. "I had thought he was less of a child."

The boy leered. "You been wrong before," he said.

———

That night they sat in the living room and read as usual. Sheppard kept himself glumly entrenched behind the Sunday New York *Times*. He wanted to recover his good humor, but every time he thought of the rejected shoe, he felt a new charge of irritation. He did not trust himself even to look at Johnson. He realized that the boy had refused the shoe because he was insecure. Johnson had been frightened by his own gratitude. He didn't know what to make of the new self he was becoming conscious of. He understood that something he had been was threatened and he was facing himself and his possibilities for the first time. He was questioning his identity. Grudgingly, Sheppard felt a slight return of sympathy for the boy. In a few minutes, he lowered his paper and looked at him.

Johnson was sitting on the sofa, gazing over the top of the encyclopedia. His expression was trancelike. He might have been listening to something far away. Sheppard watched him intently but the boy continued to listen, and did not turn his head. The poor kid is lost, Sheppard thought. Here he had sat all evening, sullenly reading the paper, and had not said a word to break the tension. "Rufus," he said.

Johnson continued to sit, stock-still, listening.

"Rufus," Sheppard said in a slow hypnotic voice, "you can be anything in the world you want to be. You can be a scientist or an architect or an engineer or whatever you set your mind to, and whatever you set your mind to be, you can be the best of its kind." He imagined his voice penetrating to the boy in the black caverns of his psyche. Johnson leaned forward but his eyes did not turn. On the street a car door closed. There was a silence. Then a sudden blast from the door bell.

Sheppard jumped up and went to the door and opened it. The same policeman who had come before stood there. The patrol car waited at the curb.

"Lemme see that boy," he said.

Sheppard scowled and stood aside. "He's been here all evening," he said. "I can vouch for it."

The policeman walked into the living room. Johnson appeared engrossed in his book. After a second he looked up with an annoyed expression, like a great man interrupted at his work.

"What was that you were looking at in that kitchen window over on Winter Avenue about a half hour ago, bud?" the policeman asked.

"Stop persecuting this boy!" Sheppard said. "I'll vouch for the fact he was here. I was here with him."

"You heard him," Johnson said. "I been here all the time."

"It ain't everybody makes tracks like you," the policeman said and eyed the clubfoot.

"They couldn't be his tracks," Sheppard growled, infuriated. "He's been here all the time. You're wasting your own time and you're wasting ours." His felt the *ours* seal his solidarity with the boy. "I'm sick of this," he said. "You people are too damn lazy to go out and find whoever is doing these things. You come here automatically."

The policeman ignored this and continued looking through Johnson. His eyes were small and alert in his fleshy face. Finally he turned toward the door. "We'll get him sooner or later," he said, "with his head in a window and his tail out."

Sheppard followed him to the door and slammed it behind him. His spirits were soaring. This was exactly what he had needed. He returned with an expectant face.

Johnson had put the book down and was sitting there, looking at him slyly. "Thanks," he said.

Sheppard stopped. The boy's expression was predatory. He was openly leering.

"You ain't such a bad liar yourself," he said.

"Liar?" Sheppard murmured. Could the boy have left and come back? He felt himself sicken. Then a rush of anger sent him forward. "Did you leave?" he said furiously. "I didn't see you leave."

The boy only smiled.

"You went up in the attic to see Norton," Sheppard said.

"Naw," Johnson said, "that kid is crazy. He don't want to do nothing but look through that stinking telescope."

"I don't want to hear about Norton," Sheppard said harshly. "Where were you?"

"I was sitting on that pink can by my ownself," Johnson said. "There wasn't no witnesses."

Sheppard took out his handkerchief and wiped his forehead. He managed to smile.

Johnson rolled his eyes. "You don't believe in me," he said. His voice was cracked the way it had been in the dark room two nights before. "You make out like you got all this confidence in me but you ain't got any. When things get hot, you'll fade like the rest of them." The crack became exaggerated, comic. The mockery in it was blatant. "You don't believe in me. You ain't got no confidence," he wailed. "And you ain't any smarter than that cop. All that about tracks—that was a trap. There wasn't any tracks. That whole place is concreted in the back and my feet were dry."

Sheppard slowly put the handkerchief back in his pocket. He dropped down on the sofa and gazed at the rug beneath his feet. The boy's clubfoot was set within the circle of his vision. The pieced-together shoe appeared to grin at him with Johnson's own face. He caught hold of the edge of the sofa cushion and his knuckles turned white. A chill of hatred shook him. He hated the shoe, hated the foot, hated the boy. His face paled. Hatred choked him. He was aghast at himself.

He caught the boy's shoulder and gripped it fiercely as if to keep himself from falling. "Listen," he said, "you looked in that window to embarrass me. That was all you wanted—to shake my resolve to help you, but my resolve isn't shaken. I'm stronger than you are. I'm stronger than you are and I'm going to save you. The good will triumph."

"Not when it ain't true," the boy said. "Not when it ain't right."

"My resolve isn't shaken," Sheppard repeated. "I'm going to save you."

Johnson's look became sly again. "You ain't going to save me," he said. "You're going to tell me to leave this house. I did those other two jobs too—the first one as well as the one I done when I was supposed to be in the picture show."

"I'm not going to tell you to leave," Sheppard said. His voice was toneless, mechanical. "I'm going to save you."

Johnson thrust his head forward. "Save yourself," he hissed. "Nobody can save me but Jesus."

Sheppard laughed curtly. "You don't deceive me," he said. "I flushed that out of your head in the reformatory. I saved you from that, at least."

The muscles in Johnson's face stiffened. A look of such repulsion hardened on his face that Sheppard drew back. The boy's eyes were like distorting mirrors in which he saw himself made hideous and grotesque. "I'll show you," Johnson whispered. He rose abruptly and started headlong for the door as if he could not get out of Sheppard's sight quick enough, but it was the door to the back hall he went through, not the front door. Sheppard turned on the sofa and looked behind him where the boy had disappeared. He heard the door to his room slam. He was not leaving. The intensity had gone out of Sheppard's eyes. They looked flat and lifeless as if the shock of the boy's revelation were only now reaching the center of his consciousness. "If he would only leave," he murmured. "If he would only leave now of his own accord."

—

The next morning Johnson appeared at the breakfast table in the grandfather's suit he had come in. Sheppard pretended not to notice but one look told him what he already knew, that he was trapped, that there could be nothing now but a battle of nerves and that Johnson would win it. He wished he had never laid eyes on the boy. The failure of his compassion numbed him. He got out of the house as soon as he could and all day he dreaded to go home in the evening. He had a faint hope that the boy might be gone when he returned. The grandfather's suit might have meant he was leaving. The hope grew in the afternoon. When he came home and opened the front door, his heart was pounding.

He stopped in the hall and looked silently into the living room. His expectant expression faded. His face seemed suddenly as old as his white hair. The two boys were sitting close together on the sofa, reading the same book. Norton's cheek rested against the sleeve of Johnson's black suit. Johnson's finger moved under the lines they were reading. The elder brother and the younger. Sheppard looked woodenly at this scene for almost a minute. Then he walked into the room and took off his coat and dropped it on a chair. Neither boy noticed him. He went on to the kitchen.

Leola left the supper on the stove every afternoon before she left and he put it on the table. His head ached and his nerves were taut. He sat down on the kitchen stool and remained there, sunk in his depression. He wondered if he could infuriate Johnson enough to make him leave of his own accord. Last night what had enraged him was the Jesus business. It might enrage Johnson, but it depressed him. Why not simply tell the boy to go? Admit defeat. The thought of facing Johnson again sickened him. The boy looked at him as if he were the guilty one, as if he were a moral leper. He knew without conceit that he was a good man, that he had nothing to reproach himself with. His feelings about Johnson now were involuntary. He would like to feel compassion for him. He would like to be able to help him. He longed for the time when there would be no one but himself and Norton in the house, when the child's simple selfishness would be all he had to contend with, and his own loneliness.

He got up and took three serving dishes off the shelf and took them to the stove. Absently he began pouring the butterbeans and the hash into the dishes. When the food was on the table, he called them in.

They brought the book with them. Norton pushed his place setting around to the same side of the table as Johnson's and moved his chair next to Johnson's chair. They sat down and put the book between them. It was a black book with red edges.

"What's that you're reading?" Sheppard asked, sitting down.

"The Holy Bible," Johnson said.

God give me strength, Sheppard said under his breath.

"We lifted it from a ten cent store," Johnson said.

"We?" Sheppard muttered. He turned and glared at Norton. The child's face was bright and there was an excited sheen to his eyes. The change that had come over the boy struck him for the first time. He looked alert. He had on a blue plaid shirt and his eyes were a brighter blue than he had ever seen them before. There was a strange new life in him, the sign of new and more rugged vices. "So now you steal?" he said, glowering. "You haven't learned to be generous but you have learned to steal."

"No he ain't," Johnson said. "I was the one lifted it. He only watched. He can't sully himself. It don't make any difference about me. I'm going to hell anyway."

Sheppard held his tongue.

"Unless," Johnson said, "I repent."

"Repent, Rufus," Norton said in a pleading voice. "Repent, hear? You don't want to go to hell."

"Stop talking this nonsense," Sheppard said, looking sharply at the child.

"If I do repent, I'll be a preacher," Johnson said. "If you're going to do it, it's no sense in doing it halfway."

"What are you going to be, Norton," Sheppard asked in a brittle voice, "a preacher too?"

There was a glitter of wild pleasure in the child's eyes. "A space man!" he shouted.

"Wonderful," Sheppard said bitterly.

"Those space ships ain't going to do you any good unless you believe in Jesus," Johnson said. He wet his finger and began to leaf through the pages of the Bible. "I'll read you where it says so," he said.

Sheppard leaned forward and said in a low furious voice, "Put that Bible up, Rufus, and eat your dinner."

Johnson continued searching for the passage.

"Put that Bible up!" Sheppard shouted.

The boy stopped and looked up. His expression was startled but pleased.

"That book is something for you to hide behind," Sheppard said. "It's for cowards, people who are afraid to stand on their own feet and figure things out for themselves."

Johnson's eyes snapped. He backed his chair a little way from the table. "Satan has you in his power," he said. "Not only me. You too."

Sheppard reached across the table to grab the book but Johnson snatched it and put it in his lap.

Sheppard laughed. "You don't believe in that book and you know you don't believe in it!"

"I believe it!" Johnson said. "You don't know what I believe and what I don't."

Sheppard shook his head. "You don't believe it. You're too intelligent."

"I ain't too intelligent," the boy muttered. "You don't know nothing about me. Even if I didn't believe it, it would still be true."

"You don't believe it!" Sheppard said. His face was a taunt.

"I believe it!" Johnson said breathlessly. "I'll show you I believe it!" He opened the book in his lap and tore out a page of it and thrust it into his mouth. He fixed his eyes on Sheppard. His jaws worked furiously and the paper crackled as he chewed it.

"Stop this," Sheppard said in a dry, burnt-out voice. "Stop it."

The boy raised the Bible and tore out a page with his teeth and began grinding it in his mouth, his eyes burning.

Sheppard reached across the table and knocked the book out of his hand. "Leave the table," he said coldly.

Johnson swallowed what was in his mouth. His eyes widened as if a vision of splendor were opening up before him. "I've eaten it!" he breathed. "I've eaten it like Ezekiel and it was honey to my mouth!"

"Leave this table," Sheppard said. His hands were clenched beside his plate.

"I've eaten it!" the boy cried. Wonder transformed his face. "I've eaten it like Ezekiel and I don't want none of your food after it nor no more ever."

"Go then," Sheppard said softly. "Go. Go."

The boy rose and picked up the Bible and started toward the hall with it. At the door he paused, a small black figure on the threshold of some dark apocalypse. "The devil has you in his power," he said in a jubilant voice and disappeared.

———

After supper Sheppard sat in the living room alone. Johnson had left the house but he could not believe that the boy had simply gone. The first feeling of release had passed. He felt dull and cold as at the onset of an illness and dread had settled in him like a fog. Just to leave would be too anticlimactic an end for Johnson's taste; he would return and try to prove something. He might come back a week later and set fire to the place. Nothing seemed too outrageous now.

He picked up the paper and tried to read. In a moment he threw it down and got up and went into the hall and listened. He might be hiding in the attic. He went to the attic door and opened it.

The lantern was lit, casting a dim light on the stairs. He didn't hear anything. "Norton," he called, "are you up there?" There was no answer. He mounted the narrow stairs to see.

Amid the strange vine-like shadows cast by the lantern, Norton sat with his eye to the telescope. "Norton," Sheppard said, "do you know where Rufus went?"

The child's back was to him. He was sitting hunched, intent, his large ears directly above his shoulders. Suddenly he waved his hand and crouched closer to the telescope as if he could not get near enough to what he saw.

"Norton!" Sheppard said in a loud voice.

The child didn't move.

"Norton!" Sheppard shouted.

Norton started. He turned around. There was an unnatural brightness about his eyes. After a moment he seemed to see that it was Sheppard. "I've found her!" he said breathlessly.

"Found who?" Sheppard said.

"Mamma!"

Sheppard steadied himself in the door way. The jungle of shadows around the child thickened.

"Come and look!" he cried. He wiped his sweaty face on the tail of his plaid shirt and then put his eye back to the telescope. His back became fixed in a rigid intensity. All at once he waved again.

"Norton," Sheppard said, "you don't see anything in the telescope but star clusters. Now you've had enough of that for one night. You'd better go to bed. Do you know where Rufus is?"

"She's there!" he cried, not turning around from the telescope. "She waved at me!"

"I want you in bed in fifteen minutes," Sheppard said. After a moment he said, "Do you hear me, Norton?"

The child began to wave frantically.

"I mean what I say," Sheppard said. "I'm going to call in fifteen minutes and see if you're in bed."

He went down the steps again and returned to the parlor. He

went to the front door and cast a cursory glance out. The sky was crowded with the stars he had been fool enough to think Johnson could reach. Somewhere in the small wood behind the house, a bull frog sounded a low hollow note. He went back to his chair and sat a few minutes. He decided to go to bed. He put his hands on the arms of the chair and leaned forward and heard, like the first shrill note of a disaster warning, the siren of a police car, moving slowly into the neighborhood and nearer until it subsided with a moan outside the house.

He felt a cold weight on his shoulders as if an icy cloak had been thrown about him. He went to the door and opened it.

Two policemen were coming up the walk with a dark snarling Johnson between them, handcuffed to each. A reporter jogged alongside and another policeman waited in the patrol car.

"Here's your boy," the dourest of the policemen said. "Didn't I tell you we'd get him?"

Johnson jerked his arm down savagely. "I was waitin for you!" he said. "You wouldn't have got me if I hadn't of wanted to get caught. It was my idea." He was addressing the policemen but leering at Sheppard.

Sheppard looked at him coldly.

"Why did you want to get caught?" the reporter asked, running around to get beside Johnson. "Why did you deliberately want to get caught?"

The question and the sight of Sheppard seemed to throw the boy into a fury. "To show up that big tin Jesus!" he hissed and kicked his leg out at Sheppard. "He thinks he's God. I'd rather be in the reformatory than in his house, I'd rather be in the pen! The Devil has him in his power. He don't know his left hand from his right, he don't have as much sense as his crazy kid!" He paused and then swept on to his fantastic conclusion. "He made suggestions to me!"

Sheppard's face blanched. He caught hold of the door facing.

"Suggestions?" the reporter said eagerly, "what kind of suggestion?"

"Immor'l suggestions!" Johnson said. "What kind of suggestions do you think? But I ain't having none of it, I'm a Christian, I'm..."

Sheppard's face was tight with pain. "He knows that's not true," he said in a shaken voice. "He knows he's lying. I did everything I knew how for him. I did more for him than I did for my own child. I hoped to save him and I failed, but it was an honorable failure. I have nothing to reproach myself with. I made no suggestions to him."

"Do you remember the suggestions?" the reporter asked. "Can you tell us exactly what he said?"

"He's a dirty atheist," Johnson said. "He said there wasn't no hell."

"Well, they seen each other now," one of the policemen said with a knowing sigh. "Let's us go."

"Wait," Sheppard said. He came down one step and fixed his eyes on Johnson's eyes in a last desperate effort to save himself. "Tell the truth, Rufus," he said. "You don't want to perpetrate this lie. You're not evil, you're mortally confused. You don't have to make up for that foot, you don't have to..."

Johnson hurled himself forward. "Listen at him!" he screamed. "I lie and steal because I'm good at it! My foot don't have a thing to do with it! The lame shall enter first! The halt'll be gathered together. When I get ready to be saved, Jesus'll save me, not that lying stinking atheist, not that..."

"That'll be enough out of you," the policeman said and yanked him back. "We just wanted you to see we got him," he said to Sheppard, and the two of them turned around and dragged Johnson away, half turned and screaming back at Sheppard.

"The lame'll carry off the prey!" he screeched, but his voice was muffled inside the car. The reporter scrambled into the front seat with the driver and slammed the door and the siren wailed into the darkness.

Sheppard remained there, bent slightly like a man who has been shot but continues to stand. After a minute he turned and went back in the house and sat down in the chair he had left. He closed his eyes on a picture of Johnson in a circle of reporters at the police station, elaborating his lies. "I have nothing to reproach myself with," he murmured. His every action had been selfless, his one aim had been to save Johnson for some decent kind of service, he had not spared himself, he had sacrificed his reputation, he had done more for Johnson than he had done for his own child. Foulness hung about him like an odor in the air, so close that it seemed to come from his own breath. "I have nothing to reproach myself with," he repeated. His voice sounded dry and harsh. "I did more for him than I did for my own child." He was swept with a sudden panic. He heard the boy's jubilant voice. Satan has you in his power.

"I have nothing to reproach myself with," he began again. "I did more for him than I did for my own child." He heard his voice as if it were the voice of his accuser. He repeated the sentence silently.

Slowly his face drained of color. It became almost gray beneath the white halo of his hair. The sentence echoed in his mind, each syllable like a dull blow. His mouth twisted and he closed his eyes against the revelation. Norton's face rose before him, empty, forlorn, his left eye listing almost imperceptibly toward the outer rim as if it could not bear a full view of grief. His heart constricted with a repulsion for himself so clear and intense that he gasped for breath. He had stuffed his own emptiness with good works like a glutton. He had ignored his own child to feed his vision of himself. He saw the clear-eyed Devil, the sounder of hearts, leering at him from the eyes of Johnson. His image of himself shrivelled until everything was black before him. He sat there paralyzed, aghast.

He saw Norton at the telescope, all back and ears, saw his arm shoot up and wave frantically. A rush of agonizing love for the child rushed over him like a transfusion of life. The little boy's face appeared to him transformed; the image of his salvation; all light. He groaned with joy. He would make everything up to him. He would never let him suffer again. He would be mother and father. He jumped up and ran to his room, to kiss him, to tell him that he loved him, that he would never fail him again.

The light was on in Norton's room but the bed was empty. He turned and dashed up the attic stairs and at the top reeled back like a man on the edge of a pit. The tripod had fallen and the telescope lay on the floor. A few feet over it, the child hung in the jungle of shadows, just below the beam from which he had launched his flight into space.

—

FLANNERY O'CONNOR (1925–1964) was born in Savannah, Georgia, and died in Milledgeville. Her stories have commanded wide respect and admiration for what her fellow Southern writer Walker Percy called the "original and stunning voice that offers them." A religious visionary, she was also a practical, down-to-earth person whose stories stir their readers, confront them long and hard.

III

CLASS AND RACE

The novelist Walker Percy once spoke this way: "I turn from the news today—so much about class and race—and I attend Hardy of yore, and our own [the South's] Flannery O'Connor, with us for such a short time: such a welcome relief, such wisdom!" So with Toni Morrison's writing for sure.

FROM *JUDE THE OBSCURE*

Thomas Hardy

For many days he haunted the cloisters and quadrangles of the colleges at odd minutes in passing them, surprised by impish echoes of his own footsteps, smart as the blows of a mallet. The Christminster "sentiment," as it had been called, ate further and further into him, till he probably knew more about those buildings materially, artistically, and historically, than any one of their inmates.

It was not till now, when he found himself actually on the spot of his enthusiasm, that Jude perceived how far away from the object of that enthusiasm he really was. Only a wall divided him from those happy young contemporaries of his with whom he shared a common mental life; men who had nothing to do from morning till night but to read, mark, learn, and inwardly digest. Only a wall—but what a wall!

Every day, every hour, as he went in search of labour, he saw them going and coming also, rubbed shoulders with them, heard their voices, marked their movements. The conversation of some of the more thoughtful among them seemed oftentimes, owing to his long and persistent preparation for this place, to be peculiarly akin to his own thoughts. Yet he was as far from them as if he had been at the antipodes. Of course he was. He was a young workman in a white blouse, and with stone-dust in the creases of his clothes and in passing him they did not even see him, or hear him, rather saw through him as through a pane of glass at their familiars beyond. Whatever they were to him, he to them was not on the spot at all; and yet he had fancied he would be close to their lives by coming there.

But the future lay ahead after all; and if he could only be so fortunate as to get into good employment he would put up with the inevitable. So he thanked God for his health and strength, and took courage. For the present he was outside the gates of everything, colleges included: perhaps some day he would be inside. Those palaces of light and leading; he might some day look down on the world through their panes....

During the next week or two he accordingly placed himself in such positions about the city as would afford him glimpses of several of the most distinguished among the Provosts, Wardens, and other Heads of Houses; and from those he ultimately selected five whose physiognomies seemed to say to him that they were appreciative and far-seeing men. To these five he addressed letters, briefly stating his difficulties, and asking their opinion on his stranded situation.

When the letters were posted Jude mentally began to criticize them; he wished they had not been sent. "It is just one of those intrusive, vulgar, pushing, applications which are so common in these days," he thought. "Why couldn't I know better than address utter strangers in such a way? I may be an impostor, an idle scamp, a man with a bad character, for all that they know to the contrary.... Perhaps that's what I am!"

Nevertheless, he found himself clinging to the hope of some reply as to his one last chance of redemption. He waited day after day, saying that it was perfectly absurd to expect, yet expecting. While he waited he was suddenly stirred by news about Phillotson. Phillotson was giving up the school near Christminster, for a larger one further south, in Mid-Wessex. What this meant; how it would affect his cousin; whether, as seemed possible, it was a practical move of the schoolmaster's towards a larger income, in view of a provision for two instead of one, he would not allow himself to say. And the tender relations between Phillotson and the young girl of whom Jude was passionately enamoured effectually made it repugnant to Jude's tastes to apply to Phillotson for advice on his own scheme.

Meanwhile the academic dignitaries to whom Jude had written vouchsafed no answer, and the young man was thus thrown back entirely on himself, as formerly, with the added gloom of a weakened hope. By indirect inquiries he soon perceived clearly, what he had long uneasily suspected, that to qualify himself for certain open scholarships and exhibitions was the only brilliant course. But to do this a good deal of coaching would be necessary, and much natural ability. It was next to impossible that a man reading on his own system, however widely and thoroughly, even over the prolonged period of ten years, should be able to compete with those who had passed their lives under trained teachers and had worked to ordained lines.

The other course, that of buying himself in, so to speak, seemed the only one really open to men like him, the difficulty being simply of a material kind. With the help of his information he began to reckon the extent of this material obstacle, and ascertained, to his dismay, that, at the rate at which, with the best of fortune, he would be able to save money, fifteen years must elapse before he could be in a position to forward testimonials to the Head of a College and advance to a matriculation examination. The undertaking was hopeless.

He saw what a curious and cunning glamour the neighbourhood of the place had exercised over him. To get there and live there, to move among the churches and halls and become imbued with the *genius loci,* had seemed to his dreaming youth, as the spot shaped its charms to him from its halo on the horizon, the obvious and ideal thing to do. "Let me only get there," he had said with the fatuousness of Crusoe over his big boat, "and the rest is but a matter of time and energy." It would have been far better for him in every way if he had never come within sight and sound of the delusive precincts, had gone to some busy commercial town with the sole object of making money by his wits, and thence surveyed his plan in true perspective. Well, all that was clear to him amounted to this, that the whole scheme had burst up, like an iridescent soap-bubble, under the touch of a reasoned inquiry. He looked back at himself along the vista of his past years, and his thought was akin to Heine's:

> "Above the youth's inspired and flashing eyes
> I see the motley mocking fool's-cap rise!"

Fortunately he had not been allowed to bring his disappointment into his dear Sue's life by involving her in this collapse. And the painful details of his awakening to a sense of his limitations should now be spared her as far as possible. After all, she had only known a little part of the miserable struggle in which he had been engaged thus unequipped, poor, and unforeseeing.

He always remembered the appearance of the afternoon on which he awoke from his dream. Not quite knowing what to do with himself, he went up to an octagonal chamber in the lantern of a singularly built theatre that was set amidst this quaint and singular city. It had windows all round, from which an outlook over the whole town and its edifices could be gained. Jude's eyes swept all the views in succession, meditatively, mournfully, yet sturdily. Those buildings and their associations and privileges were not for him. From the looming roof of the great library, into which he hardly ever had time to enter, his gaze travelled on to the varied spires, halls, gables, streets, chapels, gardens, quadrangles, which composed the *ensemble* of this unrivalled panorama. He saw that his destiny lay not with these, but among the manual toilers in the shabby purlieu which he himself occupied, unrecognized as part of the city at all by its visitors and panegyrists, yet without whose denizens the hard readers could not read nor the high thinkers live.

He looked over the town into the country beyond, to the trees which screened her whose presence had at first been the support of his heart, and whose loss was now a maddening torture. But for this blow he might have borne with his fate. With Sue as companion he could have renounced his ambitions with a smile. Without her it was inevitable that the reaction from the long strain to which he had subjected himself should affect him disastrously. Phillotson had no doubt passed through a similar intellectual disappointment to that which now enveloped him. But the schoolmaster had been since blest with the consolation of sweet Sue, while for him there was no consoler.

Descending to the streets, he went listlessly along till he arrived at an inn, and entered it. Here he drank several glasses of beer in rapid succession, and when he came out it was night. By the light of the flickering lamps he rambled home to supper, and had not long been sitting at table when his landlady brought up a letter that had just arrived for him. She laid it down as if impressed with a sense of its possible importance, and on looking at it Jude perceived that it bore the embossed stamp of one of the Colleges whose heads he had addressed. "*One*—at last!" cried Jude.

The communication was brief, and not exactly what he had expected; though it really was from the Master in person. It ran thus:

> "BIBLIOLL COLLEGE.
>
> "Sir,—I have read your letter with interest; and, judging from your description of yourself as a working-man, I venture to think that you will have a much better chance of success in life by remaining in your own sphere and sticking to your trade than by adopting any other course. That, therefore, is what I advise you to do. Yours faithfully,
>
> "T. TETUPHENAY.
>
> "To Mr. J. Fawley, Stone-mason."

This terribly sensible advice exasperated Jude. He had known all that before. He knew it was true. Yet it seemed a hard slap after ten years of labour, and its effect upon him just now was to make him rise recklessly from the table, and, instead of reading as usual, to go downstairs and into the street. He stood at a bar and tossed off two or three glasses, then unconsciously sauntered along till he came to a spot called The Fourways in the middle of the city, gazing abstractedly at the groups of people like one in a trance, till, coming to himself, he began talking to the policeman fixed there.

That officer yawned, stretched out his elbows, elevated himself an inch and a half on the balls of his toes, smiled, and looking humorously at Jude, said, "You've had a wet, young man."

"No; I've only begun," he replied cynically.

Whatever his wetness, his brains were dry enough. He only heard in part the policeman's further remarks, having fallen into thought on what struggling people like himself had stood at that Crossway, whom nobody ever thought of now. It had more history than the oldest college in the city. It was literally teeming, stratified, with the shades of human groups, who had met there for tragedy, comedy, farce; real enactments of the intensest kind. At Fourways men had stood and talked of Napoleon, the loss of America, the execution of King Charles, the burning of the Martyrs, the Crusades, the Norman Conquest, possibly of the arrival of Caesar. Here the two sexes had met for loving, hating, coupling, parting; had waited, had suffered, for each other; had triumphed over each other; cursed each other in jealousy, blessed each other in forgiveness.

He began to see that the town life was a book of humanity infinitely more palpitating, varied, and compendious than the gown life. These struggling men and women before him were the reality of Christminster, though they knew little of Christ or Minster. That was one of the humours of things. The floating population of students and teachers, who did know both in a way, were not Christminster in a local sense at all.

He looked at his watch, and, in pursuit of this idea, he went on till he came to a public hall, where a promenade concert was in progress. Jude entered, and found the room full of shop youths and girls, soldiers, apprentices, boys of eleven smoking cigarettes, and light women of the more respectable and amateur class. He had tapped the real Christminster life. A band was playing, and the crowd walked about and jostled each other, and every now and then a man got upon a platform and sang a comic song.

The spirit of Sue seemed to hover round him and prevent his

flirting and drinking with the frolicsome girls who made advances —wistful to gain a little joy. At ten o'clock he came away, choosing a circuitous route homeward to pass the gates of the College whose Head had just sent him the note.

The gates were shut, and, by an impulse, he took from his pocket the lump of chalk which as a workman he usually carried there, and wrote along the wall:

"I have understanding as well as you; I am not inferior to you: yea, who knoweth not such things as these?"—Job xii. 3.

—

THOMAS HARDY (1840–1928) published *Jude the Obscure* in 1895, and thereby confronted its readers with the aspirations and disappointments of those who are all too often disregarded by people of influence. In this work, Hardy gives us a look inward at someone too readily overlooked by certain individuals whose education and means have not made them immune to moral blindness.

The Artificial Nigger

Flannery O'Connor

Mr. Head awakened to discover that the room was full of moon-light. He sat up and stared at the floor boards—the color of silver—and then at the ticking on his pillow, which might have been brocade, and after a second, he saw half of the moon five feet away in his shaving mirror, paused as if it were waiting for his permission to enter. It rolled forward and cast a dignifying light on everything. The straight chair against the wall looked stiff and attentive as if it were awaiting an order and Mr. Head's trousers, hanging to the back of it, had an almost noble air, like the garment some great man had just flung to his servant; but the face on the moon was a grave one. It gazed across the room and out the window where it floated over the horse stall and appeared to contemplate itself with the look of a young man who sees his old age before him.

Mr. Head could have said to it that age was a choice blessing and that only with years does a man enter into that calm understanding of life that makes him a suitable guide for the young. This, at least, had been his own experience.

He sat up and grasped the iron posts at the foot of his bed and raised himself until he could see the face on the alarm clock which sat on an overturned bucket beside the chair. The hour was two in the morning. The alarm on the clock did not work but he was not dependent on any mechanical means to awaken him. Sixty years had not dulled his responses; his physical reactions, like his moral ones, were guided by his will and strong character, and these could be seen plainly in his features. He had a long tube-like face with a long rounded open jaw and a long depressed nose. His eyes were alert but quiet, and in the miraculous moonlight they had a look of composure and of ancient wisdom as if they belonged to one of the great guides of men. He might have been Vergil summoned in the middle of the night to go to Dante, or better, Raphael, awakened by a blast of God's light to fly to the side of Tobias. The only dark spot in the room was Nelson's pallet, underneath the shadow of the window.

Nelson was hunched over on his side, his knees under his chin and his heels under his bottom. His new suit and hat were in the boxes that they had been sent in and these were on the floor at the foot of the pallet where he could get his hands on them as soon as he woke up. The slop jar, out of the shadow and made snow-white in the moonlight, appeared to stand guard over him like a small personal angel. Mr. Head lay back down, feeling entirely confident that he could carry out the moral mission of the coming day. He meant to be up before Nelson and to have the breakfast cooking by the time he awakened. The boy was always irked when Mr. Head was the first up. They would have to leave the house at four to get to the railroad junction by five-thirty. The train was to stop for them at five forty-five and they had to be there on time for this train was stopping merely to accommodate them.

This would be the boy's first trip to the city though he claimed it would be his second because he had been born there. Mr. Head had tried to point out to him that when he was born he didn't have the intelligence to determine his whereabouts but this had made no impression on the child at all and he continued to insist that this was to be his second trip. It would be Mr. Head's third trip. Nelson had said, "I will've already been there twict and I ain't but ten."

Mr. Head had contradicted him.

"If you ain't been there in fifteen years, how you know you'll be able to find your way about?" Nelson had asked. "How you know it hasn't changed some?"

"Have you ever," Mr. Head had asked, "seen me lost?"

Nelson certainly had not but he was a child who was never satisfied until he had given an impudent answer and he replied, "It's nowhere around here to get lost at."

"The day is going to come," Mr. Head prophesied, "when you'll find you ain't as smart as you think you are." He had been thinking about this trip for several months but it was for the most part in moral terms that he conceived it. It was to be a lesson that the boy would never forget. He was to find out from it that he had no cause for pride merely because he had been born in a city. He was to find out that the city is not a great place. Mr. Head meant him to see everything there is to see in a city so that he would be content to stay at home for the rest of his life. He fell asleep thinking how the boy would at last find out that he was not as smart as he thought he was.

He was awakened at three-thirty by the smell of fatback frying and he leaped off his cot. The pallet was empty and the clothes boxes had been thrown open. He put on his trousers and ran into the other room. The boy had a corn pone on cooking and had fried the meat. He was sitting in the half-dark at the table, drinking cold coffee out of a can. He had on his new suit and his new gray hat pulled low over his eyes. It was too big for him but they had ordered it a size large because they expected his head to grow. He didn't say anything but his entire figure suggested satisfaction at having arisen before Mr. Head.

Mr. Head went to the stove and brought the meat to the table in the skillet. "It's no hurry," he said. "You'll get there soon enough and it's no guarantee you'll like it when you do neither," and he sat down across from the boy whose hat teetered back slowly to reveal a fiercely expressionless face, very much the same shape as the old man's. They were grandfather and grandson but they looked enough alike to be brothers and brothers not too far apart in age, for

Mr. Head had a youthful expression by daylight, while the boy's look was ancient, as if he knew everything already and would be pleased to forget it.

Mr. Head had once had a wife and daughter and when the wife died, the daughter ran away and returned after an interval with Nelson. Then one morning, without getting out of bed, she died and left Mr. Head with sole care of the year-old child. He had made the mistake of telling Nelson that he had been born in Atlanta. If he hadn't told him that, Nelson couldn't have insisted that this was going to be his second trip.

"You may not like it a bit," Mr. Head continued. "It'll be full of niggers."

The boy made a face as if he could handle a nigger.

"All right," Mr. Head said. "You ain't ever seen a nigger."

"You wasn't up very early," Nelson said.

"You ain't ever seen a nigger," Mr. Head repeated. "There hasn't been a nigger in this county since we run that one out twelve years ago and that was before you were born." He looked at the boy as if he were daring him to say he had ever seen a Negro.

"How you know I never saw a nigger when I lived there before?" Nelson asked. "I probably saw a lot of niggers."

"If you seen one you didn't know what he was," Mr. Head said, completely exasperated. "A six-month-old child don't know a nigger from anybody else."

"I reckon I'll know a nigger if I see one," the boy said and got up and straightened his slick sharply creased gray hat and went outside to the privy.

They reached the junction some time before the train was due to arrive and stood about two feet from the first set of tracks. Mr. Head carried a paper sack with some biscuits and a can of sardines in it for their lunch. A coarse-looking orange-colored sun coming up behind the east range of mountains was making the sky a dull red behind them, but in front of them it was still gray and they faced a gray transparent moon, hardly stronger than a thumbprint and completely without light. A small tin switch box and a black fuel tank were all there was to mark the place as a junction; the tracks were double and did not converge again until they were hidden behind the bends at either end of the clearing. Trains passing appeared to emerge from a tunnel of trees and, hit for a second by the cold sky, vanish terrified into the woods again. Mr. Head had had to make special arrangements with the ticket agent to have this train stop and he was secretly afraid it would not, in which case, he knew Nelson would say, "I never thought no train was going to stop for you." Under the useless morning moon the tracks looked white and fragile. Both the old man and the child stared ahead as if they were awaiting an apparition.

Then suddenly, before Mr. Head could make up his mind to turn back, there was a deep warning bleat and the train appeared, gliding very slowly, almost silently around the bend of trees about two hundred yards down the track, with one yellow front light shining. Mr. Head was still not certain it would stop and he felt it would make an even bigger idiot of him if it went by slowly. Both he and Nelson, however, were prepared to ignore the train if it passed them.

The engine charged by, filling their noses with the smell of hot metal and then the second coach came to a stop exactly where they were standing. A conductor with the face of an ancient bloated bulldog was on the step as if he expected them, though he did not look as if it mattered one way or the other to him if they got on or not. "To the right," he said.

Their entry took only a fraction of a second and the train was already speeding on as they entered the quiet car. Most of the travelers were still sleeping, some with their heads hanging off the chair arms, some stretched across two seats, and some sprawled out with their feet in the aisle. Mr. Head saw two unoccupied seats and pushed Nelson toward them. "Get in there by the winder," he said in his normal voice which was very loud at this hour of the morning. "Nobody cares if you sit there because it's nobody in it. Sit right there."

"I heard you," the boy muttered. "It's no use in you yelling," and he sat down and turned his head to the glass. There he saw a pale ghost-like face scowling at him beneath the brim of a pale ghost-like hat. His grandfather, looking quickly too, saw a different ghost, pale but grinning, under a black hat.

Mr. Head sat down and settled himself and took out his ticket and started reading aloud everything that was printed on it. People began to stir. Several woke up and stared at him. "Take off your hat," he said to Nelson and took off his own and put it on his knee. He had a small amount of white hair that had turned tobacco-colored over the years and this lay flat across the back of his head. The front of his head was bald and creased. Nelson took off his hat and put it on his knee and they waited for the conductor to come ask for their tickets.

The man across the aisle from them was spread out over two seats, his feet propped on the window and his head jutting into the aisle. He had on a light blue suit and a yellow shirt unbuttoned at the neck. His eyes had just opened and Mr. Head was ready to introduce himself when the conductor came up from behind and growled, "Tickets."

When the conductor had gone, Mr. Head gave Nelson the return half of his ticket and said, "Now put that in your pocket and don't lose it or you'll have to stay in the city."

"Maybe I will," Nelson said as if this were a reasonable suggestion.

Mr. Head ignored him. "First time this boy has ever been on a train," he explained to the man across the aisle, who was sitting up now on the edge of his seat with both feet on the floor.

Nelson jerked his hat on again and turned angrily to the window.

"He's never seen anything before," Mr. Head continued. "Ignorant as the day he was born, but I mean for him to get his fill once and for all."

The boy leaned forward, across his grandfather and toward the stranger. "I was born in the city," he said. "I was born there. This is my second trip." He said it in a high positive voice but the man across the aisle didn't look as if he understood. There were heavy purple circles under his eyes.

Mr. Head reached across the aisle and tapped him on the arm. "The thing to do with a boy," he said sagely, "is to show him all it is to show. Don't hold nothing back."

"Yeah," the man said. He gazed down at his swollen feet and lifted the left one about ten inches from the floor. After a minute he put it down and lifted the other. All through the car people began to get up and move about and yawn and stretch. Separate voices could be heard here and there and then a general hum. Suddenly Mr. Head's serene expression changed. His mouth almost closed and a light, fierce and cautious both, came into his eyes. He was looking down the length of the car. Without turning, he caught Nelson by the arm and pulled him forward. "Look," he said.

A huge coffee-colored man was coming slowly forward. He had on a light suit and a yellow satin tie with a ruby pin in it. One of his hands rested on his stomach which rode majestically under his buttoned coat, and in the other he held the head of a black walking stick that he picked up and set down with a deliberate outward motion each time he took a step. He was proceeding very slowly, his large brown eyes gazing over the heads of the passengers. He had a small white mustache and white crinkly hair. Behind him there were two young women, both coffee-colored, one in a yellow dress and one in a green. Their progress was kept at the rate of his and they chatted in low throaty voices as they followed him.

Mr. Head's grip was tightening insistently on Nelson's arm. As the procession passed them, the light from a sapphire ring on the brown hand that picked up the cane reflected in Mr. Head's eye, but he did not look up nor did the tremendous man look at him. The group proceeded up the rest of the aisle and out of the car. Mr. Head's grip on Nelson's arm loosened. "What was that?" he asked.

"A man," the boy said and gave him an indignant look as if he were tired of having his intelligence insulted.

"What kind of a man?" Mr. Head persisted, his voice expressionless.

"A fat man," Nelson said. He was beginning to feel that he had better be cautious.

"You don't know what kind?" Mr. Head said in a final tone.

"An old man," the boy said and had a sudden foreboding that he was not going to enjoy the day.

"That was a nigger," Mr. Head said and sat back.

Nelson jumped up on the seat and stood looking backward to the end of the car but the Negro had gone.

"I'd of thought you'd know a nigger since you seen so many when you was in the city on your first visit," Mr. Head continued. "That's his first nigger," he said to the man across the aisle.

The boy slid down into the seat. "You said they were black," he said in an angry voice. "You never said they were tan. How do you expect me to know anything when you don't tell me right?"

"You're just ignorant is all," Mr. Head said and he got up and moved over in the vacant seat by the man across the aisle.

Nelson turned backward again and looked where the Negro had disappeared. He felt that the Negro had deliberately walked down the aisle in order to make a fool of him and he hated him with a fierce raw fresh hate; and also, he understood now why his grandfather disliked them. He looked toward the window and the face there seemed to suggest that he might be inadequate to the day's exactions. He wondered if he would even recognize the city when they came to it.

After he had told several stories, Mr. Head realized that the man he was talking to was asleep and he got up and suggested to Nelson that they walk over the train and see the parts of it. He particularly wanted the boy to see the toilet so they went first to the men's room and examined the plumbing. Mr. Head demonstrated the ice-water cooler as if he had invented it and showed Nelson the bowl with the single spigot where the travelers brushed their teeth. They went through several cars and came to the diner.

This was the most elegant car in the train. It was painted a rich egg-yellow and had a wine-colored carpet on the floor. There were wide windows over the tables and great spaces of the rolling view were caught in miniature in the sides of the coffee pots and in the glasses. Three very black Negroes in white suits and aprons were running up and down the aisle, swinging trays and bowing and bending over the travelers eating breakfast. One of them rushed up to Mr. Head and Nelson and said, holding up two fingers, "Space for two!" but Mr. Head replied in a loud voice, "We eaten before we left!"

The waiter wore large brown spectacles that increased the size of his eye whites. "Stan' aside then please," he said with an airy wave of the arm as if he were brushing aside flies.

Neither Nelson nor Mr. Head moved a fraction of an inch. "Look," Mr. Head said.

The near corner of the diner, containing two tables, was set off from the rest by a saffron-colored curtain. One table was set but empty but at the other, facing them, his back to the drape, sat the tremendous Negro. He was speaking in a soft voice to the two women while he buttered a muffin. He had a heavy sad face and his neck bulged over his white collar on either side. "They rope them off," Mr. Head explained. Then he said, "Let's go see the kitchen," and they walked the length of the diner but the black waiter was coming fast behind them.

"Passengers are not allowed in the kitchen!" he said in a haughty voice. "Passengers are NOT allowed in the kitchen!"

Mr. Head stopped where he was and turned. "And there's good reason for that," he shouted into the Negro's chest, "because the cockroaches would run the passengers out!"

All the travelers laughed and Mr. Head and Nelson walked out, grinning. Mr. Head was known at home for his quick wit and Nelson felt a sudden keen pride in him. He realized the old man would be his only support in the strange place they were approaching. He would be entirely alone in the world if he were ever lost from his grandfather. A terrible excitement shook him and he wanted to take hold of Mr. Head's coat and hold on like a child.

As they went back to their seats they could see through the passing windows that the countryside was becoming speckled with small houses and shacks and that a highway ran alongside the train. Cars sped by on it, very small and fast. Nelson felt that there was less breath in the air than there had been thirty minutes ago. The man across the aisle had left and there was no one near for Mr. Head to hold a conversation with so he looked out the window, through his own reflection, and read aloud the names of the buildings they were passing. "The Dixie Chemical Corp!" he announced. "Southern Maid Flour! Dixie Doors! Southern Belle Cotton Products! Patty's Peanut Butter! Southern Mammy Cane Syrup!"

"Hush up!" Nelson hissed.

All over the car people were beginning to get up and take their luggage off the overhead racks. Women were putting on their coats and hats. The conductor stuck his head in the car and snarled, "Firstoppppmry," and Nelson lunged out of his sitting position, trembling. Mr. Head pushed him down by the shoulder.

"Keep your seat," he said in dignified tones. "The first stop is on the edge of town. The second stop is at the main railroad station." He had come by this knowledge on his first trip when he had got off at the first stop and had had to pay a man fifteen cents to take him into the heart of town. Nelson sat back down, very pale. For the first time in his life, he understood that his grandfather was indispensable to him.

The train stopped and let off a few passengers and glided on as if it had never ceased moving. Outside, behind rows of brown rickety houses, a line of blue buildings stood up, and beyond them a pale rose-gray sky faded away to nothing. The train moved into the railroad yard. Looking down, Nelson saw lines and lines of silver tracks multiplying and criss-crossing. Then before he could start counting them, the face in the window started out at him, gray but distinct, and he looked the other way. The train was in the station. Both he and Mr. Head jumped up and ran to the door. Neither noticed that they had left the paper sack with the lunch in it on the seat.

They walked stiffly through the small station and came out of a heavy door into the squall of traffic. Crowds were hurrying to work. Nelson didn't know where to look. Mr. Head leaned against the side of the building and glared in front of him.

Finally Nelson said, "Well, how do you see what all it is to see?"

Mr. Head didn't answer. Then as if the sight of people passing had given him the clue, he said, "You walk," and started off down the street. Nelson followed, steadying his hat. So many sights and sounds were flooding in on him that for the first block he hardly knew what he was seeing. At the second corner, Mr. Head turned and looked behind him at the station they had left, a putty-colored terminal with a concrete dome on top. He thought that if he could keep the dome always in sight, he would be able to get back in the afternoon to catch the train again.

As they walked along, Nelson began to distinguish details and take note of the store windows, jammed with every kind of equipment—hardware, drygoods, chicken feed, liquor. They passed one that Mr. Head called his particular attention to where you walked in and sat on a chair with your feet upon two rests and let a Negro polish your shoes. They walked slowly and stopped and stood at the entrances so he could see what went on in each place but they did not go into any of them. Mr. Head was determined not to go into any city store because on his first trip here, he had got lost in a large one and had found his way out only after many people had insulted him.

They came in the middle of the next block to a store that had a weighing machine in front of it and they both in turn stepped up on it and put in a penny and received a ticket. Mr. Head's ticket said, "You weigh 120 pounds. You are upright and brave and all your friends admire you." He put the ticket in his pocket, surprised that the machine should have got his character correct but his weight wrong, for he had weighed on a grain scale not long before and knew he weighed 110. Nelson's ticket said, "You weigh 98 pounds. You have a great destiny ahead of you but beware of dark women." Nelson did not know any women and he weighed only 68 pounds but Mr. Head pointed out that the machine had probably printed the number upside down, meaning the 9 for a 6.

They walked on and at the end of five blocks the dome of the terminal sank out of sight and Mr. Head turned to the left. Nelson could have stood in front of every store window for an hour if there had not been another more interesting one next to it. Suddenly he said, "I was born here!" Mr. Head turned and looked at him with horror. There was a sweaty brightness about his face. "This is where I come from!" he said.

Mr. Head was appalled. He saw the moment had come for drastic action. "Lemme show you one thing you ain't seen yet," he said and took him to the corner where there was a sewer entrance. "Squat down," he said, "and stick you head in there," and he held the back of the boy's coat while he got down and put his head in the sewer. He drew it back quickly, hearing a gurgling in the depths under the sidewalk. Then Mr. Head explained the sewer system, how the entire city was underlined with it, how it contained all the drainage and was full of rats and how a man could slide into it and be sucked along down endless pitchblack tunnels. At any minute any man in the city might be sucked into the sewer and never heard from again. He described it so well that Nelson was for some seconds shaken. He connected the sewer passages with the entrance to hell and understood for the first time how the world was put together in its lower parts. He drew away from the curb.

Then he said, "Yes, but you can stay away from the holes," and his face took on that stubborn look that was so exasperating to his grandfather. "This is where I come from!" he said.

Mr. Head was dismayed but he only muttered, "You'll get your fill," and they walked on. At the end of two more blocks he turned to the left, feeling that he was circling the dome; and he was correct for in a half-hour they passed in front of the railroad station again. At first Nelson did not notice that he was seeing the same stores twice but when they passed the one where you put your feet on the rests while the Negro polished your shoes, he perceived that they were walking in a circle.

"We done been here!" he shouted. "I don't believe you know where you're at!"

"The direction just slipped my mind for a minute," Mr. Head said and they turned down a different street. He still did not intend to let the dome get too far away and after two blocks in their new direction, he turned to the left. This street contained two- and three-story wooden dwellings. Anyone passing on the sidewalk could see into the rooms and Mr. Head, glancing through one window, saw a woman lying on an iron bed, looking out, with a sheet pulled over her. Her knowing expression shook him. A fierce-looking boy on a bicycle came driving down out of nowhere and he had to jump to the side to keep from being hit. "It's nothing to them if they knock you down," he said. "You better keep closer to me."

They walked on for some time on streets like this before he remembered to turn again. The houses they were passing now were all unpainted and the wood in them looked rotten; the street between was narrower. Nelson saw a colored man. Then another. Then another. "Niggers live in these houses," he observed.

"Well come on and we'll go somewheres else," Mr. Head said. "We didn't come to look at niggers," and they turned down another street but they continued to see Negroes everywhere. Nelson's skin began to prickle and they stepped along at a faster pace in order to leave the neighborhood as soon as possible. There were colored men in their undershirts standing in the doors and colored women rocking on the sagging porches. Colored children played in the gutters and stopped what they were doing to look at them. Before long they began to pass rows of stores with colored customers in them but they didn't pause at the entrances of these. Black eyes in black faces were watching them from every direction. "Yes," Mr. Head said, "this is where you were born—right here with all these niggers."

Nelson scowled. "I think you done got us lost," he said.

Mr. Head swung around sharply and looked for the dome. It was nowhere in sight. "I ain't got us lost either," he said. "You're just tired of walking."

"I ain't tired, I'm hungry," Nelson said. "Give me a biscuit."

They discovered then that they had lost the lunch.

"You were the one holding the sack," Nelson said. "I would have kepaholt of it."

"If you want to direct this trip, I'll go on by myself and leave you right here," Mr. Head said and was pleased to see the boy turn white. However, he realized they were lost and drifting farther every minute from the station. He was hungry himself and beginning to be thirsty and since they had been in the colored neighborhood, they had both begun to sweat. Nelson had on his shoes and he was unaccustomed to them. The concrete sidewalks were very hard. They both wanted to find a place to sit down but this was impossible and they kept on walking, the boy muttering under his breath, "First you lost the sack and then you lost the way," and Mr. Head growling from time to time, "Anybody wants to be from this nigger heaven can be from it!"

By now the sun was well forward in the sky. The odor of dinners cooking drifted out to them. The Negroes were all at their doors to see them pass. "Whyn't you ast one of these niggers the way?" Nelson said. "You got us lost."

"This is where you were born," Mr. Head said. "You can ast one yourself if you want to."

Nelson was afraid of the colored men and he didn't want to be laughed at by the colored children. Up ahead he saw a large colored woman leaning in a doorway that opened onto the sidewalk. Her hair stood straight out from her head for about four inches all around and she was resting on bare brown feet that turned pink at the sides. She had on a pink dress that showed her exact shape. As they came abreast of her, she lazily lifted one hand to her head and her fingers disappeared into her hair.

Nelson stopped. He felt his breath drawn up by the woman's dark eyes. "How do you get back to town?" he said in a voice that did not sound like his own.

After a minute she said, "You in town now," in a rich low tone that made Nelson feel as if a cool spray had been turned on him.

"How do you get back to the train?" he said in the same reedlike voice.

"You can catch you a car," she said.

He understood she was making fun of him but he was too paralyzed even to scowl. He stood drinking in every detail of her. His eyes traveled up from her great knees to her forehead and then made a triangular path from the glistening sweat on her neck down and across her tremendous bosom and over her bare arm back to where her fingers lay hidden in her hair. He suddenly wanted her to reach down and pick him up and draw him against her and then he wanted to feel her breath on his face. He wanted to look down and down into her eyes while she held him tighter and tighter. He had never had such a feeling before. He felt as if he were reeling down through a pitchblack tunnel.

"You can go a block down yonder and catch you a car take you to the railroad station, Sugarpie," she said.

Nelson would have collapsed at her feet if Mr. Head had not pulled him roughly away. "You act like you don't have any sense!" the old man growled.

They hurried down the street and Nelson did not look back at the woman. He pushed his hat sharply forward over his face which was already burning with shame. The sneering ghost he had seen in the train window and all the foreboding feelings he had on the way returned to him and he remembered that his ticket from the scale had said to beware of dark women and that his grandfather's had said he was upright and brave. He took hold of the old man's hand, a sign of dependence that he seldom showed.

They headed down the street toward the car tracks where a long yellow rattling trolley was coming. Mr. Head had never boarded a streetcar and he let that one pass. Nelson was silent. From time to time his mouth trembled slightly but his grandfather, occupied with his own problems, paid him no attention. They stood on the corner and neither looked at the Negroes who were passing, going about their business just as if they had been white, except that most of them stopped and eyed Mr. Head and Nelson. It occurred to Mr. Head that since the streetcar ran on tracks, they could simply follow the tracks. He gave Nelson a slight push and explained that they would follow the tracks on into the railroad station, walking, and they set off.

Presently to their great relief they began to see white people again and Nelson sat down on the sidewalk against the wall of a building. "I got to rest myself some," he said. "You lost the sack and the direction. You can just wait on me to rest myself."

"There's the tracks in front of us," Mr. Head said. "All we got to do is keep them in sight and you could have remembered the sack as good as me. This is where you were born. This is your old home town. This is your second trip. You ought to know how to do," and he squatted down and continued in this vein but the boy, easing his burning feet out of his shoes, did not answer.

"And standing there grinning like a chim-pan-zee while a nigger woman gives you direction. Great Gawd!" Mr. Head said.

"I never said I was nothing but born here," the boy said in a shaky voice. "I never said I would or wouldn't like it. I never said I wanted to come. I only said I was born here and I never had nothing to do with that. I want to go home. I never wanted to come in the first place. It was all your big idea. How you know you ain't following the tracks in the wrong direction?"

This last had occurred to Mr. Head too. "All these people are white," he said.

"We ain't passed here before," Nelson said. This was a neighborhood of brick buildings that might have been lived in or might not. A few empty automobiles were parked along the curb and there was an occasional passerby. The heat of the pavement came up through Nelson's thin suit. His eyelids began to droop, and after a few minutes his head tilted forward. His shoulders twitched once or twice and then he fell over on his side and lay sprawled in an exhausted fit of sleep.

Mr. Head watched him silently. He was very tired himself but they could not both sleep at the same time and he could not have slept anyway because he did not know where he was. In a few minutes Nelson would wake up, refreshed by his sleep and very cocky, and would begin complaining that he had lost the sack and the way. You'd have a mighty sorry time if I wasn't here, Mr. Head thought; and then another idea occurred to him. He looked at the sprawled figure for several minutes; presently he stood up. He justified what he was going to do on the grounds that it is sometimes necessary to teach a child a lesson he won't forget, particularly when the child is always reasserting his position with some new impudence. He walked without a sound to the corner about twenty feet away and sat down on a covered garbage can in the alley where he could look out and watch Nelson wake up alone.

The boy was dozing fitfully, half conscious of vague noises and black forms moving up from some dark part of him into the light.

His face worked in his sleep and he had pulled his knees up under his chin. The sun shed a dull dry light on the narrow street; everything looked like exactly what it was. After a while Mr. Head, hunched like an old monkey on the garbage can lid, decided that if Nelson didn't wake up soon, he would make a loud noise by bamming his foot against the can. He looked at his watch and discovered that it was two o'clock. Their train left at six and the possibility of missing it was too awful for him to think of. He kicked his foot backwards on the can and a hollow boom reverberated in the alley.

Nelson shot up onto his feet with a shout. He looked where his grandfather should have been and stared. He seemed to whirl several times and then, picking up his feet and throwing his head back, he dashed down the street like a wild maddened pony. Mr. Head jumped off the can and galloped after but the child was almost out of sight. He saw a streak of gray disappearing diagonally a block ahead. He ran as fast as he could, looking both ways down every intersection, but without sight of him again. Then as he passed the third intersection, completely winded, he saw about half a block down the street a scene that stopped him altogether. He crouched behind a trash box to watch and get his bearings.

Nelson was sitting with both legs spread out and by his side lay an elderly woman, screaming. Groceries were scattered about the sidewalk. A crowd of women had already gathered to see justice done and Mr. Head distinctly heard the old woman on the pavement shout, "You've broken my ankle and your daddy'll pay for it! Every nickel! Police! Police!" Several of the women were plucking at Nelson's shoulder but the boy seemed too dazed to get up.

Something forced Mr. Head from behind the trash box and forward, but only at a creeping pace. He had never in his life been accosted by a policeman. The women were milling around Nelson as if they might suddenly all dive on him at once and tear him to pieces, and the old woman continued to scream that her ankle was broken and to call for an officer. Mr. Head came on so slowly that he could have been taking a backward step after each forward one, but when he was about ten feet away, Nelson saw him and sprang. The child caught him around the hips and clung panting against him.

The women all turned on Mr. Head. The injured one sat up and shouted, "You sir! You'll pay every penny of my doctor's bill that your boy has caused. He's a juve-nile deliquent! Where is an officer? Somebody take this man's name and address!"

Mr. Head was trying to detach Nelson's fingers from the flesh in the back of his legs. The old man's head had lowered itself into his collar like a turtle's; his eyes were glazed with fear and caution.

"Your boy has broken my ankle!" the old woman shouted. "Police!"

Mr. Head sensed the approach of the policeman from behind. He stared straight ahead at the women who were massed in their fury like a solid wall to block his escape. "This is not my boy," he said. "I never seen him before."

He felt Nelson's fingers fall out of his flesh.

The women dropped back, staring at him with horror, as if they were so repulsed by a man who would deny his own image and likeness that they could not bear to lay hands on him. Mr. Head walked on, through a space they silently cleared, and left Nelson behind. Ahead of him he saw nothing but a hollow tunnel that had once been the street.

The boy remained standing where he was, his neck craned forward and his hands hanging by his sides. His hat was jammed on his head so that there were no longer any creases in it. The injured woman got up and shook her fist at him and the others gave him pitying looks, but he didn't notice any of them. There was no policeman in sight.

In a minute he began to move mechanically, making no effort to catch up with his grandfather but merely following at about twenty paces. They walked on for five blocks in this way. Mr. Head's shoulders were sagging and his neck hung forward at such an angle that it was not visible from behind. He was afraid to turn his head. Finally he cut a short hopeful glance over his shoulder. Twenty feet behind him, he saw two small eyes piercing into his back like pitchfork prongs.

The boy was not of a forgiving nature but this was the first time he had ever had anything to forgive. Mr. Head had never disgraced himself before. After two more blocks, he turned and called over his shoulder in a high desperately gay voice, "Let's us go get us a Co' Cola somewheres!"

Nelson, with a dignity he had never shown before, turned and stood with his back to his grandfather.

Mr. Head began to feel the depth of his denial. His face as they walked on became all hollows and bare ridges. He saw nothing they were passing but he perceived that they had lost the car tracks. There was no dome to be seen anywhere and the afternoon was advancing. He knew that if dark overtook them in the city, they would be beaten and robbed. The speed of God's justice was only what he expected for himself, but he could not stand to think that his sins would be visited upon Nelson and that even now, he was leading the boy to his doom.

They continued to walk on block after block through an endless section of small brick houses until Mr. Head almost fell over a water spigot sticking up about six inches off the edge of a grass plot. He had not had a drink of water since early morning but he felt he did not deserve it now. Then he thought that Nelson would be thirsty and they would both drink and be brought together. He squatted down and put his mouth to the nozzle and turned a cold stream of water into his throat. Then he called out in the high desperate voice, "Come on and getcher some water!"

This time the child stared through him for nearly sixty seconds. Mr. Head got up and walked on as if he had drunk poison. Nelson, though he had not had water since some he had drunk out of a paper cup on the train, passed by the spigot, disdaining to drink where his grandfather had. When Mr. Head realized this, he lost all hope. His face in the waning afternoon light looked ravaged and abandoned. He could feel the boy's steady hate, traveling at an even pace behind him and he knew that (if by some miracle they escaped being murdered in the city) it would continue just that way for the rest of his life. He knew that now he was wandering into a black strange place where nothing was like it had ever been before, a long old age without respect and an end that would be welcome because it would be the end.

As for Nelson, his mind had frozen around his grandfather's treachery as if he were trying to preserve it intact to present at the final judgment. He walked without looking to one side or the other, but every now and then his mouth would twitch and this was when he felt, from some remote place inside himself, a black mysterious form reach up as if it would melt his frozen vision in one hot grasp.

The sun dropped down behind a row of houses and hardly noticing, they passed into an elegant suburban section where mansions were set back from the road by lawns with birdbaths on them. Here everything was entirely deserted. For blocks they didn't pass even a dog. The big white houses were like partially submerged icebergs in the distance. There were no sidewalks, only drives, and these wound around and around in endless ridiculous circles. Nelson made no move to come nearer to Mr. Head. The old man felt that if he saw a sewer entrance he would drop down into it and let himself be carried away; and he could imagine the boy standing by, watching with only a slight interest, while he disappeared.

A loud bark jarred him to attention and he looked up to see a fat man approaching with two bulldogs. He waved both arms like someone shipwrecked on a desert island. "I'm lost!" he called. "I'm lost and can't find my way and me and this boy have got to catch this train and I can't find the station. Oh Gawd I'm lost! Oh hep me Gawd I'm lost!"

The man, who was bald-headed and had on golf knickers, asked him what train he was trying to catch and Mr. Head began to get out his tickets, trembling so violently he could hardly hold them. Nelson had come up to within fifteen feet and stood watching.

"Well," the fat man said, giving him back the tickets, "you won't have time to get back to town to make this but you can catch it at the suburb stop. That's three blocks from here," and he began explaining how to get there.

Mr. Head stared as if he were slowly returning from the dead and when the man had finished and gone off with the dogs jumping at his heels, he turned to Nelson and said breathlessly, "We're going to get home!"

The child was standing about ten feet away, his face bloodless under the gray hat. His eyes were triumphantly cold. There was no light in them, no feeling, no interest. He was merely there, a small figure, waiting. Home was nothing to him.

Mr. Head turned slowly. He felt he knew now what time would be like without seasons and what heat would be like without light and what man would be like without salvation. He didn't care if he never made the train and if it had not been for what suddenly caught his attention, like a cry out of the gathering dusk, he might have forgotten there was a station to go to.

He had not walked five hundred yards down the road when he saw, within reach of him, the plaster figure of a Negro sitting bent over on a low yellow brick fence that curved around a wide lawn. The Negro was about Nelson's size and he was pitched forward at an unsteady angle because the putty that held him to the wall had cracked. One of his eyes was entirely white and he held a piece of brown watermelon.

Mr. Head stood looking at him silently until Nelson stopped at a little distance. Then as the two of them stood there, Mr. Head breathed, "An artificial nigger!"

It was not possible to tell if the artificial Negro were meant to be young or old; he looked too miserable to be either. He was meant to look happy because his mouth was stretched up at the corners but the chipped eye and the angle he was cocked at gave him a wild look of misery instead.

"An artificial nigger!" Nelson repeated in Mr. Head's exact tone.

The two of them stood there with their necks forward at almost the same angle and their shoulders curved in almost exactly the same way and their hands trembling identically in their pockets. Mr. Head looked like an ancient child and Nelson like a miniature old man. They stood gazing at the artificial Negro as if they were faced with some great mystery, some monument to another's victory that brought them together in their common defeat. They could both feel it dissolving their differences like an action of mercy. Mr. Head had never known before what mercy felt like because he had been too good to deserve any, but he felt he knew now. He looked at Nelson and understood that he must say something to the child to show that he was still wise and in the look the boy returned he saw a hungry need for that assurance. Nelson's eyes seemed to implore him to explain once and for all the mystery of existence.

Mr. Head opened his lips to make a lofty statement and heard himself say, "They ain't got enough real ones here. They got to have an artificial one."

After a second, the boy nodded with a strange shivering about his mouth, and said, "Let's go home before we get ourselves lost again."

Their train glided into the suburb stop just as they reached the station and they boarded it together, and ten minutes before it was due to arrive at the junction, they went to the door and stood ready to jump off if it did not stop; but it did, just as the moon, restored to its full splendor, sprang from a cloud and flooded the clearing with light. As they stepped off, the sage grass was shivering gently in shades of silver and the clinkers under their feet glittered with a fresh black light. The treetops, fencing the junction like the protecting walls of a garden, were darker than the sky which was hung with gigantic white clouds illuminated like lanterns.

Mr. Head stood very still and felt the action of mercy touch him again but this time he knew that there were no words in the world that could name it. He understood that it grew out of agony, which is not denied to any man and which is given in strange ways to children. He understood it was all a man could carry into death to give his Maker and he suddenly burned with shame that he had so little of it to take with him. He stood appalled, judging himself with the thoroughness of God, while the action of mercy covered his pride like a flame and consumed it. He had never thought himself a great sinner before but he saw now that his true depravity had been hidden from him lest it cause him despair. He realized that he was forgiven for sins from the beginning of time, when he had conceived in his own heart the sin of Adam, until the present, when he had denied poor Nelson. He saw that no sin was too monstrous for him to claim as his own, and since God loved in proportion as He forgave, he felt ready at that instant to enter Paradise.

Nelson, composing his expression under the shadow of his hat brim, watched him with a mixture of fatigue and suspicion, but as the train glided past them and disappeared like a frightened serpent into the woods, even his face lightened and he muttered, "I'm glad I've went once, but I'll never go back again!"

FROM *THE BLUEST EYE*

Toni Morrison

School has started, and Frieda and I get new brown stockings and cod-liver oil. Grown-ups talk in tired, edgy voices about Zick's Coal Company and take us along in the evening to the railroad tracks where we fill burlap sacks with the tiny pieces of coal lying about. Later we walk home, glancing back to see the great carloads of slag being dumped, red hot and smoking, into the ravine that skirts the steel mill. The dying fire lights the sky with a dull orange glow. Frieda and I lag behind, staring at the patch of color surrounded by black. It is impossible not to feel a shiver when our feet leave the gravel path and sink into the dead grass in the field.

Our house is old, cold, and green. At night a kerosene lamp lights one large room. The others are braced in darkness, peopled by roaches and mice. Adults do not talk to us—they give us directions. They issue orders without providing information. When we trip and fall down they glance at us; if we cut or bruise ourselves, they ask us are we crazy. When we catch colds, they shake their heads in disgust at our lack of consideration. How, they ask us, do you expect anybody to get anything done if you all are sick? We cannot answer them. Our illness is treated with contempt, foul Black Draught, and castor oil that blunts our minds.

When, on a day after a trip to collect coal, I cough once, loudly, through bronchial tubes already packed tight with phlegm, my mother frowns. "Great Jesus. Get on in that bed. How many times do I have to tell you to wear something on your head? You must be the biggest fool in this town. Frieda? Get some rags and stuff that window."

Frieda restuffs the window. I trudge off to bed, full of guilt and self-pity. I lie down in my underwear, the metal in my black garters hurts my legs, but I do not take them off, for it is too cold to lie stockingless. It takes a long time for my body to heat its place in the bed. Once I have generated a silhouette of warmth, I dare not move, for there is a cold place one-half inch in any direction. No one speaks to me or asks how I feel. In an hour or two my mother comes. Her hands are large and rough, and when she rubs the Vicks salve on my chest, I am rigid with pain. She takes two fingers' full of it at a time, and massages my chest until I am faint. Just when I think I will tip over into a scream, she scoops out a little of the salve on her forefinger and puts it in my mouth, telling me to swallow. A hot flannel is wrapped about my neck and chest. I am covered up with heavy quilts and ordered to sweat, which I do—promptly.

Later I throw up, and my mother says, "What did you puke on the bed clothes for? Don't you have sense enough to hold your head out the bed? Now, look what you did. You think I got time for nothing but washing up your puke?"

The puke swaddles down the pillow onto the sheet—green-gray, with flecks of orange. It moves like the insides of an uncooked egg. Stubbornly clinging to its own mass, refusing to break up and be removed. How, I wonder, can it be so neat and nasty at the same time?

My mother's voice drones on. She is not talking to me. She is talking to the puke, but she is calling it my name: Claudia. She wipes it up as best she can and puts a scratchy towel over the large wet place. I lie down again. The rags have fallen from the window crack, and the air is cold. I dare not call her back and am reluctant to leave my warmth. My mother's anger humiliates me; her words chafe my cheeks, and I am crying. I do not know that she is not angry at me, but at my sickness. I believe she despises my weakness for letting the sickness "take holt." By and by I will not get sick; I will refuse to. But for now I am crying. I know I am making more snot, but I can't stop.

My sister comes in. Her eyes are full of sorrow. She sings to me: "When the deep purple falls over sleepy garden walls, someone thinks of me...." I doze, thinking of plums, walls, and "someone."

But was it really like that? As painful as I remember? Only mildly. Or rather, it was a productive and fructifying pain. Love, thick and dark as Alaga syrup, eased up into that cracked window. I could smell it—taste it—sweet, musty, with an edge of wintergreen in its base—everywhere in that house. It stuck, along with my tongue, to the frosted windowpanes. It coated my chest, along with the salve, and when the flannel came undone in my sleep, the clear, sharp curves of air outlined its presence on my throat. And in the night, when my coughing was dry and tough, feet padded into the room, hands repinned the flannel, readjusted the quilt, and rested a moment on my forehead. So when I think of autumn, I think of somebody with hands who does not want me to die....

HEREISTHEFAMILYMOTHERFATHER
DICKANDJANETHEYLIVEINTHEGREE
NANDWHITEHOUSETHEYAREVERYH

The Breedloves did not live in a storefront because they were having temporary difficulty adjusting to the cutbacks at the plant. They lived there because they were poor and black, and they stayed there because they believed they were ugly. Although their poverty was traditional and stultifying, it was not unique. But their ugliness was unique. No one could have convinced them that they were not relentlessly and aggressively ugly. Except for the father, Cholly, whose ugliness (the result of despair, dissipation, and violence directed toward petty things and weak people) was behavior, the rest of the family—Mrs. Breedlove, Sammy Breedlove, and Pecola Breedlove—wore their ugliness, put it on, so to speak, although it did not belong to them. The eyes, the small eyes set closely together under narrow foreheads. The low, irregular hairlines, which seemed even more irregular in contrast to the straight, heavy eyebrows which nearly met. Keen but crooked noses, with insolent nostrils. They had high cheekbones, and their ears turned forward. Shapely lips which called attention not to themselves but to the rest of the face. You looked at them and wondered why they were so ugly; you looked closely and could not find the source. Then you realized that it came from conviction, their conviction. It was as though some mysterious all-knowing master had given each one a cloak of ugliness to wear, and they had each accepted it without question. The master had said, "You are ugly people." They had looked about themselves and saw nothing to contradict the statement; saw, in fact, support for it leaning at them from every billboard, every movie, every glance. "Yes," they had said. "You are right." And they took the ugliness in their hands, threw it as a mantle over them, and went about the world with it. Dealing with it each according to his way. Mrs. Breedlove handled hers as an actor does a prop: for the articulation of character, for support of a role she frequently imagined was hers—martyrdom. Sammy used his as a weapon to cause others pain. He adjusted his behavior to it, chose his companions on the basis of it: people who could be fascinated, even intimidated by it. And Pecola. She hid behind hers. Concealed, veiled, eclipsed—peeping out from behind the shroud very seldom, and then only to yearn for the return of her mask.

This family, on a Saturday morning in October, began, one by one, to stir out of their dreams of affluence and vengeance into the anonymous misery of their storefront. . . .

Geraldine, Louis, Junior, and the cat lived next to the playground of Washington Irving School. Junior considered the playground his own, and the schoolchildren coveted his freedom to sleep late, go home for lunch, and dominate the playground after school. He hated to see the swings, slides, monkey bars, and seesaws empty and tried to get kids to stick around as long as possible. White kids; his mother did not like him to play with niggers. She had explained to him the difference between colored people and niggers. They were easily identifiable. Colored people were neat and quiet; niggers were dirty and loud. He belonged to the former group: he wore white shirts and blue trousers; his hair was cut as close to his scalp as possible to avoid any suggestion of wool, the part was etched into his hair by the barber. In winter his mother put Jergens Lotion on his face to keep the skin from becoming ashen. Even though he was light-skinned, it was possible to ash. The line between colored and nigger was not always clear; subtle and telltale signs threatened to erode it, and the watch had to be constant.

Junior used to long to play with the black boys. More than anything in the world he wanted to play King of the Mountain and have them push him down the mound of dirt and roll over him. He wanted to feel their hardness pressing on him, smell their wild blackness, and say "Fuck you" with that lovely casualness. He wanted to sit with them on curbstones and compare the sharpness of jackknives, the distance and arcs of spitting. In the toilet he wanted to share with them the laurels of being able to pee far and long. Bay Boy and P. L. had at one time been his idols. Gradually he came to agree with his mother that neither Bay Boy nor P. L. was good enough for him. He played only with Ralph Nisensky, who was two years younger, wore glasses, and didn't want to *do* anything. More and more Junior enjoyed bullying girls. It was easy making them scream and run. How he laughed when they fell down and their bloomers showed. When they got up, their faces red and crinkled, it made him feel good. The nigger girls he did not pick on very much. They usually traveled in packs, and once when he threw a stone at some of them, they chased, caught, and beat him witless. He lied to his mother, saying Bay Boy did it. His mother was very upset. His father just kept on reading the Lorain *Journal*.

When the mood struck him, he would call a child passing by to come play on the swings or the seesaw. If the child wouldn't, or did and left too soon, Junior threw gravel at him. He became a very good shot.

Alternately bored and frightened at home, the playground was his joy. On a day when he had been especially idle, he saw a very black girl taking a shortcut through the playground. She kept her head down as she walked. He had seen her many times before, standing alone, always alone, at recess. Nobody ever played with her. Probably, he thought, because she was ugly.

Now Junior called to her. "Hey! What are you doing walking through my yard?"

The girl stopped.

"Nobody can come through this yard 'less I say so."

"This ain't your yard. It's the school's."

"But I'm in charge of it."

The girl started to walk away.

"Wait." Junior walked toward her. "You can play in it if you want to. What's your name?"

"Pecola. I don't want to play."

"Come on. I'm not going to bother you."

"I got to go home."

"Say, you want to see something? I got something to show you."

"No. What is it?"

"Come on in my house. See, I live right there. Come on. I'll show you."

"Show me what?"

"Some kittens. We got some kittens. You can have one if you want."

"Real kittens?"

"Yeah. Come on."

He pulled gently at her dress. Pecola began to move toward his house. When he knew she had agreed, Junior ran ahead excitedly, stopping only to yell back at her to come on. He held the door open for her, smiling his encouragement. Pecola climbed the porch stairs and hesitated there, afraid to follow him. The house looked dark. Junior said, "There's nobody here. My ma's gone out, and my father's at work. Don't you want to see the kittens?"

Junior turned on the lights. Pecola stepped inside the door.

How beautiful, she thought. What a beautiful house. There was a big red-and-gold Bible on the dining-room table. Little lace doilies were everywhere—on arms and backs of chairs, in the center of a large dining table, on little tables. Potted plants were on all the windowsills. A color picture of Jesus Christ hung on a wall with the prettiest paper flowers fastened on the frame. She wanted to see everything slowly, slowly. But Junior kept saying, "Hey, you. Come on. Come on." He pulled her into another room, even more beautiful than the first. More doilies, a big lamp with green-and-gold base and white shade. There was even a rug on the floor, with enormous dark-red flowers. She was deep in admiration of the flowers when Junior said, "Here!" Pecola turned. "Here is your kitten!" he screeched. And he threw a big black cat right in her face. She sucked in her breath in fear and surprise and felt fur in her mouth. The cat clawed her face and chest in an effort to right itself, then leaped nimbly to the floor.

—

TONI MORRISON was born in Lorain, Ohio, in 1931. She is the author of many essays and novels, and in 1993 was the recipient of the Nobel Prize in literature. She teaches at Princeton University.

IV

PERSONAL EXPERIENCE AND

COMMENTARY

Following the affecting, strenuous lead of James Agee, we who worked on this book step forward.

FROM *LET US NOW PRAISE FAMOUS MEN*
EDUCATION

James Agee

In every child who is born, under no matter what circumstances, and of no matter what parents, the potentiality of the human race is born again: and in him, too, once more, and of each of us, our terrific responsibility towards human life; towards the utmost idea of goodness, of the horror of error, and of God.

Every breath his senses shall draw, every act and every shadow and thing in all creation, is a mortal poison, or is a drug, or is a signal or symptom, or is a teacher, or is a liberator, or is liberty itself, depending entirely upon his understanding: and understanding,* and action proceeding from understanding and guided by it, is the one weapon against the world's bombardment, the one medicine, the one instrument by which liberty, health, and joy may be shaped or shaped towards, in the individual, and in the race.

---

*Active "understanding" is only one form, and there are suggestions of "perfection" which could be called "understanding" only by definitions so broad as to include diametric reversals. The peace of God surpasses all understanding; Mrs. Ricketts and her youngest child do, too; "understanding" can be its own, and hope's, most dangerous enemy.

This is no place to dare all questions that must be asked, far less to advance our tentatives in this murderous air, nor even to qualify so much as a little the little which thus far has been suggested, nor even either to question or to try to support my qualifications to speak of it at all: we are too near one of the deepest intersections of pity, terror, doubt, and guilt; and I feel that I can say only, that "education," whose function is at the crisis of this appalling responsibility, does not seem to me to be all, or even anything, that it might be, but seems indeed the very property of the world's misunderstanding, the sharpest of its spearheads in every brain: and that since it could not be otherwise without destroying the world's machine, the world is unlikely to permit it to be otherwise.

In fact, and ignorant though I am, nothing, not even law, nor property, nor sexual ethics, nor fear, nor doubtlessness, nor even authority itself, all of which it is the business of education to cleanse the brain of, can so nearly annihilate me with fury and with horror; as the spectacle of innocence, of defenselessness, of all human hope, brought steadily in each year by the millions into the machineries of the teachings of the world, in which the man who would conceive of and who would dare attempt even the beginnings of what "teaching" must be could not exist two months clear of a penitentiary: presuming even that his own perceptions, and the courage of his perceptions, were not a poison as deadly at least as those poisons he would presume to drive out: or the very least of whose achievements, supposing he cared truly not only to hear himself speak but to be understood, would be a broken heart.*

For these and other reasons it would seem to me mistaken to decry the Alabama public schools, or even to say that they are "worse" or "less good" than schools elsewhere: or to be particularly wholehearted in the regret that these tenants are subjected only to a few years of this education: for they would be at a disadvantage if they had more of it, and at a disadvantage if they had none, and they are at a disadvantage in the little they have; and it would be hard

---

*It may be that the only fit teachers never teach but are artists, and artists of the kind most blankly masked and least didactic.

and perhaps impossible to say in which way their disadvantage would be greatest.

———

School was not in session while I was there. My research on this subject was thin, indirect, and deductive. By one way of thinking it will seem for these reasons worthless: by another, which I happen to trust more, it may be sufficient.

I saw, for instance, no teachers: yet I am quite sure it is safe to assume that they are local at very least to the state and quite probably to the county; that most of them are women to whom teaching is either an incident of their youth or a poor solution for their spinsterhood; that if they were of much intelligence or courage they could not have survived their training in the State Normal or would never have undertaken it in the first place; that they are saturated in every belief and ignorance which is basic in their country and community; that any modification of this must be very mild indeed if they are to survive as teachers; that even if, in spite of all these screenings, there are superior persons among them, they are still again limited to texts and to a system of requirements officially imposed on them; and are caught between the pressures of class, of the state, of the churches, and of the parents, and are confronted by minds already so deeply formed that to liberate them would involve uncommon and as yet perhaps undiscovered philosophic and surgical skill. I have only sketched a few among dozens of the facts and forces which limit them; and even so I feel at liberty to suggest that even the best of these, the kindly, or the intuitive, the so-called natural teachers, are exceedingly more likely than not to be impossibly handicapped both from without and within themselves, and are at best the servants of unconscious murder; and of the others, the general run, that if murder of the mind and spirit were statutory crimes, the law, in its customary eagerness to punish the wrong person,* might spend all its ingenuity in the invention of deaths by de-

———

*This is not to suggest there is a "right person" or that punishment can ever be better than an enhancement of error.

layed torture and never sufficiently expiate the enormities which through them, not by their own fault, have been committed.

Or again on the curriculum: it was unnecessary to make even such search into this as I made to know that there is no setting before the students of "economic" or "social" or "political" "facts" and of their situation within these "facts," no attempt made to clarify or even slightly to relieve the situation between the white and negro races, far less to explain the sources, no attempt to clarify psychological situations in the individual, in his family, or in his world, no attempt to get beneath and to revise those "ethical" and "social" pressures and beliefs in which even a young child is trapped, no attempt, beyond the most nominal, to interest a child in using or in discovering his senses and judgment, no attempt to counteract the paralytic quality inherent in "authority," no attempt beyond the most nominal and stifling to awaken, to protect, or to "guide" the sense of investigation, the sense of joy, the sense of beauty, no attempt to clarify spoken and written words whose power of deceit even at the simplest is vertiginous, no attempt, or very little, and ill taught, to teach even the earliest techniques of improvement in occupation ("scientific farming," diet and cooking, skilled trades), nor to "teach" a child in terms of his environment, no attempt, beyond the most suffocated, to awaken a student either to "religion" or to "irreligion," no attempt to develop in him either "skepticism" or "faith," nor "wonder," nor mental "honesty" nor mental "courage," nor any understanding of or delicateness in "the emotions" and in any of the uses and pleasures of the body save the athletic; no attempt either to relieve him of fear and of poison in sex or to release in him a free beginning of pleasure in it, nor to open within him the illimitable potentials of grief, of danger, and of goodness in sex and in sexual love, nor to give him the beginnings at very least of a knowledge, and of an attitude, whereby he may hope to guard and increase himself and those whom he touches, no indication of the damages which society, money, law, fear and quick belief have set upon these matters and upon all things in human life, nor of their causes, nor of the alternate ignorances and possibilities of ruin or of joy, no fear of doubtlessness, no fear of the illusions of knowledge, no fear of compromise:—and here again I have scarcely begun, and am confronted immediately with a serious problem: that is: by my naming of the lack of such teaching, I can appear too easily to recommend it, to imply, perhaps, that if these things were "taught," all would be "solved": and this I do not believe: but insist rather that in the teaching of these things, infinitely worse damage could and probably would result than in the teaching of those subjects which in fact do compose the curriculum: and that those who would most insist upon one or another of them can be among the deadliest enemies of education: for if the guiding hand is ill qualified, an instrument is murderous in proportion to its sharpness. Nothing I have mentioned but is at the mercy of misuse; and one may be sure a thousand to one it will be misused; and that its misuse will block any more "proper" use even more solidly than unuse and discrediting could. It could be said, that we must learn a certitude and correlation in every "value" before it will be possible to "teach" and not to murder; but that is far too optimistic. We would do better to examine, far beyond their present examination, the extensions within ourselves of doubt, responsibility, and conditioned faith and the possibilities of their more profitable union, to a degree at least of true and constant terror in even our tentatives, and if (for instance) we should dare to be "teaching" what Marx began to open, that we should do so only in the light of the terrible researches of Kafka and in the opposed identities of Blake and Céline.

All I have managed here, and it is more than I intended, is to give a confused statement of an intention which presumes itself to be good: the mere attempt to examine my own confusion would consume volumes. But let what I have tried to suggest amount to this alone: that not only within present reach of human intelligence, but even within reach of mine as it stands today, it would be possible that young human beings should rise onto their feet a great deal less dreadfully crippled than they are, a great deal more nearly capable of living well, a great deal more nearly aware, each of them, of their own dignity in existence, a great deal better qualified, each within his limits, to live and to take part toward the creation of a world in which good living will be possible without guilt toward every neighbor: and that teaching at present, such as it is, is almost entirely either irrelevant to these possibilities or destructive of them, and is, indeed, all but entirely unsuccessful even within its own "scales" of "value."

———

Within the world as it stands, however, the world they must live in, a certain form of education is available to these tenant children; and the extent to which they can avail themselves of it is of considerable importance in all their future living.

A few first points about it:

They are about as poorly equipped for self-education as human beings can be. Their whole environment is such that the use of the intelligence, of the intellect, and of the emotions is atrophied, and is all but entirely irrelevant to the pressures and needs which involve almost every instant of a tenant's conscious living: and indeed if these faculties were not thus reduced or killed at birth they would result in a great deal of pain, not to say danger. They learn the work they will spend their lives doing, chiefly of their parents, and from their parents and from the immediate world they take their conduct, their morality, and their mental and emotional and spiritual key. One could hardly say that any further knowledge or consciousness is at all to their use or advantage, since there is nothing to read, no reason to write, and no recourse against being cheated even if one is able to do sums; yet these forms of literacy are in general held to be desirable: a man or woman feels a certain sort of extra helplessness who lacks them: a truly serious or ambitious parent hopes for even more, for a promising child; though what "more" may be is, inevitably, only dimly understood.

———

School opens in middle or late September and closes the first of May. The country children, with their lunches, are picked up by busses at around seven-thirty in the morning and are dropped off again towards the early winter darkness. In spite of the bus the children of these three families have a walk to take. In dry weather it is shortened a good deal; the bus comes up the branch road as far as the group of negro houses at the bottom of the second hill and the Ricketts children walk half a mile to meet it and the Gudger children walk three quarters. In wet weather the bus can't risk leaving the highway and the Ricketts walk two miles and the Gudgers a mile and a half in clay which in stretches is knee-deep on a child.

There was talk during the summer of graveling the road, though most of the fathers are over forty-five, beyond road-age. They can hardly afford the time to do such work for nothing, and they and their negro neighbors are in no position to pay taxes. Nothing had come of it within three weeks of the start of school, and there was no prospect of free time before cold weather.

Southern winters are sickeningly wet, and wet clay is perhaps the hardest of all walking. "Attendance" suffers by this cause, and by others. Junior Gudger, for instance, was absent sixty-five and Louise fifty-three days out of a possible hundred-and-fifty-odd, and these absences were "unexcused" eleven and nine times respectively, twenty-three of Junior's and a proportionate number of Louise's absences fell in March and April, which are full of work at home as well as wetness. Late in her second year in school Louise was needed at home and missed several consecutive school days, including the final examinations. Her "marks" had been among the best in her class and she had not known of the examination date, but no chance was given her to make up the examinations and she had to take the whole year over. The Ricketts children have much worse attendance records and Pearl does not attend at all.

School does not begin until the children shall have helped two weeks to a month in the most urgent part of the picking season, and ends in time for them to be at work on the cotton-chopping.

The bus system which is now a routine of country schools is helpful, but not particularly to those who live at any distance from tax-maintained roads.

The walking, and the waiting in the cold and wetness, one day after another, to school in the morning, and home from schools in the shriveling daylight, is arduous and unpleasant.

Schooling, here as elsewhere, is identified with the dullest and most meager months of the year, and, in this class and country, with the least and worst food and a cold noonday lunch: and could be set only worse at a disadvantage if it absorbed the pleasanter half of the year.

The "attendance problem" is evidently taken for granted and, judging by the low number of unexcused absences, is "leniently" dealt with: the fact remains, though, that the children lose between a third to half of each school year, and must with this handicap keep up their lessons and "compete" with town children in a contest in which competition is stressed and success in it valued and rewarded.

———

The schoolhouse itself is in Cookstown; a recently built, windowy, "healthful" red brick and white-trimmed structure which perfectly exemplifies the American genius* for sterility, unimagination, and general gutlessness in meeting any opportunity for "reform" or "improvement." It is the sort of building a town such as Cookstown is proud of, and a brief explanation of its existence in such country will be worth while. Of late years Alabama has "come awake" to "education," illiteracy has been reduced; texts have been modernized; a good many old schools have been replaced by new ones. For this latter purpose the counties have received appropriations in proportion to the size of their school population. The school population of this county is five black to one white, and since not a cent of the money has gone into negro schools, such buildings as this are possible: for white children. The negro children, meanwhile, continue to sardine themselves, a hundred and a hundred and twenty strong, into stove-heated one-room pine shacks which might comfortably accommodate a fifth of their number if the walls, roof, and windows were tight.† But then, as one prominent landlord said and as many

———

*So well shown forth in "low-cost" housing.

†Aside from discomfort, and unhealthfulness, and the difficulty of concentrating, this means of course that several "grades" are in one room, reciting and studying by rotation, each using only a fraction of each day's time. It means hopeless boredom and waste for the children, and exhaustion for the teacher.

more would agree: "I don't object to nigrah education, not up through foath a fift grade maybe, but not furdern dat: I'm too strong a believah in white syewpremcy."

This bus service and this building the (white) children are schooled in, even including the long and muddy walk, are of course effete as compared to what their parents had.* The schooling itself is a different matter, too: much more "modern." The boys and girls alike are subjected to "art" and to "music," and the girls learn the first elements of tap dancing. Textbooks are so cheap almost anyone can afford them: that is, almost anyone who can afford anything at all; which means that they are a stiff problem in any year to almost any tenant. I want now to list and suggest the contents of a few textbooks which were at the Gudger house, remembering, first, that they imply the far reaches of the book-knowledge of any average adult tenant.

> *The Open Door Language Series: First Book: Language Stories and Games.*
> *Trips to Take.* Among the contents are poems by Vachel Lindsay, Elizabeth Madox Roberts, Robert Louis Stevenson, etc. Also a story titled: "Brother Rabbit's Cool Air Swing," and subheaded: "Old Southern Tale."
> *Outdoor Visits:* Book Two of *Nature and Science Readers.* (Book One is *Hunting.*) Book Two opens: "Dear Boys and Girls: in this book you will read how Nan and Don visited animals and plants that live outdoors."
> *Real Life Readers: New Stories and Old: A Third Reader.* Illustrated with color photographs.
> *The Trabue-Stevens Speller.* Just another speller.
> *Champion Arithmetic.* Five hundred and ten pages: a champion psychological inducement to an interest in numbers. The final problem: "Janet bought 1 ¼ lbs. of salted peanuts and ½ lb. of salted almonds. Altogether she bought ? lbs. of nuts?"

---

*Their parents would have walked to one-room wooden schoolhouses. I'm not sure, but think it more likely than not, that many of the white children still do today.

Dear Boys and Girls indeed!

Such a listing is rich as a poem; twisted full of contents, symptoms, and betrayals, and these, as in a poem, are only reduced and diluted by any attempt to explain them or even by hinting. Personally I see enough there to furnish me with bile for a month: yet I know that any effort to make clear in detail what is there, and why it seems to me so fatal, must fail.

Even so, see only a little and only for a moment.

These are books written by "adults." They must win the approval and acceptance of still other "adults," members of school "boards"; and they will be "taught" with by still other "adults" who have been more or less "trained" as teachers. The intention is, or should be, to engage, excite, preserve, or develop the "independence" of, and furnish with "guidance," "illumination," "method," and "information," the curiosities of children.

Now merely re-examine a few words, phrases and facts:

The Open Door: open to whom. That metaphor is supposed to engage the interest of children.

Series: First Book. Series. Of course The Bobsey Twins is a series; so is The Rover Boys. Series perhaps has some pleasure associations to those who have children's books, which no tenant children have: but even so it is better than canceled by the fact that this is so obviously not a pleasure book but a schoolbook, not even well disguised. An undisguised textbook is only a little less pleasing than a sneaking and disguised one, though. *First Book:* there entirely for the convenience of adults; it's only grim to a child.

Language: it appears to be a *modern* substitution for the word "English." I don't doubt the latter word has been murdered; the question is, whether the new one has any life whatever to a taught child or, for that matter, to a teacher.

Stories and Games: both, modified by a school word, and in a school context. Most children prefer pleasure to boredom, lacking our intelligence to reverse this preference: but you must use your imagination or memory to recognize how any game can be poisoned by being "conducted": and few adults have either.

Trips to Take. Trips indeed, for children who will never again travel as much as in their daily bus trips to and from school. Children like figures of speech or are, if you like, natural symbolists and poets: being so, they see through frauds such as this so much the more readily. No poem is a "trip," whatever else it may be, and suffers by being lied about.

The verse. I can readily imagine that "educators" are well pleased with themselves in that they have got rid of the Bivouac of the Dead and are using much more nearly contemporary verse. I am quite as sure, knowing their kind of "knowledge" of poetry, that the pleasure is all theirs.

These children, both of town and country, are saturated southerners, speaking dialects not very different from those of negroes. *Brother* Rabbit! *Old Southern Tale!*

Outdoor Visits. Nature and Science. Book One: *Hunting.* Dear Boys and Girls. In this book you will read (oh, I will, will I?). Nan and Don. Visit. Animals and Plants that Live Outdoors. Outdoors. You will pay formal calls on Plants. They live outdoors. "Nature." "Science." Hunting. Dear Boys and Girls. Outdoor Visits.

Real Life. "Real" "Life" "Readers." Illustrated by *color* photographs.

Or back into the old generation, a plainer title: *The Trabue-Stevens Speller.* Or the *Champion Arithmetic,* weight eighteen pounds, an attempt at ingratiation in the word champion, so broad of any mark I am surprised it is not spelled *Champeen.*

Or you may recall the page of geography text I have quoted elsewhere: which, I must grant, tells so much about education that this chapter is probably unnecessary.

———

I give up. Relative to my memory of my own grade-schooling, I recognize all kinds of "progressive" modifications: Real Life, color photographs, Trips to Take (rather than Journey to Make), games, post-kindergarten, "Language," Nan and Don, "Nature and Science," Untermeyer-vintage poetry, "dear boys and girls"; and I am sure of only one thing: that it is prepared by adults for their own self-flattery and satisfaction, and is to children merely the old set retouched, of afflictions, bafflements, and half-legible insults more or less apathetically submitted to.

—

Louise Gudger is fond of school, especially of geography and arithmetic, and gets unusually good "marks": which means in part that she has an intelligence quick and acquisitive above the average, in part that she has learned to parrot well and to respect "knowledge" as it is presented to her. She has finished the third grade. In the fourth grade she will learn all about the history of her country. Her father and much more particularly her mother is excited over her brightness and hopeful of it: they intend to make every conceivable effort by which she may continue not only through the grades but clear through high school. She wants to become a teacher, and quite possibly she will; or a trained nurse; and again quite possibly she will.

Junior Gudger is in the second grade because by Alabama law a pupil is automatically passed after three years in a grade. He is still almost entirely unable to read and write, and is physically fairly skilful. It may be that he is incapable of "learning": in any case "teaching" him would be a "special problem." It would be impossible in a public, competitive class of mixed kinds and degrees of "intelligence"; and I doubt that most public-school teachers are trained in it anyhow.

Burt and Valley Few are too young for school. I foresee great difficulty for Burt, who now at four is in so desperate a psychological situation that he is capable of speaking any language beyond gibberish (in which he has great rhythmic and syllabic talent) only after he has been given the security of long and friendly attention, of a sort which markedly excludes his brothers.

Pearl Woods, who is eight, may have started to school this fall (1936); more likely not, though, for it was to depend on whether the road was graveled so she would not have the long walk to the bus alone or within contamination of the Ricketts children. She is extremely sensitive, observant, critical and crafty, using her mind and her senses much more subtly than is ever indicated or "taught" in school: whether her peculiar intelligence will find engagement or ruin in the squarehead cogs of public schooling is another matter.

Thomas is three years too young for school. As a comedian and narcist dancer he has natural genius; aside from this I doubt his abilities. Natural artists, such as he is, and natural craftsmen, like Junior, should not necessarily have to struggle with reading and writing; they have other ways of learning, and of enlarging themselves, which however are not available to them.

Clair Bell is three years young for school and it seems probable that she will not live for much if any of it, so estimates are rather irrelevant. I will say, though, that I was so absorbed in her physical and spiritual beauty that I was not on the lookout for signs of "intelligence" or the lack of it, and that education, so far as I know it, would either do her no good or would hurt her.

Flora Merry Lee and Katy are in the second grade. Katy, though she is so shy that she has to write out her reading lessons, is brighter than average; Flora Merry Lee, her mother says, is brighter than Katy; she reads and writes smoothly and "specially delights in music." Garvrin and Richard are in the fourth grade. Garvrin doesn't take to schooling very easily though he tries hard; Richard is bright but can't get interested; his mind wanders. In another year or two they will be big enough for full farm work and will be needed for it, and that will be the end of school.

Margaret quit school when she was in the fifth grade because her eyes hurt her so badly every time she studied books. She has forgotten a good deal how to read. Paralee quit soon after Margaret did because she was lonesome. She still reads fairly easily, and quite possibly will not forget how.

The Ricketts are spoken of disapprovingly, even so far away as the county courthouse, as "problem" children. Their attendance record is extremely bad; their conduct is not at all good; they are always fighting and sassing back. Besides their long walk in bad weather, here is some more explanation. They are much too innocent to understand the profits of docility. They have to wear clothes and shoes which make them the obvious butts of most of the children. They come of a family which is marked and poor even among the poor whites, and are looked down on even by most levels of the tenant class. They are uncommonly sensitive, open, trusting, easily hurt, and amazed by meanness and by cruelty, and their ostracism is of a sort to inspire savage loyalty among them. They are indeed "problems"; and the "problem" will not be simplified as these "over"sexed and anarchic children shift into adolescence. The two girls in particular seem inevitably marked out for incredibly cruel misunderstanding and mistreatment.

———

Mrs. Ricketts can neither read nor write. She went to school one day in her life and her mother got sick and she never went back. Another time she told me that the children laughed at her dress and the teacher whipped her for hitting back at them, but Margaret reminded her that that was the dress she had made for Flora Merry Lee and that it was Flora Merry Lee and Katy who had been whipped, and she agreed that that was the way it was.

Fred Ricketts learned quickly. He claims to have learned how to read music in one night (he does, in any case, read it), and he reads language a little less hesitantly than the others do and is rather smug about it—"I was readn whahl back na Pgressive Fahmuh—" He got as far as the fifth grade and all ways was bright. When his teacher said the earth turned on a axle, he asked her was the axle set in posts, then. She said yes, she reckoned so. He said well, wasn't hell supposed to be under the earth, and if it was wouldn't they be all the time trying to chop the axle post out from under the earth? But here the earth still was, so what was all this talk about axles. "Teacher never did bring up nothn bout no axles after that. No sir, she never did bring up nothin about no durn axles after that. No sir-ree, she shore never did brang up nufn baout no dad blame axles attah dayut."

Woods quit school at twelve when he ran away and went to work in the mines. He can read, write, and figure; so can his wife. Woods understands the structures and tintings of rationalization in money, sex, language, religion, law, and general social conduct in a sour way which is not on the average curriculum.

George Gudger can spell and read and write his own name; beyond that he is helpless. He got as far as the second grade. By that time there was work for him and he was slow minded anyway. He feels it is a terrible handicap not to be educated and still wants to learn to read and write and to figure, and his wife has tried to learn him, and still wants to. He still wants to, too, but he thinks it is unlikely that he will ever manage to get the figures and letters to stick in his head.

Mrs. Gudger can read, write, spell, and handle simple arithmetic, and grasps and is excited by such matters as the plainer facts of astronomy and geology. In fact, whereas many among the three families have crippled but very full and real intelligences, she and to a perhaps less extent her father have also intellects. But these intellects died before they were born; they hang behind their eyes like fetuses in alcohol.

———

It may be that more are born "incapable of learning," in this class, or in any case "incapable of learning," or of "using their intelligences," beyond "rudimentary" stages, than in economically luckier classes. If this is so, and I doubt the proportion is more than a little if at all greater, several ideas come to mind: Incapable of learning what? And capable of learning what else, which is not available either to them or, perhaps, in the whole field and idea of education? Or are they incapable through incompetent teaching, or through blind standards, or none, on the part of educators, for measuring what "intelligence" is? Or incapable by what pressures of past causes in past generations? Or should the incapability be so lightly (or sorrowfully) dismissed as it is by teachers and by the middle class in general?

But suppose a portion are born thus "incapable": the others, nevertheless, the great majority, are born with "intelligences" potentially as open and "healthful," and as varied in pattern and in charge, as any on earth. And by their living, and by their education, they are made into hopeless and helpless cripples, capable exactly and no more of doing what will keep them alive: by no means so well equipped as domestic and free animals: and that is what their children are being made into, more and more incurably, in every year, and in every day.

"Literacy" is to some people a pleasing word: when "illiteracy" percentages drop, many are pleased who formerly were shocked, and think no more of it. Disregarding the proved fact that few doctors of philosophy are literate, that is, that few of them have the remotest idea how to read, how to say what they mean, or what they mean in the first place, the word literacy means very little even as it is ordinarily used. An adult tenant writes and spells and reads painfully and hesitantly as a child does and is incapable of any save the manifest meanings of any but the simplest few hundred words, and is all but totally incapable of absorbing, far less correlating, far less critically examining, any "ideas" whether true or false; or even physical facts beyond the simplest and most visible. That they are, by virtue of these limitations, among the only "honest" and "beautiful" users of language, is true, perhaps, but it is not enough. They are at an immeasurable disadvantage in a world which is run, and in which they are hurt, and in which they might be cured, by "knowledge" and by "ideas": and to "consciousness" or "knowledge" in its usages in personal conduct and in human relationships, and to those unlimited worlds of the senses, the remembrance, the mind and the heart which, beyond that of their own existence, are the only human hope, dignity, solace, increasement, and joy, they are all but totally blinded. The ability to try to understand existence, the ability to try to recognize the wonder and responsibility of one's own existence, the ability to know even fractionally the almost annihilating beauty, ambiguity, darkness, and horror which swarm every instant of every consciousness, the ability to try to accept, or the ability to try to defend one's self, or the ability to dare to try to assist others; all such as these, of which most human beings are cheated of their potentials, are, in most of those who even begin to discern or wish for them, the gifts or thefts of economic privilege, and are available to members of these leanest classes only by the rare and irrelevant miracle of born and surviving "talent."

Or to say it in another way: I believe that every human being is potentially capable, within his "limits," of fully "realizing" his potentialities; that this, his being cheated and choked of it, is infinitely the ghastliest, commonest, and most inclusive of all the crimes of which the human world can accuse itself; and that the discovery and use of "consciousness," which has always been and is our deadliest enemy and deceiver, is also the source and guide of all hope and cure, and the only one.

———

I am not at all trying to lay out a thesis, far less to substantiate or to solve. I do not consider myself qualified. I know only that murder is being done, against nearly every individual in the planet, and that there are dimensions and correlations of cure which not only are not being used but appear to be scarcely considered or suspected. I know there is cure, even now available, if only it were available, in science and in the fear and joy of God. This is only a brief personal statement of these convictions: and my self-disgust is less in my ignorance, and far less in my "failure" to "defend" or "support" the statement, than in my inability to state it even so far as I see it, and in my inability to blow out the brains with it of you who take what it is talking of lightly, or not seriously enough.

A Few Notes

Most of you would never be convinced that much can be implied out of little: that everything to do with tenant education, for instance, is fully and fairly indicated in the mere list of textbooks. I have not learned how to make this clear, so I have only myself to thank. On the other hand there are plenty of people who never get anything into their heads until they are brained by twenty years' documentation: these are the same people who so scrupulously obey, insist on, and interpret "the facts," and "the rules."

I have said a good deal more here on what ought to be than on what is: but God forbid I should appear to say, "I know what ought to be, and this is it." But it did and does seem better to shout a few obvious facts (they can never be "obvious" enough) than to meech. The meechers will say, Yes, but do you realize all (or any) of the obstacles, presuming you are (in general) a little more right than merely raving? The answer is, I am sure I don't realize them all, but I realize more of them, probably, than you do. Our difference is that you accept and respect them. "Education" as it stands is tied in with every bondage I can conceive of, and is the chief cause of these bondages, including acceptance and respect, which are the worst bondages of all. "Education," if it is anything short of crime, is a recognition of these bondages and a discovery of more and a deadly enemy of all of them; it is the whole realm of human consciousness, action, and possibility; it has above all to try to recognize and continuously to suspect and to extend its understanding of its own nature. It is all science and all conduct; it is also all religion. By which I mean, it is all "good" or "wise" science, conduct, and religion. It is also all individuals; no less various. It cannot be less and be better than outrageous. Its chief task is fearfully to try to learn what is "good" and "why" (and when), and how to communicate, and its own dimensions, and its responsibility.

Oh, I am very well aware how adolescent this is and how easily laughable. I will nevertheless insist that any persons milder, more obedient to or compromising* with "the obstacles as they are," more "realistic," contented with the effort for less, are dreamy and insufficiently skeptical. Those are the worst of the enemies, and always have been.

———

I don't know whether negroes or whites teach in the negro schools; I presume negroes. If they are negroes, I would presume for general

*One of the researches most urgently needed is into the whole problem of compromise and noncompromise. I am dangerously and mistakenly much against compromise: "my kind never gets anything done." The (self-styled) "Realists" are quite as dangerously ready to compromise. They seem never sufficiently aware of the danger; they much too quickly and easily respect the compromise and come at rest in it. I would suppose that nothing is necessarily wrong with compromise of itself, except that those who are easy enough to make it are easy enough to relax into and accept it, and that it thus inevitably becomes fatal. Or more nearly, the essence of the trouble is that compromise is held to be a virtue of itself.

reasons that many of them, or most, are far superior to the white teachers. By and large only the least capable of whites become teachers, particularly in primary schools, and more particularly in small towns and in the country: whereas with so little in the world available to them, it must be that many of the most serious and intelligent negroes become teachers. But you would have to add: They are given, insofar as they are given any, a white-traditioned education, and are liable to the solemn, meek piousness of most serious and educated negroes in the south; to a deep respect for knowledge and education as they have worked for it; to a piteous mah-people or Uncle Tom attitude towards all life. Even those who are aware of more dangerous attitudes would in the south have to be careful to the point of impotence. Moreover they would be teaching only very young children, in the earliest years of school, in overcrowded classrooms.

———

Note on all grade-school teachers: that at best they are exceedingly ill-paid, and have also anxiety over their jobs: with all the nervousness of lack of money and of insecurity even in that little: not a good state of mind for a teacher of the young. Nor is the state of mind resulting of sexlessness, or of carefully spotless moral rectitude, whether it be "innate," or self-enforced for the sake of the job. Nearly all teachers and clergymen suffocate their victims through this sterility alone.

———

It would be hard to make clear enough the deadliness of vacuum and of apathy which is closed over the very nature of teaching, over teachers and pupils alike: or in what different worlds words and processes leave a teacher, and reach a child. Children, taught either years beneath their intelligence or miles wide of relevance to it, or both: their intelligence becomes hopelessly bewildered, drawn off its centers, bored, or atrophied. Carry it forward a few years and recognize how soft-brained an american as against a european "college graduate" is. On the other side: should there be any such thing as textbooks in any young life: and how many "should" learn to read at all?

———

As a whole part of "psychological education" it needs to be remembered that a neurosis can be valuable; also that "adjustment" to a sick and insane environment is of itself not "health" but sickness and insanity.

———

I could not wish of any one of them that they should have had the "advantages" I have had: a Harvard education is by no means an unqualified advantage.

———

Adults writing to or teaching children: in nearly every word within these textbooks, for instance, there is a flagrant mistake of some kind. The commonest is this: that they simplify their own ear, without nearly enough skepticism as to the accuracy of the simplification, and with virtually no intuition for the child or children; then write or teach to satisfy that ear; discredit the child who is not satisfied, and value the child who, by docile or innocent distortions of his intelligence, is.

———

In school a child is first plunged into the hot oil bath of the world at its cruelest: and children are taught far less by their teachers than by one another. Children are, or quickly become, exquisitely sensitive to social, psychologic, and physical meanings and discriminations. The war is bloody and pitiless as that war alone can be in which every combatant is his own sole army, and is astounded and terrified in proportion to the healthfulness of his consciousness. What clothes are worn, for one simple thing alone, is of tremendous influence upon the child who wears them. A child is quickly and frightfully instructed of his situation and meaning in the world; and that one stays alive only by one form or another of cowardice, or brutality, or deception, or other crime. It is all, needless to say, as harmful to the "winners" (the well-to-do, or healthful, or extraverted) as to the losers.

———

The "esthetic" is made hateful and is hated beyond all other kinds of "knowledge." It is false-beauty to begin with; it is taught by sick women or sicker men; it becomes identified with the worst kinds of femininity and effeminacy; it is made incomprehensible and suffocating to anyone of much natural honesty and vitality.

———

The complete acquaintance of a child with "music" is the nauseating little tunes you may remember from your own schooltime. His "art" has equally little to do with "art." The dancing, as I have said, is taught to girls: it is the beginning of tap dancing. The spectacle of a tenant's little daughter stepping out abysmal imitations of Eleanor Powell has a certain charm, but it is somehow decadent, to put it mildly. This is not at all to say that madrigals, finger-painting, or morris-dancing are to be recommended: I wish to indicate only that in either case the "teaching" of "the esthetic" or of "the arts" in Cookstown leaves, or would leave, virtually everything still to be desired.

———

It is hardly to Louise's good fortune that she "likes" school, school being what it is. Dressed as she is, and bright as she is, and serious and dutiful and well-thought-of as she is, she already has traces of a special sort of complacency which probably must, in time, destroy all in her nature that is magical, indefinable, and matchless: and this though she is one of the stronger persons I have ever known.

———

Perhaps half the people alive are born with the possibility of moral intuitions far more subtle and excellent than those laid down by law and custom, and most of the others might learn a great deal. As it is they are more than sufficiently destroyed. If beginning at the age of six they were subjected to a daily teaching of law, the damage would be so much the worse. There is a fair parallel in "consciousness," in "intelligence": and the standards of education, which seem even more monstrous than those of law, are thus imposed as law is not, and are made identical with knowledge.

———

No equipment to handle an abstract idea or to receive it: nor to receive or handle at all complex facts: nor to put facts and ideas together and strike any fire or meaning from them. They are like

revolutionists who must fight fire and iron and poison gas with barrel staves and with bare hands: except that they lack even the idea
of revolution.

It would be the narrative task of many pages even scarcely to
suggest how slowed, blinded, and helpless-minded they are made.
Just as with food, they cannot conceive of or be interested in what
they have never tasted or heard of. All except the simplest knowledge of immediate materials and of the senses is completely irrelevant to the life they are living. Perhaps fortunately, the one thing
the adults could most surely receive and understand is what a good
revolutionist could tell them about their immediate situation and
what is to be done about it: certainly one would be a fool, and an in-
sulting one, who tried much else, or who tried much else before
that was accomplished. The children could learn this and much
more.

For various reasons I am not a good revolutionist, and much as I
wanted to, could bear in my "conscience," or in my respect for what
they were as they stood, to do almost none of this, beyond deter-
mining what in general they might learn if they were rightly given
it. Moreover, though there are revolutionists whom I totally respect, and before the mere thought of whom I hold myself in contempt, I go blind to think what crimes others would commit upon
them, and instill into them; and by every appearance and proba-
bility these latter, who for all their devotion and courage seem to
me among the most dangerous and hideous persons at large, are
greatly in the majority, and it is they who own and will always be-
tray all revolutions.

———

"Sense of beauty": Is this an "instinct" or a product of "training." In
either case there appears to be almost no such thing among the
members of these three families, and I have a strong feeling that the
"sense of beauty," like nearly everything else, is a class privilege. I
am sure in any case that its "terms" differ by class, and that the
"sense" is limited and inarticulate in the white tenant class almost
beyond hope of description. (This quite aside from the fact that in
other classes, where it is less limited, it is almost a hundred per cent

corrupted.) They live on land, and in houses, and under skies and seasons, which all happen to seem to me beautiful beyond almost anything else I know, and they themselves, and the clothes they wear, and their motions, and their speech, are beautiful in the same intense and final commonness and purity: but by what chance have I this "opinion" or "perception" or, I might say, "knowledge"? And on the other hand, why do they appear so completely to lack it? This latter, there seem good reasons for. Habit. No basis of comparison. No "sophistication" (there can be a good meaning of the word). No reason nor glimmer of reason to regard anything in terms other than those of need and use. Land is what you get food out of: houses are what you live in, not comfortably: the sky is your incalculable friend or enemy: all nature, all that is built upon it, all that is worn, all that is done and looked to, is in plain and powerful terms of need, hope, fear, chance, and function. Moreover, the profoundest and plainest "beauties," those of the order of the stars and of solitude in darkened and empty land, come at least partly of awe, and such in a simple being is, simply, unformulable fear. It is true that in what little they can obtain of them, they use and respect the rotted prettinesses of "luckier" classes; in such naïvety that these are given beauty: but by and large it seems fairly accurate to say that being so profoundly members in nature, among man-built things and functions which are almost as scarcely complicated "beyond" nature as such things can be, and exist on a "human" plane, they are little if at all more aware of "beauty," nor of themselves as "beautiful," than any other member in nature, any animal, anyhow. It is very possible, I would believe probable, that many animals are sensitive to beauty in terms of exhilaration or fear or courting or lust; many are, for that matter, accomplished and obvious narcisists: in this sense I would also guess that the animals are better equipped than the human beings. I would say too that there is a purity in this existence *in* and *as* "beauty," which can so scarcely be conscious of itself and its world as such, which is inevitably lost in consciousness, and that this is a serious loss.

But so are resourcefulness against deceit and against strangling: and so are pleasure, and joy, and love: and a human being who is deprived of these and of this consciousness is deprived almost of existence itself.

———

JAMES AGEE (1909–1955) wrote nonfiction for *Fortune* and *Time,* even as he offered the world poems, essays, and movie reviews. His 1936 venture south to Alabama, accompanied by the photographer Walker Evans, prompted the documentary classic *Let Us Now Praise Famous Men,* which offers a soliloquy of sorts on education.

A Witness to Public Education

Robert Coles

In my junior year of college I had the great good luck to study with Perry Miller, whose American literature courses and seminars taught us so very much about this country. He wanted to get to know us and invited us to his Widener Library study. I recall getting into a spirited conversation with him once about Emerson and Thoreau—I was taken aback, actually, by the moral energy he displayed himself as he spoke of the moral energy those two Concordians possessed. I also remember talking with him about the tutoring I was doing in Boston as part of my community service work at Phillips Brooks House. I was trying to be of assistance to high-schoolers who were having trouble with their school lessons. I helped students as they struggled with their grammar and spelling, and their math. I also got to know them as young men and women who had no interest, by and large, in attending college. They told me they aspired to be carpenters, electricians, plumbers, steamfitters, nurses, or secretaries. I remember noticing the academic ability of a particular youth, encouraging him or her to think of college, only to be turned down with the shake of a head or a look of surprise meant to give me pause, second thoughts. I also remember discussing such experiences with Professor Miller. I kept speaking of the "potential" in one or another youth, the considerable and evident intelligence, the untapped "promise"—and once he, in turn and unforgettably, remonstrated with me wryly, quietly: "It's quite possible to be bright and not want to go to college." I had, of course, been pushing that outcome with my tutees and, on their behalf, with Miller; and he had clearly decided with that remark to initiate a discussion with me—which we had at some length, and which I've never wanted to forget. In essence, a distinguished Harvard professor was reminding me of "class" and its relationship to the outlook of young, mid-century Americans. He was also, by indirection, commenting on the dangers of a smug parochialism and, too, a condescension masked as ostensible good will. He wanted me to realize that even though I happened to be in college, and was brought up to want to get to that place, there was no reason to assume that such a hope, such a destination or outcome, was "normal" or "natural" or expectable or desirable.

He saw how puzzled I looked as he gave voice to such observations; and, as a consequence, he amplified his remarks, gave me a disquisition (I can hear his voice, see his gestures and mannerisms) on the "working class world," in England (when it then reigned supreme) and in this country—on the pride and dignity, the feisty spirit of such a world. He wasn't romanticizing a segment of our 1950s nation, nor was he gratuitously critical of me for wanting "more" for my tutees, for (as he put it) "aspiring on their behalf." He simply wanted me to understand the complexity of a particular human involvement—what I brought out of my life to those young people, what they believed and felt out of their experiences at home and in a neighborhood. Once, memorably, he put the matter this way: "You're trying hard to teach them—but let them be your teachers, too."

That plea for a certain humility, for a willingness to subordinate one's own thinking life to that of others, was not easily heard, I fear—indeed, Professor Miller was the first to understand the difficulty his advice posed for someone like me, and for some of his other students as well. Again and again, in his Classics of the Christian Tradition course, he reminded us of the provocations to be found in the New Testament, as in, "The last shall be first, the first last"—an unsettling message for young ones quite pleased to be where they were, in that famous Yard, and at a time when their nation's power was triumphant.

I tried to remember my teacher's counsel, but readily slipped into the habit of exhorting the high-schoolers I was tutoring; if they worked harder and did better in their classroom work, they, too, could be like me, a college student—but they were as little inclined to hear me as I was to hear my teacher, Perry Miller. Once, one of my most promising students, a young man named Hank, whom I remember well for his outspoken candor as well as his intelligence, turned the tables on me, let me know that he was quite happy with his future prospects (he wanted to be a carpenter, like his father), and decidedly uninterested in "going beyond high school," as he put it. I recall that phrase, frankly, because what followed it in explanation proved unforgettable. "I'm happy with my life—I know where I'm headed and I'm glad." This same youth had also told me how much he liked to go to the library, to browse through magazines and books. Surely with that strong inclination, he was a fit candidate for college—so I suggested. But he objected—and again, he put the matter in such a way that I had a hard time, in turn, putting his words out of my mind: "I like to read a book and enjoy it, but in school they make it into a big deal, and it's not fun anymore."

I had yet to know much, at least academically, about human psychology, nor was Professor Miller especially interested in psychiatry or psychoanalysis, but I did tell him about Hank and his comments with some sense that they had struck a significant chord or two in my mind, and my listening teacher most forcefully and explicitly let me know what he made of what had transpired. I myself was having a lot of trouble figuring out what I wanted to do with my life—especially so because I was in the pre-medical school science course, and it was rife with fierce competition, to put it mildly. Moreover, I didn't like the way a particular English professor was dealing with the novels we were reading. He gave us frequent spot quizzes on "name identification," and he offered the densest kind of explication, interpretation, which we, then, had to offer back when we took the hour exams and the final. Professor Miller had heard me sing of my woes in both those respects, and so (without the mannerisms of the clinic, thank God) he tactfully let me know tersely and trenchantly that "the fellow [Hank] may be a step ahead of us." Again, a moment that remains fixed in my head—a shrewdly knowing teacher who was willing to link himself with his student, and acknowledge on their joint behalf a measure of irony, at the very least.

I've often harkened back to those particular experiences, moments of awareness—for me, they are the college education I was lucky to receive: a professor who himself resisted the temptations of complacent smugness, of self-satisfaction, and who let a student know about certain hazards that go with trying to learn about others and to help them. A decade later, finally out of school myself, a child psychiatrist in the military, in accordance with the "doctors draft" that had all of us physicians give two years to our country (I sure was reluctant then; I now think it was the best thing that ever happened to me) I stumbled into Ruby Bridges, a six-year-old girl in New Orleans who was just starting her experience with school. In fact Ruby had to fight her way past a mob every day to get to a classroom, where she studied on her own because all the other children had been withdrawn by their parents. This was the start of school desegregation in the Deep South—a great ordeal for public education in our nation. I would end up observing that ordeal for years; I got to know the African-American and white children who went through it and, too, their teachers, and learned thereby a little of what happens in schools when the world in which they belong makes new and serious demands on them—in this case, the initiation of a complex kind of human relatedness hitherto outlawed: the classroom as a color-blind scene. As I kept trying to learn how those children in Louisiana (and later in Georgia and Mississippi and Alabama and North Carolina) all managed under stressful circumstances, to say the least, I only gradually learned to stop imposing my own educational experiences (and the assumptions they had prompted in me) in favor of a more tentative kind of watchfulness, worthy of what Professor Miller had suggested. In fact I went back several times during the early part of my seven-year stay in the South to visit this important teacher in my life (he died in 1963) and told him what I was seeing and hearing in the South's public schools. In 1962, thoroughly unsure of what to make of an exceedingly complex social and racial landscape, and of the psychological ironies and ambiguities that were hard to fathom, I was about to throw my hands up in surrender and return north. But I was told this in a Widener Library study:

> You're getting an education about education! I think you are trying too hard to get a fix on a research project. You keep telling me about what you're trying to find out about these kids, all their "problems," all the psychopathology. Fair enough—but I think they've got you confused, and that's a good thing. Your ideas aren't adequate to them, to the whole story of their lives, which you've yet to learn. Why don't you give some thought to what you are trying to unearth in this "research" of yours? Why don't you make those children and their parents and their teachers your colleagues—better, your professors? Ask them what they think is important, really important, for you to know.

By then I was tape-recording conversations in schools and homes—even the one I had with my former college professor. I thought I had figured out a so-called "methodology," a manner of doing my work: the use of children's drawings and paintings to get at their inner life, as well as, of course, interviews with them and "direct observation," as Anna Freud put it, of their school and home life. But Professor Miller's comments prompted me to make a shift in the way I conducted those interviews—I began to share some of my thoughts with the children; I began to ask them for their thoughts on schooling, on the racial tensions in their communities, putting emphasis on their social and cultural perceptions rather than on an exclusive interest in their psychology. I began to learn from these boys and girls (and their parents and teachers) throughout the South, in a time of social upheaval, what happens in our public schools for the good and the bad.

The results of that research (it was extended to rural as well as urban school children, for example, the sons and daughters of migrant farmworkers and Appalachian families, and those who attend schools on our Indian reservations and in Alaska) were a surprise to me: some children (especially those under the worst stresses) often enough mustered an impressive quality of mind and heart, if given half a chance, and thereby did far better educationally and psychologically than I expected. For years, actually, I tried to understand the reasons for such an outcome, until, one day, the girl who had experienced, maybe, the most fearful time of it, with her very life at stake for a while, looked back (she was eight) at what she had experienced a couple of years earlier:

> It was bad, yes, a lot bad; but I had this goal to outlast those folks screaming; and I had the teacher, giving me plenty to do, and you know, at first I had her all to myself. I wanted to learn the best I could, so I wouldn't disappoint my folks, and my people here in New Orleans [its African-American citizens]. I knew everyone was watching, and that's why I kept saying to myself: let them see what you can do—you show them! It was tough, but when you win and it's been a long battle, then you're proud. My mom says, if things come too easy, you don't get as much out of what you're doing! I'd come home, and I did extra work so I could keep ahead, and no saying "I told you so, she just can't make the grade." I hope I'll keep on moving up, and I hope I'll be able to prove Judge Wright right [J. Skelley Wright, the federal judge who ordered school desegregation to begin].

She smiled as she considered the rhyme of Wright/right; she wrote out both words for me—thus showing me what I already knew, how well she was doing at spelling. But, in fact, she had in her own unprepossessing, beguiling way given me a full educational textbook in those few sentences. She had pointed out what others call the "variables" or "factors" that go to make a successful public education, even one pursued under the most threatening of conditions. She may have met mobs on her way to and from school, but she had a lot to keep her going while there: a teacher who worked closely with her; a sense of purpose and direction; and a sense, also, of achievement measured daily by her willingness and ability to persist, no matter the difficulties confronting her. Moreover, her family and the neighborhood where she lived rallied around her— for many this child was a hero, applauded as a brave pioneer. For such a child, for others like her across the South during the 1960s, school attendance became a closely observed, highly sanctioned effort as well as a perilous and much-opposed one. No wonder these children by and large did so well both academically and personally. Vulnerable with respect to their background and their daily situation as participants in a controversial political and racial, as well as educational, initiative, these students were nevertheless given respect, attention, support, even acclaim. They faced angry crowds, but they were not by any means lost; quite the contrary: they received the kind of individual assistance in their studies at home and at school (from those who supported what they were doing) that any quite well-to-do children can take for granted in private schools.

Eventually I came back to my native New England to teach at Harvard, first in Erik H. Erikson's course, and then on my own, at the College and at the Medical School. At that time, the early 1970s, Boston also experienced an educational crisis not unlike, in certain respects, the ones I'd watched across the South where African-American parents were determined to find more adequate schools for their children. I rode on a bus for a year with some of those boys and girls—they were leaving Roxbury for a less-crowded, better-equipped school in the Back Bay. Now I was getting into the midst of an educational struggle that wasn't prompted by segregationist defiance, but rather, by the workings of class as well as race in a northern city known, ironically, for its long-standing abolitionist history. Now I was talking with children who weren't being individually celebrated as protagonists of progress, but who were regarded by themselves and others as victims of a flawed educational system—one whose inadequacies (and worse) had to do with the way our social and economic system works: those with money and power find thoroughly adequate schools, public or private, for their sons and daughters, whereas those who are poor, no matter their skin color, are far less able to command such an outcome for their children. In time, I concluded my "study" of northern children going through their kind of educational crisis and settled into a different relationship to such young people—I started working as a volunteer teacher in an elementary school (named after Martin Luther King) right near Harvard and in high schools in Boston (the Jeremiah Burke and Brighton High School). So doing, this past decade and more, I have been a witness to public education and its well-known and persisting problems as they, alas, help shape the lives of countless children who live in Cambridge and Boston, not far from many important colleges and universities. I often meet young people who strike me as intelligent, alert, knowing in many ways, yet indifferent to school work, even scornful of it. I meet others who don't know how to do their lessons very well, who need encouragement and assistance that, for the most part, is not forthcoming. I meet still others, in high school, who actually pose a threat to their classmates, not to mention their teachers. I also meet, I'm sorry to say, teachers who have long ago lost the enthusiasm and dedication that are needed to keep a class going well, especially under the circumstances that prevail in many urban schools. Yet there are more hopeful moments, and they are truly memorable.

Even in the toughest high school classes there are always—yes, always—some youths who are really trying to grab hold of that proverbial ladder and climb their way out of the ghetto life they have known so long. Often I wonder what makes for the difference: why are some in my classes so unruly, so provocative, or so bored and indifferent and sullen, or so irritable and restless and smart-alecky, whereas others are quietly industrious, respectful, anxious to learn, eager to take part in the various projects I try to initiate? I wish I could answer such a question in a clear-cut psychological and sociological manner, the approach I myself for so long have assumed to be the correct and desirable one. Always, that is, I have tried to understand the children in those classrooms as troubled because of this or that aspect of their home life, their street life, even their previous school life; or alternatively as the beneficiaries of one or another set of experiences or influences that have favored them as students, members of a classroom. Such an observation is, of course, true—yet the complexity of things, the constant presence of irony, has to be mentioned. That is, I know youngsters who are bright, who have received some valuable encouragement (and love) at home, but who have turned out to be rowdy troublemakers in and outside of the school building. Conversely, I have marveled at certain students before me—they have had a devastating time of it, day in and day out, since their earliest years, and still they have somehow found the capacity and will to take hold as students, to give an educational life a chance, and as a consequence, to improve mightily their prospects.

As I search for the explanations we all understandably crave, I come back again and again, to what George Eliot emphasized in *Middlemarch*—the impact of luck and chance and circumstance upon young lives, their susceptibility to fateful moments, for the good and the bad alike. Put differently, I have met schoolchildren whose destinies have been decisively affected, if not determined, by particular encounters, experiences, events—accidents and incidents that have figured importantly in the way they have lived their lives in and out of the classroom. Here, for instance, is a tough, intimidating gangleader who was for awhile disruptive in my tenth-grade English class, and who one day came to see me after class in hopes that we would "rap"—and so we did, several times, whereupon this declaration:

> Since my cousin lost his legs [in a shooting that caused hemiplegia], I've stopped myself from hanging out with the guys. I go to the movies in the afternoon and sometimes I don't watch the show, I just sit and think. I used to hate being alone. Now that's the best time—you're able to figure out stuff, and you're not being pushed to get lost by falling in with someone who has himself a knife and a gun

and a big mouth and some dough and some buddies to stand by and guard him. While the people in the movie do their thing, I "weigh things," that's what my cousin thought he was so good at, but he wasn't: he got cut down. I think I'm going to start school and be serious at it. See what I mean?

I told him I did—I saw on his face his "meaning," his fear and his melancholy, and his consequent intent to shift his mind's angle of moral vision. He didn't become, overnight, a successful student, nor did he altogether surrender his swagger, his truculent, dismissive "cool" that, often enough, caused me irritation or frustration or fear or anger, or all the above. But he gradually did become a more-or-less participating member of the class, as opposed to a looming, scary, antagonistic presence in it—and by the end of the year I could honestly feel that he was really learning in the class, and glad that such was the case. On the last day of the school, ever so poignantly and tersely, he thanked a couple of us teachers for "showing up," and then added another thank-you: "I guess I should thank my cousin, too. [If it] wasn't for him I'd be walking down a different road for sure."

His head was lowered, and twice he shook it. I saw him then as the immensely hurt and worried youth he always was—now without the posturing and braggadocio meant to hide from others (and not least, himself) the great objective and subjective jeopardy of his young life. I recall thinking that his name was legion—that here, before me, in a particular life, was an educational story of America at the end of this century, this millennium: our inner-city youth in all their marginality, vulnerability, discontent, but also with the possibilities and potential capabilities that bespeak their humanity. No question our schools will not in and of themselves rescue many of our troubled youth—especially because resources, including human resources, have a way of gravitating toward wealth and power, and so those most in need of small classes and the best-trained, most experienced teachers are least likely to get them. Indeed, when I go into some schools and take note of the number of children in the classrooms, and the equipment and reading material in those rooms, I get all too quickly discouraged. Still, as I well know from sitting in the classes of other teachers, and occasionally from my own teaching, there are plenty of young people, even in tough neighborhoods and understaffed, inadequately supported schools, who manage to take good advantage of the education offered them. Many more, though, are doomed by the life they bring to school, and by no means rescued from that downward tug once inside a room of students and teachers.

So often, I hear this or that teacher think aloud—say that it could be otherwise: with more money and with more and better teachers, more students could be reached, touched, connected in mind and heart to the intellectual and moral energy generated in a given day-to-day educational life. As I listen to such expressed hopefulness and idealism, often tentatively or wistfully rendered, I go back in my mind to my own college years—when, for instance, "The Quiet One" was made, a film by James Agee and Helen Levitt that told of a Harlem boy's slow transformation, by learned psychological understanding on the part of his elders in an institutional setting. Now, alas, we have learned to be less hopeful about such children, and not without good reason.

Hope, actually, requires a commitment of time and money if it is to be translated into a continually felt social reality—something there, awaiting those in distress or danger. In "The Quiet One" a writer and a cinematographer dared to dream of a future when hurt children will be accorded the disciplined, wise commitment of a cadre of alert, lively, self-aware and idealistic adults, willing to guide and teach by word and deed, by constant example. All our recent knowledge notwithstanding—all our educational techniques, newly acquired and touted (neurobiology, "social engineering," and important technological breakthroughs)—the way to the waywardness of the children I meet in our public schools is, finally, through their minds and hearts: they can be stirred and touched by teachers and athletic coaches and counselors and school nurses—by us grown-ups who are part of the world of children, and are able to offer various talents and skills to these young fellow-citizens so much in need of them. Come the next century, that will still be what will spare many of our country's youth one or another kind of educational, social, psychological perdition: the human connection that little Ruby in New Orleans and others have known to matter so very much.

Feeling for a Story

Trevor B. Hall

For three years I had the opportunity to be the teaching fellow for the graduate course Writers in the Classroom, but already I must offer an apologetic caveat. With the title "teaching fellow" comes an implied separation between that teacher and the other men and women who made up the seminar course, as though I was there to teach the others, to instruct—that could not be further from the truth. Instead, it was these stories—the opportunity they provided for reflection—and the details of each of our life experiences that were our primary teachers.

The short stories, poems, essays, and novel excerpts that comprise this collection need no assistance standing as resourceful instructors, offering lessons taken from everyday moments by these ever-observing authors. Nonetheless, at the start of every semester I was given an assumed authority over the reason to attend these particular stories, and was often asked the same questions: "Can you tell us what the 'thread' is between all these stories?" "What is the 'theme' of the course?" Then: "What 'theories' will you draw upon to analyze the texts?"

My hesitation to address these reasonable inquiries was not for lack of an answer, but because I knew I could only give them *my* answer, *my* reason for caring about these stories, and *my* take on the very personal way they inspire my own reflections on teaching and learning. So, instead of offering my own reply, I looked to the words of one of the authors whose stories inhabited the course syllabus. In 1961 Flannery O'Connor received a similar request for definition regarding her story "A Good Man Is Hard to Find." A group of students from Rice University had apparently spent a great deal of time analyzing O'Connor's story, and had gathered together to write to her in search of an explanation—a theory—for the story's various twists. Apoplectic, O'Connor wrote back, and in a few simple, telling sentences said so much: "The meaning of a story should go on expanding for the reader the more he thinks about it.... Too much interpretation is certainly worse than too little, and where feeling for a story is absent, theory will not supply it."*

The opportunity to take a story to heart, to feel for its characters as you might for a friend, and the willingness to use that sensibility as a catalyst and guide in searching through the complexities of teaching and learning (or just about anything else life throws our way) seem to me the reasons these stories have been gathered together. I remember one student stopping me after a class to put it another way. On a cold January day when I was walking home from one of the first class meetings, I heard the patter of sneakers coming quickly from behind me. I turned around to find a slightly out-of-breath, flushed young man of about thirty. He was eager to tell me how excited he was about the course and all that we were going to read. Then he offered this.

> "I used to work as a garbage man. I liked riding on the back of the truck, watching people go about their lives as we collected their trash. I would see so many things that made me want to write, so I would scribble notes on whatever scraps of paper I could find, sometimes even on my hands. Later, I would turn my hastily jotted

Letters of Flannery O'Connor: The Habit of Being, edited by Sally Fitzgerald (New York: Farrar, Strauss and Giroux, 1979), 437.

notes into stories. Words were everything to me, and I wanted to find a way to share my love of stories with others. That's what turned me on to teaching: the chance to pore over words and stories and the subtle details of life as a way to make sense of the world."

So it was. Together, we watched Leo Tolstoy become humbled in the face of his students' relentless imaginations; we read along as James Agee revealed the might of frustration and self-doubt (and the ability to stay the course in the face of both); we paid close attention as Tillie Olsen and Toni Morrison turned our thoughts toward the way we all can sort and separate ourselves from others, hurt one another out of fear; we followed as Raymond Carver explored the everyday implications of the phrase "the blind leading the blind"; we stopped with wonder as Charles Baxter presented the phrase "imaginary fact"; we followed Flannery O'Connor into the streets of Atlanta and into the dangers of unwittingly handing down our prejudices and pain to children; and on it went with each writer's offering. In the end, of course, we could not help but put forth our own stories as companions and comparisons to those we read. In so doing, we took our time together as a chance to listen, to love, and very important, to laugh!

Stories have long guided my own teaching, my own learning. During my time with the stories and students (myself included) of Writers in the Classroom, I have witnessed what can happen when people allow a well-crafted narrative to become a source of reflection and wonder—a lens through which to examine their own lives as teachers and learners. For me, heeding the words of a demanding group of authors, holding their lessons close as I enter this or that classroom, has given me inspiration when I lacked it, company when I needed it, and pause when I drifted astray. Simply put, the stories in this collection are, in the redemptive words of Raymond Carver's character Bub: "really something."

THE POWER OF NARRATIVE

Ernest Patterson

I was introduced to the stories in this collection in the fall of 1996, and they have been constant companions in my personal and professional life ever since. As an educator taking a year off to reflect on the art of teaching, I enrolled in the class Writers in the Classroom to learn how the works comprising the course syllabus might inform my classroom teaching. What I took away from the course, however, went much further than that. These stories inspired and changed the way that I approach teaching, and even changed my roles as husband, father, and citizen.

Although I was excited about the prospect of reading and discussing these works, it was not immediately evident to me how they were going to help me become a better teacher and, ultimately, a better person. I had assigned a fair amount of reading and facilitated many classroom discussions over the course of my young teaching career, and I now sought to bring student participation, and my instruction of literature, to the next level. I knew that merely assigning or reading great literature was just the beginning and that classroom participation based on literary analysis and intellectual discussion did not often allow for much more than a cursory examination of the material. This collection of stories taught me that in order to fully uncover the richness and possibilities of literature in the classroom, one must strive for the courage and resourcefulness to honor the emotional response of the readers. Through this course I was inspired to take my work with literature deeper and to make it more personal than I had before.

The Writers in the Classroom seminar was comprised of teachers who had been trained to focus on issues centered around teaching and education. We were well versed in using literature to teach skills and standards and to fulfill scope and sequence requirements. However, a different kind of preparation, presence, and personal expectation was necessary to engage effectively with the evocative narratives contained in these stories. Notes in the margins identifying meaningful transitions and literary/theoretical allusions were a necessary element, but they only told a fragment of the story. The pieces in this collection provided all of us with the courage to move from formal interpretation to considering the emotional lives of our students, and an integration of our own affective responses into the discussions of the material.

These stories unlocked something in me and allowed me to freely offer personal anecdotes about my life experiences and how they correlated with the moral and psychological challenges of teaching. Rather than immediately offering a crafty calculated response, I was inspired to open myself and engage more fully with the moral ambiguities and the humanity of the stories' characters. I specifically remember several vignettes in Charles Baxter's "Gryphon" that were central to the shift in my contributions to classroom discussions. The story is a deeply emotional rendering of a young boy's experience of being taught by an unorthodox substitute teacher, and the boy's attempts to recount the power of the interactions with this teacher—and her "substitute facts"—to his mother. I was greatly moved by Baxter's descriptions of the young man's sense that there might be something more to school than the recitation of facts, and more to home life than the completion of chores. Baxter brought me back to the elementary-school classrooms and after-school discussions of my past, and allowed me to feel the boy's excitement and bewilderment right along with him. Through reading the story, I began to develop and express a conviction in the power of compassion, empathy, even redemption— responses that all of these stories and novel excerpts elicited from many of us in the class that semester.

When the first writing assignment came along, rather than writing an analysis of Baxter's work and how it informed my practice of teaching, I felt compelled to write a short story, something I had not done since middle school. Despite my hope that this was a useful exercise in integrating the course's ideas and materials, as soon as I submitted that story, a wave of regret, even terror, washed over me. I was chastising myself for not writing a more scholarly, analytical, "real" piece of literary criticism. My pangs of self-doubt proved to be for naught. When I got the piece back and eagerly tore through it to read the written comments, they were all very positive, concluding with, "Hey, Ernie, you have turned this opportunity to display abstract, conceptual skills into an excuse for imaginative storytelling. I mean, what gives, fellah?! This is a big-shot place—we only take clever 'interpretations' here!" I found myself laughing out loud—both with relief that my feeble story was not shot down, and with excitement that my attempt to process the emotional connections that Baxter's story elicited in me had found a sympathetic audience.

Seven years later, I am cast in new roles as head of a school, husband, and father. What I continue to take away from these stories has very little to do with a particular teaching technique, but rather is a deep conviction in the power that narrative has on an individual's presence—in the classroom and in every other aspect of life. I now teach these stories and encourage others to use them in their classrooms, because of what they have done for me personally and professionally, and because of the transformation they provided for the students in the Writers in the Classroom seminar. These stories serve us teachers well: They help us to see what it is that we really need to teach young people, and they give us powerful tools to employ in teaching what we are required to deliver to our students.

Although we all need to know the hard skills that will enable us to be successful in the professional world, we also need to keep in mind the moral ambiguities that are so often near at hand—and these stories help in that larger regard, help us teachers engage students in the dilemmas presented by life's ambiguities and ironies. Baxter's Miss Ferenczi provided me with a clear example of how to engage students in life's bigger questions, and so, to this day, I am compelled to use one of her "substitute facts" now and again, when necessary.

Tolstoy Teaching
Today's Young Americans

Michael Coles

While at college I worked with high schoolers who lived literally across a river, and too, across the proverbial railroad tracks. Those youngsters came from poor families, and the streets they knew were dangerous—crimes common and drugs easily obtained. I went to a school to do tutoring, and sometimes things went further than teaching, than learning and listening: we'd talk about "life," and what was ahead, what the young man or woman wanted to do and where.

I'd bring with me to the school some books I thought might catch the attention of those with whom I was meeting—a story, a poem, a photograph that would stir a response, a thought, a question. Some of the youth weren't "into the school thing," as a seventeen-year-old man, eagerly hoping to graduate, then join the army, let me know, as we talked about his future: "I'd like to see the world, and being a soldier would be my ticket. Here in school it's talk, talk, talk; but I'd like to *do* something—I'd like to stand up and be ready to fight for my country. My dad says lots of people pay lip service to America—but no, they won't do service-time and they figure out how to stay out—of wearing a uniform and trying their best to keep our country safe, and strong."

As I saw his lowered head across the desk table where we both were sitting, talking, I felt my own head beginning to lower—and my eyes fasten on the book of Tolstoy's educational essays, which I'd taken to the schools. We both sat silently, when suddenly I hear these words come my way: "That guy Tolstoy, you like him? We looked him up in the dictionary—he died when this century was just starting, and now it's nearing the end (that's over ninety years). What he says—the way he starts [an essay] with a question—that says everything! A lot of teachers, they get to believe in them-selves—'Mr. Know-it-all,' we call the guy, or 'Miss I-know-every-thing,' we call the lady."

Now silence as we both consider what had been so forcefully ex-pressed. Now a further observation: "This guy [Tolstoy] is telling you by asking you. If you're going to teach, you sure better be ready to learn from the folks you're trying to teach. Also you should be straight-up with kids you're teaching—we can spot phony-baloney talk in a couple of seconds, as soon as we hear it. The best part of the Tolstoy stuff you read to us [in the classroom] was when we heard Tolstoy reminding us that you can be a hypocrite, a two-faced person who isn't really honest, is just a pretender, saying good-sounding 'honest' things, but not living up to what's being said. 'Practice what you preach,' my mom says, and Tolstoy is sec-onding her all the way when he says you should get in the habit of being truthful—the time when he really levels with you through the bases-loaded home run he hits in his essay." The expression "honest convictions" is, for me, absolutely meaningless; there are honest habits, not honest convictions.

So it went in a Boston school—a youth harkening to a writer's insistence on the nature of a lived life as the true measure of its worth; and summoning as well a writer's interest in the vividly compelling truth—of fact examined through the mind's imagina-tion: "Along with a number of unrealizable fantasies, I always im-agine a series of pictures, or stories, written to fit the proverbs." Wisdom learned through the mind's alert eyes, attentive ears, offering evidence to a person, stirring her or him to thought, to a consideration of what takes place in the world. "I think Tolstoy is telling teachers like himself to be humble, to be open to learning and learning from those they teach," a Boston boy declared one day during the afternoon, and his words connected long and hard and strong with the tutor there to be of help to him, but in a moment he became his long remembering, grateful student.

V

POSTLUDE

We conclude with insistent, even arresting observations from three master teachers, two of whom worked as child psychoanalysts with teachers, as well as healed the young, and one of whom takes us vividly back to his own time of learning, even as he now continues to teach.

REMARKS,
COTUIT, MASSACHUSETTS, 1965

Erik H. Erikson

For so many Americans, school is a place of possible ascent—or, of course, decline: capability rewarded, or limitations, even troubles of the mind and spirit, expressed painfully. The teacher's task is to bring all of a classroom's children together—so that the youngsters work as a willing (a willful) community: no small achievement when it happens!

———

ERIK H. ERIKSON (1902–1994) was a child psychoanalyst and the author of *Childhood and Society,* as well as *Young Man Luther* and *Gandhi's Truth.*

REMARKS,
NEW HAVEN, CONNECTICUT, 1971

Anna Freud

When I go back in my mind, hoping to find a proper way to do justice to all that happens in a classroom, I think of the many different classrooms that exist in one classroom—for each child a particular world, which he or she views through a lens, shaped by his or her life, and for the teacher a world to observe, understand, persuade, exhort. So much goes into what gets called "instruction," or "teaching!" So many dreams and hopes, nightmares and worries or fears, hover over a class, while the young learn their letters and numbers, and their teachers do *their* learning (as to how to help others learn well). I should mention one danger that can befall us who teach (and so doing, learn): a certain self-righteousness may come our way— we explain and explain, then we may start exhorting (a sign sometimes that we're tempted to leave the teacher's desk for a pulpit!).

—

ANNA FREUD (1895–1982) extended the psychoanalytic work of her father to the study of children, and wrote at great length about their inner life—their strivings and concerns. She worked with many schoolchildren and teachers.

FROM *TEACHER*

Mark Edmundson

In America, the story of the great good teacher is told over and over again. It is the story of the man or woman who comes upon a hapless group of kids and helps them remake their lives. In the standard version, in the myth, that teacher is always fired by the highest of motives, chief among which is a love for the students that is unequivocal and that begins the day they walk through his door. The love never falters and never ends. Years later you can go back and visit the great teacher; he will remember everything about you. He will exult in your accomplishments. Your defeats he will put in proper perspective.

This great good teacher of popular legend is full of broad, generous, and generally applicable truths, which he dispenses to all. In these truths there is, of course, nothing shocking. They are things we all know on some level—put your family before your career; try to enjoy the little things—but in our hustle and bustle have forgotten. The great good teacher is happy and one with himself, and he wants us to be the same. He will die with a smile on his face.

MARK EDMUNDSON is a professor of English at the University of Virginia. He has published a number of works, including *Literature Against Philosophy* and *Plato and Derrida*.

ROBERT COLES is a professor of psychiatry and medical humanities at Harvard Medical School and a research psychiatrist for the Harvard University Health Services. He is also the James Agee Professor of Social Ethics at Harvard. His many books include the Pulitzer Prize–winning, five-volume *Children of Crisis* and the best-selling *The Moral Intelligence of Children, The Spiritual Life of Children,* and *Bruce Springsteen's America.* He lives in Massachusetts.

TREVOR B. HALL founded a nonprofit company, *The Call Academy,* which provides educational summer programs for low-income high school students, combining literature, the documentary arts, and adventure and travel. He is also president of the SNAP Foundation, an organization dedicated to inspiring young people to tell their stories through photography and writing.

ERNEST PATTERSON is currently Head of School at the Telluride Mountain School in Telluride, Colorado, where he lives with his wife and young daughter. He has served as a teacher of the humanities and sciences, and as a school administrator in independent schools across the country.

MICHAEL COLES is a photographer, teacher, and writer. He lives in Missoula, Montana.

A NOTE ON THE TYPE

The principal text of this Modern Library edition
was set in a digitized version of Janson, a typeface that
dates from about 1690 and was cut by Nicholas Kis,
a Hungarian working in Amsterdam. The original matrices have
survived and are held by the Stempel foundry in Germany.
Hermann Zapf redesigned some of the weights and sizes for
Stempel, basing his revisions on the original design.